STREETWISE®
FINANCE and ACCOUNTING for ENTREPRENEURS

Set Budgets. Manage Costs.

Suzanne Caplan

Adams Media
Avon, Massachusetts

Published by Adams Media, an F+W Publications Company
57 Littlefield Street
Avon, MA 02322
www.adamsmedia.com

ISBN 10: 1-59337-609-X
ISBN 13: 978-1-59337-609-3

Printed in United States of America.

J I H G F E D C B A

Library of Congress Cataloging-in-Publication Data

Caplan, Suzanne.
  Streetwise finance & accounting for entrepreneurs / by Suzanne Caplan.
     p. cm.
  Includes index.
  ISBN 1-59337-609-X
  1. Small business--Finance. 2. Small business--Accounting. 3. New business enterprises--Finance. I. Title. II. Title: Streetwise finance and accounting for entrepreneurs. III. Title: Finance & accounting for entrepreneurs.

  HG4027.7.C3644 2006
  658.15--dc22

                                        2006014732

This book is available at quantity discounts for bulk purchases.
For information, please call 1-800-289-0963.

Dedication

As before, this book is dedicated to Tom Nunnally,
my lifelong mentor and friend.

■ ■ ■

CONTENTS

Acknowledgments

Words of gratitude to Sherry Truesdell who has been with me since book one and we have continued to meet deadlines. To my agent Laurie Harper, who always knows what I should do, even when I don't.

And to Mary Jane and George Iksic and Jane Menchyk who make the tedious explanations all worthwhile. I am motivated by you.

Introduction

Finance & Accounting Is the Heart of Any Business

Multiple elements contribute to the success of any business venture, whether the company started just months ago or has been operating for decades. Most entrepreneurs focus on the service they provide, the products they sell, or the skills to bring in new customers. Meeting the needs and expectations of clients is the core of what makes and keeps a company vibrant. But is that really your only central role?

I was the CEO of a family manufacturing company for twenty-one years, and for at least half of that time, I saw myself as the chief sales cheerleader. I charmed the customers and motivated the troops, always expecting that someone else would handle the responsibilities that didn't interest me. Two of the things that didn't interest me were the accounting and finance. My bookkeeper kept records and my accountant filed tax returns, both of which I couldn't even begin to understand. When times got tough, I learned, in the line of fire, what I should have known before I started: understanding and running a company by the numbers is absolutely *essential*. The customers and sales people may be the soul of the company, but the finances are the heart—the thing that pumps the necessary life blood (money) through the entire system. Most entrepreneurs do not handle the day-to-day function of finance, and that's okay. But, whether you have a clerk or a controller, oversight and review is an important part of your job description, too, and here are just a few reasons why.

1. The Bottom Line Is the Bottom Line

Profitability is the key factor to success. Achieving a sufficient level of profit starts with understanding costs, and then pricing your products or services according to the needs of your particular operation. Of course, there is a competitive component to the selling price, but the basis is your costs. After that, you need to continually monitor costs. When they go up, you need to be aware that they went up, and to then incorporate the increased costs into your selling price.

2. Finance Drives the Planning Process

When money is needed for new equipment, increased inventory, additional employees, or an aggressive marketing campaign, the business owner is the one who must find the capital and make sure that it will be enough to pay your debts. Knowing in advance what your needs will be allows you to access the available resources for money.

3. Unexpected Surprises Can Destroy a Business

Many symptoms can alert the owner that the business is headed in the wrong direction. Good business owners watch more than just sales figures. They monitor profit margins and increasing short-term debt (vendor credit) as well. Once a financial crunch has begun, choices become limited and time pressure increases.

The start of financial management is understanding the basics of accounting. You want to know where the numbers come from as well as what they mean. This does not imply that you need to be the company bookkeeper, but you do need to know how the recordkeeping is set up and how it is organized. It is important to know how the reports are generated and what they tell you about the performance of your company. When profits are down or cash is short, you need to know why this happened and what options you have to make corrections.

Being in business is a profitable way to earn a living, but it isn't all product and sales. The accounting and finance may seem like hard work to you at first. However, once you master these tasks, the pressures of finances will be reduced, and all of the other aspects of running your business will be easier.

Understanding Your Accounting System and Keeping Track

The General Ledger: Entry and Storage of Financial Data

A company's financial records are stored in a filing system called a general ledger. Each transaction—whether a sale, expense, asset, or liability—flows through this system. All of the detailed information necessary to produce a Profit and Loss Statement or a Balance Sheet will be found in this central "book." The company's history is a permanent part of the general ledger system and remains available for review and analysis as the business progresses. All types of accounting systems (whether manual or computerized) will have sub-ledgers as well. You will find an account for cash, accounts receivable, or accounts payable in sub-ledgers. As a transaction takes place, the entries are posted in the general ledger and recorded in the sub-ledger. For example, when a credit sale that is posted in the accounts receivable sub-ledger turns into cash because of a payment, the transaction will be posted to the general ledger as well as the Cash and Accounts receivable sub-ledger. Simply put, an accounting system is a tracking system developed to record and report the progress of the company's transactions.

Where Transactions Begin Their Journey

There are times when transactions go directly into the general ledger without any sub-posting. These are primarily capital financial transactions that have no operational sub-ledgers. These may include items such as loan proceeds and principal repayments as well as proceeds from asset sales. What differentiates these transactions from those that have sub-ledgers, is that these are linked to the Balance Sheet (your record of assets and liabilities), but *not* to your Profit and Loss Statement. Purchasing new equipment or borrowing money is a good example of this type of transaction.

Setting Up the General Ledger

Two primary areas that you need to understand are the link between the general ledger and your financial reports, and that each account needs to have an opening balance. Even on the first day you open for business, not all of these accounts will have a zero balance.

A company generates two primary financial documents, the *Balance Sheet* and the *Profit and Loss Statement,* both of which are drawn directly from the general ledger. The order of how the balances appear is determined by the Chart of Accounts (more on that later), but all of the transactions entered will appear. The general ledger accrues the balances that make up the line items in these reports, and all changes will be reflected on both the Profit and Loss Statement and the Balance Sheet.

The General Ledger Creates an Audit Trail

The dreaded word "*audit*" strikes fear in the hearts of most business owners, but it really shouldn't. The chances of a tax audit (which is usually the main concern of business owners) are very small. Even so, having a trail to all of the transactions allows you to locate the original documentation that is valuable to you. Then, if you are ever audited, you will be prepared.

An internal audit track means that errors can be traced to their source and corrected. Perhaps there was a double billing by a vendor. In that case, you can locate the original invoices to verify and correct any mistakes, which will save the company money. On the other hand, if a customer underpaid an invoice, you can track the original invoice and collect what is owed on the bill. Everyone makes an occasional mistake, but mistakes are a lot more painful when they cost *you* money. You are not likely to be notified by the person who has been *over*paid (or *under*charged).

How Entries Are Made and Tracked

Whether you made a sale, collected money, purchased inventory, or paid for something, each transaction will be entered in the general ledger, and then will show up on the appropriate sub-ledger. If you are doing it manually on a spreadsheet, you will enter the name, the type of transaction, and the amount. Then the sale becomes revenue.

Most companies use some version of computerized accounting, which creates an invoice that links directly to the general ledger, and then shows up on the income statement as revenue. This same transaction will also show up as either an account receivable or as available cash in your bank. Automated systems will post all the appropriate sub-ledgers from the single originating transaction.

Keeping Source Documents

The general ledger will provide the data on where any original transaction comes from, but you should still require that the original paperwork establishes the details. These detailed files are called source documents, and even if your system is substantially electronic, you will want to keep a paper trail. This trail may include original invoices or receipts, or just a hard copy of a transaction done in the system. Develop a method that verifies each transaction that has been entered into your system, and then files the original away in case you need to copy or refer to it later. We have not become a paperless society yet!

The Standard Chart of Accounts

Financial recordkeeping has a variety of purposes. It provides information to management as a tool for decision-making, as well as providing the information required to file all necessary tax returns. The key to this tracking is found in the Chart of Accounts.

This chart is actually a numbering system that keeps everything in the proper category. If you were using a set of folders, or even shoe boxes, to hold receipts for all of the company's transactions, this number system would simply be the names of the folders or shoeboxes. There is an account number for each type of transaction, including the source of income and the type of expense that you might incur. At the end of each reporting period (month, quarter, or year) you will add the dollar amount in each category (as generated by your computer), and from these numbers, you can produce a Profit and Loss Statement and a Balance Sheet.

The Typical Chart Number System

Most often, the Chart of Accounts is numbered from 100 (or 1000) through 800 (8000). Each number within the range is a more detailed category within that range. The general headings are as follows:

1000 Asset Accounts—Typically the first half of these numbers cover current assets and the second half (1500+) cover fixed or long-term assets.

2000 Liabilities—Current liabilities (such as accounts payable and taxes due) will be listed in the first half of these numbers, and long-term liabilities such as deferred payments in the second half (2500+).

3000 Equity Accounts—These accounts contain the original and added capital contributions; owners draw from equity and retained earnings.

4000 Revenue or Income Accounts—The revenue is primarily generated by sales, but you may also collect taxes or fees that will be remitted to a third party. These funds can be tracked in this account.

5000 Costs of Goods Sold—Here is where you post the direct costs (such as materials and labor) associated with your sales. These are your variable costs and the correct categorization is critical. This topic will be discussed further throughout the book.

6000 Expenses (General and Administrative)—All of the other (non-direct) costs from advertising to telephones will be included in this category.

7000 Other Revenue—This may include interest paid to the company or sale of assets.

8000 Other Expenses—Items here may be things such as income tax payments.

Change the Chart Descriptions to Fit Your Business

Most accounting software comes with a preset Chart of Accounts, but this should only be used as a guideline. The categories offered must be fully reviewed and then modified to meet the nature of your specific business. You can add numbers and edit the wording fairly easily. This may be the responsibility of your bookkeeper, your controller, or perhaps the company accountant. But this exercise should be done with the input of the company CEO, and perhaps some key managers. You are the ones who will be making decisions based on the information provided both on the sales side and on the expense side. You must identify what information is valuable to your analysis.

Customizing Your Chart of Accounts to Provide Useable Information

Every company needs to keep detailed records on its sales income (what is active and what is not) as well as its expense allocation (where the money is going and how well it is being spent). You can find such detailed information simply by customizing your Chart of Accounts. In the following list, you will see a very generic Chart of Accounts.

Current Assets

1000	Petty cash
1020	Checking accounts
1060	Money market accounts
1080	Savings account
1100	Accounts receivable
1200	Inventory
1400	Prepaid expenses
1410	Employee advances
1420	Notes receivable current
1430	Work in progress
1440	Utility deposits
1470	Miscellaneous current assets

Long-Term Assets

1500 Furniture and fixtures
1510 Equipment
1520 Automobiles
1540 Leasehold improvements
1550 Buildings
1600 Land
1700 Accumulated depreciation—furniture
1710 Accumulated depreciation—equipment
1720 Accumulated depreciation—auto
1730 Accumulated depreciation—other
1740 Accumulated depreciation—leaseholds
1750 Accumulated depreciation—building

Current Liabilities

2000 Accounts payable
2100 Accrued expense
2200 Accrued rent
2210 Sales tax payable
2220 Wages payable
2330 Wage tax payable
2340 Unemployment tax
2350 Income tax
2360 Local wage tax
2400 Current portion—SBA loan
2410 Line of credit—bank
2420 Note payable—stockholder
2430 Other current liabilities

Long-Term Liabilities

2600 Loan payable, non-current portion
2610 Mortgage payable
2700 Other long-term liabilities

Equity

3500 Common stock
3600 Paid in capital
3701 Retained earnings
3710 Dividends

Income

4000 Sales revenue
4400 Rental income
4500 Interest income
4600 Other revenue
4700 Shipping charges reimbursed
4800 Sales returns and allowances
4810 Sales discounts

Expense

5000 Direct labor
5010 Union benefits
5020 Health insurance
5100 Equipment
5200 Subcontracts
5300 Freight insurance
5400 Purchase returns and allowance

Expense (General and Administrative)

6000 Advertising expense
6010 Accounting expense
6020 Amortization
6100 Auto and truck
6150 Bad debt expense
6200 Bank charges
6210 Cash over and short
6300 Chartable contributions
6350 Sponsorships
6400 Commissions

6450 Fees

6500 Depreciation

6600 Employment benefits

6650 Income tax

6700 Insurance—liability

6710 Insurance—workers' compensation

6720 Insurance—health

6730 Insurance—disability

6740 Insurance—life

6800 Interest expense

6850 Laundry and cleaning

6900 Legal and professional

6950 Licenses expense

Office Expense

7000 Maintenance

7050 Meals and entertainment

7100 Office expense

7200 Real estate taxes

7300 Water and sewage

7310 Estimated taxes

7320 Pension/profit-sharing plan

7360 Postage

7400 Rent expense

7450 Repairs

7500 Officers' salaries

7550 Office wage expense

7560 Office supplies

7700 Telephone

7750 Internet

7760 Web site maintenance

7800 Travel

7850 Utilities

8000 Miscellaneous expense

9000 Gain or loss sales of assets

9010 Corporate income tax

Learn About Hidden Costs from Your Chart of Accounts

Looking over a basic Chart of Accounts is a meaningful learning experience for the new or early-stage business owner. You will likely recognize and understand most of the costs that will be incurred. Some expenses may take you by surprise, though. Do not ignore the ones you hadn't thought about—for example, all of the various insurances you will need to pay. Take the time to investigate the costs of running your company and to find out what effect these expenses will have on your bottom line. Your awareness could help to keep your funds in line from day one, which can only add to your profitability. By customizing your own Chart of Accounts, you will be able to track the income and expenses your own business has.

One More Word on the Value of a Custom Chart

Every year, you will file a tax return and, if you have any bank loans, you will give your lender your prepared Profit and Loss Statement as well as your Balance Sheet on a regular basis. The numbers in your Chart will determine how income and expense is classified. It is always a good idea to include the most important information for your lenders, but it is even more important that you understand the information and find it valuable to operating your company. If a cost seems too high, investigate it—the amount may be posted to the wrong account. If your sales in one area seem soft, check out the details. This is the information about your company that you will use to control the present and to plan for the future.

Equity Accounts and Retained Earnings

As you are working hard and building your business, you will also want to know how you should build net worth by creating a valuable asset. You will find this information in the 3000 Account, and it will begin with Paid in Capital (the money you contributed to start the venture). Add to that any extraordinary windfalls, and the primary contribution will be the accumulation of your earnings (which are called *retained*). They will

My Own Income Account

These days, my business is in the sector of professional services. In addition to my work as a writer, I am also a speaker. I create and present seminars and do various types of consulting. I am comfortable with a computerized accounting system, so even though my one (and sometimes two) person venture is easy to track and control, I still use a full accounting program. The first year, I categorized all of my revenue under a single 4000 Income account. I did not need more detail for tax or banking purposes. But, I had little information on how I was really earning my money, so these days my Income account looks like this:

4000	Sales—general consulting
4010	Loan packaging
4020	Turnaround consulting
4030	Exit strategy planning
4100	Speakers' fees
4110	Reimbursed travel
4120	Seminar presentation
4130	Seminar design
4200	Book advance
4210	Book royalties
4220	Book development fees
4300	Miscellaneous income
4400	Real estate income

Now I can track how I am doing in every aspect of my work and where my marketing dollars need to be spent. I can also see what my most profitable work is and where I might be spending too much of my time and capital. I add categories as I add areas of interest.

build the balance in this account; however, this account will also shrink if those earnings are negative (that is, if you lose money).

The retained earnings are profits that are not distributed by dividends, but rather kept as part of the equity. If you have had a good run of luck, you will accrue a healthy retained earnings balance. But periods of loss will erode this number, making it impossible to determine whether the business has had stable or erratic performance on the profit side not just this year, but over the recent past. Whether you are planning to sell or retain your company, profits add to the cash flow and make the work a lot more fun.

▶▶ TEST DRIVE

Whether you are starting up a business or running an established one, ask yourself the following questions. If you answer no to any question, consider what you can do to turn that no into a yes.

✓ **1.** Are you contributing to the implementation of your company's accounting system?

✓ **2.** Can you determine how a transaction goes through the general ledger and then to a sub-ledger?

✓ **3.** Do you understand the need for an audit trail?

✓ **4.** Can you identify the numbers that make up the Chart of Accounts?

— **5.** Have you reviewed your Chart of Accounts recently and made changes to make it more relevant?

Create a Complete Customer Database

The accounting process activity often begins when sales transactions take place. After all, you are in business to provide goods or services to customers, so these transactions put many other actions into motion. Customers are important to your business now and, hopefully, in the future, too. Knowing as much as you can about the habits and trends of your clients is vital to your success.

Of course, you start every record with the name, address, and contact information of the customer. For business customers, you'll want to record who is authorized to make purchases as well as who is responsible for issuing payments. At the same time, you should also be setting up an effective collection system, and the contact information is critical for payment follow ups. Payments may be delayed if documents are sent to the wrong person.

The most valuable information in your customer database are your customers' sales history (what types of goods or services they have bought and how often) and their payment record. You will want to set a credit limit and ask to be alerted when the customer is approaching, or has exceeded, this amount. From this information, you can develop an entire strategy on how to better serve your customer—how to keep their business as well as expect their prompt payments.

What You Know About Your Customers Will Increase Sales

Much has been written and taught in recent years about "relationship selling." The importance of creating familiarity with your customers cannot be overstated. Using a database management system to help you do this makes sense. Knowing what is selling and trying to stock the product that is most frequently ordered so that you can deliver quickly, meets the needs of your best customers. You should also use the same customer management system to determine when clients have been inactive for a while. Make reconnecting with such customers a priority, and don't find out after the fact that you have lost long-time clients. One way to reconnect include sending customers a "tickler" message on a regular basis. You could also call to tell them about new items that they might be interested in or about the special sales that you are having. You can customize your contacts to make them very personal, to make all your customers feel that they are valuable to you.

 RTA mailers (handwritten note)

Sales Information Should Include Payment Terms

On most computerized accounting systems, as you enter each new customer contact, you can enter credit terms (net 30 days—2%, 10 days, etc.) and an established credit limit as well. This allows these terms to appear on each invoice; the posted invoice will also appear on a past due listing on your aging (more on that in Chapter 6) once the terms have expired. You will be alerted when the current sale has taken the customer over their credit limit. This information is an important management tool for creating good cash flow. Don't automatically shut off good customers because they are purchasing more; just make a personal inquiry and a solid credit decision. On the other hand, be prepared to stop selling to any customers who don't pay their bills. You depend on your cash flow, and you don't want to be a banker to troubled customers.

Create Adjustments to Revenue and <u>Inventory</u>

A sale becomes revenue because it is income to the company. The important concern for the management of your accounting records is this: which product or service was sold. There are several issues to consider. From a marketing point of view, you want to know what type of products are selling well so you can focus on the promotion of more sales in that area, or perhaps shift promotion to kick up your sales in other categories that may be more profitable. All of this will be done through the creation of an effective Chart of Accounts on the revenue category (4000–4999). Establishing these details allows you to get as much detailed information as you need.

Another one of your major concerns on the revenue side is whether the sale is taxable. For some businesses, all of their sales are either taxable or not, so filing the tax return and paying collected taxes is a simple matter. For other businesses, however, some transactions are charged sales tax and some are not. This varies on a state-by-state basis, but your accounting systems should track and make that information easily accessible. This backup information is likely to be critical in case of an audit.

A Sale Posts to Cash or Accounts Receivables

Once a product or service has been sold, delivered, or performed, the amount of that sale is posted to the revenue account (4000–4999). There is a second corresponding account that will also show a change; this is your cash account or the accounts receivable. Making a sale is not a complete transaction—there must also be an exchange of money or at least the promise of an exchange of cash.

Each credit purchase will also show up on your accounts receivable (A/R) listing. If this is in a continuing tally of credit transactions from one customer, their total A/R balance may exceed the amount of the single sale.

The sale will show up on your Profit and Loss Statement as Income, and the cash, or A/R, becomes an asset on your Balance Sheet. Until the money is collected and is spent to pay an expense, this adds to the overall value of your business. There may also be a corresponding withdrawal from inventory reflecting the cost of the merchandise that has been sold and therefore is no longer available.

A Cash Sale Should Always Be Tracked

Some companies that do a substantial amount of cash business use only an income account titled Cash Sale to record these transactions. From a record-keeping standpoint, that may be adequate. But you will lose the chance to track valuable customer data, which may have serious marketing possibilities. The more information you have on who is buying what and on how often, the better you can direct advertising and marketing to increase your level of sales. This data may be collected by issuing "frequent buyer" cards that give the customers incentives to keep coming back. These cards allow your business to follow customers' buying patterns. Even with cash sales, it is possible to record internal data.

Vendor Data Includes Category of Cost

Virtually every day that you are in business, you will be spending money on some expense, whether it is inventory purchases, wages, taxes, utilities,

Know Your Customers

One of my clients operates a very popular restaurant, which makes almost two million dollars of business per year. He was always looking for ways to be efficient in buying and preparing food so he could keep the costs down and the profits up. Every new point of sale database he could add to the cash registers refined the available information more and more. He then had no problem in finding out exactly how many prime rib dinners were sold a week ago on Tuesday. This really was a valuable asset to the kitchen planning.

But each sale was merely calculated as a cash sale, and the only customer data that was retained was from the credit card receipts. That seemed to work very well—for a while at least. After a particularly bad spell of late fall weather, business didn't bounce back as quickly as it had before and everyone was concerned. All of a sudden, having a good customer database seemed very important; perhaps an incentive would encourage people to come back.

The instant solution was a large glass container at the manager's stand advertising a weekly drawing for a free meal. Quickly, names were entered into a retained customer list. Then they offered the guests who signed up a special incentive for their birthdays. A frequent diner's card was instituted not long after that. While this restaurant owner continues to place newspaper ads and other promotions, his targeted direct mail campaign toward existing customers always brings the greatest response. You can see how important sales data can be.

advertising, or a laundry list of other types of bills. The amount and, most important, the type of these expenditures become essential parts of the details of your operation. Whether the bill is paid by cash, credit, or a third-party charge card, it must be expensed to the proper account. Knowing who your vendors are and how much business you are doing will become valuable information as you grow your company.

Make Sure Vendor Transactions Are by Name

Most expense accounts are listed by the vendor's name, but if you are one of the growing number of companies using a corporate credit or debit card, you must take extra care. If you list the credit card company as the vendor, the purchase may not default into the proper category (subledger). For example, years ago, an American Express Card was considered a "travel" card, and all purchases on that card were expensed under the travel and entertainment category. These days, companies purchase office supplies, trucking services, and even large material purchases with an AMEX, as well as Visa and MasterCard. Not entering the correct vendor will seriously diminish the accuracy of your Profit and Loss Statement.

The following is an overview of what information you need to keep in a Vendor Data File:

- Name of supplier
- Address
- Contact in purchasing
- Contact in accounting
- Normal account terms offered
- Discount offered (if any)
- Type of purchase made (account number)
- Terms of sale (cash or credit)

The initial posting enters into the system on the purchase side. You will enter the name of the vendor and the type and amount of the transaction. In some computerized accounting systems, if this is a cash purchase you can skip this initial step and go directly to the money transaction (writing the check). Then, that step will automatically default the purchase to the expense account based on the vendor that you paid. If that vendor supplies in more than one expense area, you must enter this information manually.

Creating and Monitoring Accounts Payable

When you purchase an item on credit, you will also create a payable (or a debt) to the vendor from whom you made your purchase. The single act of posting a purchase creates an expense line item on your Profit and Loss Statement and a short-term debt on your Balance Sheet. You can begin to see how interactive an accounting system really is, and how it is not that complicated, once you take the time to understand it.

The final process that takes place on the vendor (or purchase) side will be the payment for the goods or services you have purchased. If you have the sufficient cash flow to pay bills as they are due, then on that date, your system will alert you to write a check. This will cancel the debt to the vendor and withdraw cash from your bank account.

Cross Reference All Transactions

Whether you are keeping your records manually or on a computer, you want to remember to cross reference your transactions by putting purchase order numbers on checks and check numbers on vendor invoices when you stamp them paid. ▶▶ **Although we are quickly moving toward a paperless society, source documents remain important and should be retained.** You should keep original purchase orders, invoices, copies of credits, etc. If there is a dispute later on, you will need hard copies of the transactions. Keep the hard copies on file, unless you are able to retain them on your desktop with proper backups, and able to print when you need to.

Making Journal Entries

There are certain times when you should make entries directly into the General Journal without any other Profit and Loss transactional consequences. The ideal time will be when you are setting up your books at the start of the business. You will enter any applicable beginning balances. Few companies begin with zero balances.

For example, perhaps you have borrowed money to buy assets such as machinery and inventory. You will have a beginning balance in current assets for the various types of inventory you own, and you will have a beginning balance in long-term assets for the equipment. The debt will also be on the beginning balance, so as you pay it off, you will be creating equity.

As the business continues, there will be other journal entries, such as the sale of any asset. This is not typical business income that posts to a sub-ledger; instead, it will post to the asset account carrying the item that is being liquidated. You may have a gain or a loss from the sale of that asset, depending on whether you sell it at a higher price than it is maintained on the books or not.

▶▶ TEST DRIVE

Within the accounting system of your company, there are many sources of data that can directly add to your bottom line. Consider how many you are using:

1. Are you target marketing existing customers based on their previous purchases? ✓

2. Are you utilizing inventory control based on your prior usage of goods? ✓

3. Do you review outstanding invoices to make sure pricing is correct? ✓

4. Are you using accounting data to manage your cash flow? ✓

Single-Entry and Double-Entry Systems

Most accounting terms are used on a regular basis by the professionals in the field. We hear them often, yet many business owners do not know what they mean. More of a concern is that few of us are interested enough to learn. By not bringing ourselves up to speed on this discipline, we are not able to use a common language with our own accountants, and, even more important, with our bankers. ▶▶ **We need to learn the terms professionals use to discuss and analyze businesses, because often it is our business that needs their advice.** What follows are some commonly used terms and simple explanations.

Let's go back to the non-automated system of shoeboxes and folders. Assume that you make a sale and you put the receipt in a folder. That is all you do. Or, you make a purchase and put that box in another folder and nothing else. At the end of the year, you total all the accounts with nothing to compare them against. You are using a *single-entry system*.

Now, what if you put the receipt for the sale in one folder and the credit card receipt for the cash received in another? You would be using a very basic *double-entry system*. You total up the cash and the credit card slips and they should equal the sales. Then, perhaps you have also been accepting some IOUs. (They comprise your Accounts Receivable.) These are also a part of the sales receipt folder.

In financial record keeping, every action has a counteraction. A *sale* is revenue that becomes cash or money due. An *expenditure* is a cost that either reduces cash or creates a bill. This is a check and balance system that makes sure that you tie in all of the transactions. In a single-entry system, you might be able to inadvertently record a sale with the wrong amount. With the second entry, you would also have to account for either the payment or the charge, and that gives you a second chance to verify the original amount.

Checkbook accounting, whether manual or automated, is often a single-entry system. Your deposit reflects the value of your sales with no second look at the actual amount of the full sale. It's the same on the expense side, where you account for what you pay regardless of whether it is the full amount of the bill. This allows for many opportunities to make mistakes.

Cash vs. Accrual Accounting

The second level of detail in your financial setup is whether you are working on a cash basis or an accrual basis. Some automated systems will allow you to do either, and it is important to decide which set-up you will use. Let's begin with some basic definitions.

Cash Basis Accounting

This method shows income (or revenue) at the time of the payment—a credit sale will not show up on the revenue side until the bill is paid. An expense is also recorded only when a payment is made, so a purchase on credit will not show up as a transaction until the bill is paid. You can purchase all of the items that you want, but if you don't pay for the items, the sale will not show up as a transaction. Cash basis is something like not opening your bills. Actually, it's a little *too* much like not opening the envelopes, in addition to not considering all of your *outstanding* bills.

Accrual Basis Accounting

This method recognizes income whenever the transaction is completed, whether cash is received or not. A credit sale is still shown as revenue when the sale is made. On the expense side, any commitment of purchase (as well as any regular charge such as taxes and utilities) is an expense whether paid now or later. All transactions during a particular period are recorded regardless of their type. The issue is *timing* not type.

The Pros and Cons of Cash Basis

Cash basis is an easy system to set up and run and, if you are using a manual system, this system can work well. However, only very small businesses with low volume and few transactions—particularly a service business that receives and pays mostly by cash, check, or debit card—is a good candidate for this system. For example, a restaurant that pays for food when it is delivered, and then takes in mostly cash, may be a candidate for this system. There are a few other retail or service businesses that fall under this category.

On the negative side, cash basis does not match income and expense in the same period. When you make a large purchase (which you may do to pay freight or get a quantity break), and you do not sell all of the inventory, a cash basis system will show a loss from the sale on any of the products not sold. The leftover inventory will not show up anywhere as an available asset.

With income occurring in one month and the expense perhaps not showing up until a month later, you do not get a good grasp of how you are doing in the short term. This may catch up over the longer term, like over a quarter, but only if you are paying your bills in a reasonable amount of time. And your bills are not posted where they can be easily reviewed.

The biggest danger of the cash basis system is found with a company that is not doing very well. Unpaid bills could pile up without being recorded, and the mounting debt may jeopardize the future of the business without the owner knowing. (Or really wanting to know, for that matter—those unopened envelopes again). Sometimes, office managers, perhaps not wanting to upset the hardworking owner, will keep these in a drawer unseen.

The Pros and Cons of Accrual Basis

In this system, revenue and expense are recorded as soon as the transaction takes place, so the activities match for any given period. This system allows comparisons to the same period from the previous year, which is an analysis that business owners should consider doing.

The accrual method allows management to keep on top of all financial changes quickly and to take the necessary actions. If customers are not paying their bills or your business is falling behind in paying your vendors, the information will be easily available so changes can be made.

Companies that have substantial hard assets need to use accrual basis as a way to record depreciation, and to use it as an offset on taxes. You have no depreciation in a cash basis system.

On the other hand, this system can be more difficult to set up and operate, and it can actually be almost too laborious to do in a manual system. These days, however, it is not much of a cost to buy a computer and a boxed accounting software system. Both of these products are very user-friendly, and they allow for more accurate record keeping. Unless there is a compelling reason for a business not to, I recommend an accrual system.

The Tax Implications of Cash vs. Accrual System

Aside from being able to use depreciation as a tax deferment, there are a number of other tax planning strategies that can be used in an accrual system. Like most business owners, you probably know before the year has ended whether or not it has been a profitable year. You can then make some decisions that will affect the outcome of the year (this one or next) that is likely to incur more of the tax burden.

If you have a sale scheduled to bill late in the year, you can decide to bill it after January 1 and account for the revenue into the following year. If you are expecting substantial profits this year, you may want to stock up on printing and supplies. With an accrual system, you don't even have to pay for them—just post the invoice when it comes in. Remember, if you buy materials or inventory, that will show up as assets and not expenses. A large down payment on equipment or insurance can also be posted in the current period. This is referred to as *timing*, and you can discuss it fully with your accountant.

Direct and Variable Costs

The costs that are directly related to producing your product or providing your service are described as your direct costs. If you are involved in manufacturing, they will include the materials used and the production labor costs. In a restaurant, this will include the cost of food and beverage along with people directly involved in cooking and service. A service business will count the labor directly involved in providing the service. Contractors have materials and direct labor, and often some of the labor costs such as union dues and insurance.

Direct costs are also referred to as *variable costs*. The reason is clear— the higher the volume (the more sales), the more these costs will increase. They will vary according to activity going on in the business. If you aren't selling many widgets, you don't need a lot of widget materials and widget makers. Knowing what percentage of variable costs is normal and being committed to sticking to that percentage gives you an indication when to decrease purchases and production. Variable costs also signal when it is time for increasing purchases and production.

Responding to Change

The most serious mistake business owners make is to cut back too slowly when business begins to get soft. The initial reaction is to hope that a slow day or two is only a temporary fluke. So you don't slow production because you don't want to get hit with new orders unprepared. It is never easy to cut back hours of valuable employees or hold up orders to longtime vendors. However, the sooner the situation is assessed and action is taken, the better overall financial health will be. Direct costs must be modified to reflect any changes in revenue or the projection of changes down the road. If your business is soft over the holiday season, start making plans in November.

Gross Profits

This term represents the profit derived from the total revenue after deducting the direct cost of producing or providing the company product or service. It is also referred to as the operating income, because it describes the fact that this leftover profit is the money your business will have available to pay all other operating bills, such as rent, insurance, and salaries. Refer to the Chart of Accounts and you will find these bills listed under accounts numbered 6000 and 7000. There are several ways to increase the total dollar amount of gross profits available in your company—raise unit prices, lower direct costs, and increase the total overall volume. You absolutely need to know what this term represents. In future chapters, you will learn strategies about making sure that your gross margins are sufficient to run the company.

Indirect and Fixed Costs

These are the costs that are incurred and ongoing—the ones you need to open the doors of your business each day to operate. They remain fixed whether your sales are vibrant or whether they are slow. They are only indirectly connected to the sales volume. It's true, for example, that you would have no sales if you didn't have a place of business, but the cost of having a place to do business doesn't directly determine how high or low the volume of business done there will be.

There are two categories of costs that you must account for in the area of fixed costs. The first is *overhead* such as the following:

- Rent
- Utilities
- Insurance
- Interest
- Legal and professional services
- Repairs
- Taxes

Certain Costs Are Semivariable

Some of the costs that are listed as indirect and fixed are, at the very least, semivariable and will fluctuate according to your sales level. As volume increases, so will the cost of printing, postage, telephone, and travel. The more customers you service, the more money you spend to handle their needs. You may even have to hire additional personnel to meet the volume of a growing business. These costs will not automatically go down as business slows up, but you must keep an eye on them.

The other expenses are *sales and marketing-driven costs* such as the following:

- Advertising
- Commission
- Internet and Web site services
- Travel and entertainment
- Postage and printing

Inside Track	Fixed Costs Can Get Out of Hand

Recently, many old-economy companies—for example, the legend airlines such as United and Delta, as well as the American automotive companies—have gone into great financial stress because of the high costs of health care and pensions. These are costs that started low, but the benefits were generous and they grew over the years.

As a consultant, I often see the same problems. I have often come into a business that is experiencing some financial trouble, and I can figure out quickly, as an outsider, how their fixed costs are unbalanced. The space they have rented is too large or fancy and the occupancy costs are high. Top-of-the-line office equipment has been leased (usually very easily) and, many times, luxury cars as well. Also, the travel expenses are often high. The assumption is made that the cash flow of the business will pay for these expenses. The only available revenue flow for the purpose of covering fixed overhead (which includes location costs as well as employee benefits) is the gross profit. When running a business, you need to conserve your operating cash, so it is essential that you get a handle on how much will be available during normal operating times. This information is critical to success and, sometimes, even to survival. Direct costs should be covered first from normal operating income and never be allowed to grow in excess of the revenue growth.

For the most part, all of these costs will continue even during your business's very slow times. Often you will have agreements, such as leases, that establish these costs on a monthly or annualized basis. A new company should be cautious about high-priced agreements before the sales volume and profit margins are adequate to support the overhead easily. In the early days when you are projecting robust sales, it is very easy to spend generously, only to regret it later.

▶▶ TEST DRIVE

Learning the basics of what is included in an accounting system is the first step to understanding the critical documents that it will require. Ask yourself the following questions.

1. Is your system single-entry or double-entry?
2. Can your business be operated on a cash basis? Why should you use an accrual system?
3. Do you plan ahead to minimize taxes?
4. Are your direct costs accounted for?
5. Do you monitor and control fixed costs?
6. Do you budget according to sales projections?

The Checkbook Programs

Most business owners, even the sole proprietors, need to use computers in some aspect of their work. These days, it takes far more time and energy to track paper than to learn how to use a computer. Computers almost run themselves, and they have become necessary for communication with customers and vendors. Adding accounting programs is a natural step, but selecting one that fits your needs is important. You don't just want to store your numbers; you also want calculations and reports that will help you manage more efficiently.

Many of us began by tracking our personal finances with a basic checkbook program like Quicken or Microsoft Money. You can enter your income (dollars actually earned), pay bills, and track expenses with these basic tools. You can print checks as well, which gives you another level of security. You can even pay bills online and have the amounts automatically deducted from your checkbook balance. However, this tracking method is not sufficient to run even the most basic business. But, if you can learn how to use an automated checkbook, you can readily move up to a small accounting package, which will cost less than $100 to purchase in the entry level version.

Checkbook Bookkeeping Services

If you really do not have the time or the resources to manage your business accounting in-house, there are several checkbook bookkeeping services you can hire as outside contractors; some accounting firms run their own. These accounting firms (not necessarily CPAs) will take your check stubs, invoices, and bills and do all of the computing at their facilities. Some will actually write your checks as well. Then, on a monthly basis, you will receive a financial statement showing how your business is doing. The one thing that isn't often included is the advisory service offered by most accountants. But the information is compiled in a format ready to be reviewed by a professional. And, if you have given the firms all of the information, what you get back should be reliable. One caution here is that these firms often use cash basis accounting, unless you specifically ask them to compute your books on an accrual basis.

QuickBooks and Their Specialized Versions

Virtually as easy as using Quicken is the first level of QuickBooks. This program, called Simple Start, is also in the $100 price range. You can enter, expenses, and pay bills, as well as create customer invoices and track their payments to you. At the end of each month, you will be able to compile a bank reconciliation so you can balance your cash. The system will also allow you to create some simple but essential reports, such as a Profit and Loss Statement and sales reports. It's a good program for a beginner. Most general office workers can learn to use this software, even if they have no basic accounting background.

The Next Step: QuickBooks Basic and Pro

Even at the more advanced levels of QuickBooks Basic or Pro, you are spending less than $300, and the Pro will allow for up to five users for about $750. Once you have learned the way to set up the details of your company and navigate through the menus, the appearance of the screens will be very similar and user friendly. In the case of both Basic and Pro, you can now monitor inventory and create purchase orders when materials are needed. Your invoices will be generated, customer accounts will be posted, and you can track incoming payments. Based on the information you are inputting you can also:

- Create a budget for future costs based on past trends.
- Assess your company's performance with a comparison of current performance to past performance from the same period.
- Track employee time and job costs.
- Generate general payroll in-house.

The software at these levels will give a small company most of the tools it needs to manage every aspect of its financial business. An important extra element to the success of the operation is that the employee designated to be in charge has more than basic computer skills; at least some accounting understanding is desirable. The company owner or CEO also must understand how the reports are generated and how to read them, and how to interpret the information generated. In business, numbers are the score, and you want to know whether you are winning.

QuickBooks Premier Edition

At a higher cost, the basic QuickBooks program has a more sophisticated edition called Premier. A single user system costs about $500 and the multiple-user version about three times as much.

Beyond the basic functions already described in Basic and Pro, the analysis capability of the Premier program is quite sophisticated. You will be able to use your data to produce future performance trends, and even do comparisons with others in your industry.

This edition also provides you with the tools to create a Business Plan incorporating both the descriptive sections and the required financial spreadsheets. This is a valuable tool for your own planning, and it is often a necessary part of any loan package. At this level, the training of your internal bookkeeper needs to be at a higher level.

Industry Specific Versions of QuickBooks

There are vast differences between the financial concerns of a service business, a retail or wholesale distribution business, and a contractor. Questions of how complex, direct costs must be kept, inventory must be managed, or unallocated costs must be tracked, are all keys to successful financial management. Here is a short review of what you may be able to find in the QuickBooks Industry Specific Editions.

1. Contractor's Edition

Job costing is the premier add-on to this package. This function begins with the ability to estimate accurately and continues through the completion of the job. Whether it is the cost of materials, labor, or incidental materials, everything can be tracked by an individual job number so the company knows which jobs showed a profit and how close the company was to the estimated goal. Be sure to review and account for any unassigned expenses.

An updated job status report is available, which allows an overview of all open projects. The managerial benefit of this report is that personnel assignments can be made on a more effective basis, and materials can be ordered in a more timely fashion.

2. Manufacturing Edition (Wholesale Distribution)

One of the most critical issues for both manufacturers and wholesalers is inventory management. QuickBooks allows various reports of inventory by vendor or product type. In addition to tracking the quantity on hand, you can track what is on order and a history of the previous sales of the item. A just-in-time purchase system may be established to cut the cost of inventory. This is about a separate version of Quickbooks, not the general one.

The in-depth sales analysis allows any manufacturer or wholesaler to plan growth in profitable areas based on history by product, territories, sales reps, or customer types.

The job cost feature on this edition also has a Cost As Built feature that is valuable but needs good operator attention.

3. Professional Services Edition

Most professional service firms work on multiple projects at one time, and tracking the time involved in each project can be a challenge. This specialized version allows unbilled hour tracking by more than one person in any specific job. All outside expenses and sub-contractors can also be allocated to any specific project so that when it is time to bill, you have included all reimbursable costs. You can also track expenses that are not assigned to projects to verify or to re-track as general overhead expense. Some professionals, such as lawyers, require a higher level of time sheet tracking in order to submit bills.

4. Retail Edition

Closely tracking sales and profitability on a regular basis is a critical tool for any retail operation. Daily reports of sales allows for data that can be utilized to determine when special sales incentives should go into place. This edition also tracks sales tax collected and due; in most states, taxes must be paid on a monthly basis. You can generate reports that transfer directly to the tax returns so that the report can be created in-house.

As in most of the specialized editions, you can generate a comparison Profit and Loss Statement by dollars as well as by percentage.

Many of your sales reports will export easily into Excel graphs to give a visual display of your progress.

5. Nonprofit Edition

Nonprofit agencies have some unique accounting demands; these will not be covered in depth in this book. The concern of such agencies is not about profitability, but rather about tracking grants and budgets to meet the reporting requirements of founders and taxing authorities. This edition allows for that type of tracking.

QuickBooks Seminars Are Easy to Find

The Small Business Development Centers have more than 1,000 university- and college-based programs throughout the United States. Most of them offer QuickBooks classes on a regular basis, as do many community colleges. You can send your office manager to learn a higher level of skill; you may need to attend one of the seminars yourself in order to fully understand how your records are being kept. There are also trainers who will come into your office and run a class. Most business owners monitor the cash in the bank, the current level of sales, and little else. Changing your knowledge base is not an easy thing to accomplish, but it is necessary.

Peachtree Accounting Programs

Although it is not as widely used as QuickBooks, Peachtree (a division of Sage Software) provides a wide range of accounting programs that are just as easy to use and provide very valuable management data. In the opinion of many who work with businesses in the field, Peachtree is a more accounting-based program than QuickBooks is. This system can only be used on an accrual basis, and it has far more access to journal entries as well as the ability to track entries that have been made incorrectly and gone astray.

The ledger and sub-ledgers track well, and entries may be modified but not deleted. Perhaps one of the most valuable features of Peachtree is the ability to generate Crystal Reports that can be customized with specific charts, graphs, and logos. These visual representations are excellent for detailed analyses of a company. Sophisticated lenders like to see these types of reports because they can establish specific results and trends for a growing company.

Crystal Reports are a third-party software that can interface with your Peachtree Accounting system. The main design difference between QuickBooks and Peachtree is that one is a more proprietary system and the other is an open architecture. That is what it takes to be able to access many of the third-party add-ons.

Crystal reports can be as simple as merging your customer data onto a mailing list without first going to an Excel spreadsheet. But there are sophisticated usage and costs reports that can be designed for your specific company. Your Peachtree accounting system can expand in these valuable ways.

Peachtree Starts Out with a Basic System

Similar to the beginner versions of QuickBooks, Peachtree has a basic system called First Accounting. Very user-friendly, this program will also teach basic accounting instead of bookkeeping to its user.

From this start, there is a regular Peachtree Accounting package, Complete Accounting, and Premium Accounting. The last two will allow for multiple users. The pricing on all of these software packages are competitive, starting around the $100 range and going to the $1,000-plus range for multiple-user systems. Premium is a very powerful tool, allowing for department financials and a budgeting feature of up to three years. Crystal Reports are included in this version.

The Key to Understanding the Books

Keeping accurate books in a company should be a fairly simple task—as long as day-to-day attention is paid. Understanding the reports that are generated is a bit more complicated. If your company is expecting substantial growth or has multiple product lines and sources of income, your knowledge of accounting needs to start now. Peachtree may be the answer to this process. You can find an experienced consultant to install and help to set up report groups that you will need. Fairly accurate Cash Flow Projections can be automated. Creating the appropriate Crystal Reports will be very valuable for analysis as well as loan proposals.

Peachtree Premium Additions

As with QuickBooks, Peachtree has also issued industry specific editions. Most of them are parallel, with one major exception—there is a specific package for Manufacturing, and another one for Distribution. This allows for more powerful tools in each.

The advanced assembly tools in the Manufacturing edition are extremely useful for creating work tickets and excellent inventory tracking. Distribution has some advanced pricing features, as well as drop ship and back order information, which is very valuable to this specific type of business.

Peachtree is a powerful management tool in the hands of someone who will use its features. If you can work with an accounting firm that uses this program, you can grow a powerful operating system. You can link with ACT, which is one of the most popular contact management softwares in the market. There is also an entire series of Web enabling and Web based add-ons.

Multiple-User Systems

Both QuickBooks and Peachtree sell systems that they describe as multiple-user. In short, that means that you get a license for more than one computer to install and use the software. They all continue to operate off of a single server and multiple operators cannot be in the same module without conflict. If you are growing, you likely might be outgrowing the off-the-shelf software.

QuickBooks has an Enterprise Series that minimizes some of these conflicts. But, at an initial installation cost of $3,500, plus a good consultant to set it up, you are likely at a point that you need to look at other customized alternatives. The parent corporation of Peachtree (Sage Software) also has alternatives for when the time comes.

Garbage In, Garbage Out

One of my clients purchased a QuickBooks system and hired someone to install the program and input all of his data, some of which had been kept manually and some of which was in reports from his payroll service. The process took weeks, and even though the software had a reasonable cost, the consultant charged $20 per hour. By the time she was finished, she had put almost 100 hours into the task of getting the system up and running. My client kept out of her way while she was doing it. He was a contractor, and he was not interested in this area of business.

The first set of reports were done, and their inaccuracy was truly alarming. Sales had been double entered, a substantial number of payments were missing, and more. This was the often described *garbage in-garbage out phenomenon*. It had cost $2,500 to do, another $1,500 to undo, and I am not sure if the system was ever accurate. Buying accounting software and installing it is only one step in growing a well-managed business. Running the system carefully is very critical. This takes the attention of the business owner to monitor how the Chart of Accounts is being set up and how the data is being coded. The good news is that, once the system is up and running, these issues no longer are day-to-day concerns.

▶▶ TEST DRIVE

The choice of software is an important one; all of your company's records will be kept there and the reports will be generated for your analysis. Have you reviewed what you need? Ask yourself the following questions.

1. Is there someone already in-house who can use accounting software?
2. Do you require close scrutiny on inventory control?
3. Are you tracking and collecting all of the money that is owed to you?
4. Are you growing so rapidly that starting small with your software program may inhibit that growth?

2

Understanding the Reports That Are Generated

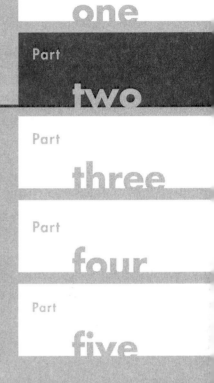

Your Monthly Income Statement

At the end of each month, your company should be able to generate a Profit and Loss Statement, also referred to as an Income Statement. If you are using any standard type of software to do your accounting, this will be as easy as the click of a mouse. You go under the heading of reports and choose the selection under company financials. There you will locate the report that can be designed for the month or year to date. You need to look at your own statements often and begin to understand what things look like when the company is doing well. And, if the company isn't doing well, you need to know where you need to make changes. Are your gross profits high enough, but your sales a bit soft? Or, are sales growing at a steady pace, yet your profits are shrinking? The general format of monthly statements is as follows.

> Gross sales
> > less returns
> > = net sales
> > less cost of goods (direct costs)
> > = gross profit
> > less general and administrative costs
> > = net (before tax) profit

Analyzing Sales Data

Here is where the Chart of Accounts creates the categories that are listed individually in your report. If you have not customized your Chart, you will see categories like the following:

- Revenue—sales
- Work in progress
- Interest income
- Shipping charges reimbursed
- Miscellaneous income (a category that should be used as little as possible)

This may tell you where the sales revenue comes from, but it will do little to inform you about where the *income* actually originated. Let's look at expanding this information with more specific categories. For example, if your business is a women's boutique, the Chart of Accounts might look like this:

4000 Sales—clothing
4100 Sales—shoes
4200 Sales—small leather goods
4300 Sales—purses
4400 Sales—jewelry
4500 Sales—accessories

The next step would be to develop a detailed sales breakdown by type of product or manufacturer, so that you know at a glance exactly what has been selling. Your new, more defined sales breakdown may look something like this:

4000 Sales—clothing, ABC design
4010 Sales—clothing, Ralph Lauren
4020 Sales—clothing, Tommy Hilfiger
4030 Sales—clothing, other manufacturers
4100 Sales—shoes, Nine West
4110 Sales—shoes, Enzo
4120 Sales—shoes, Joan and David
4130 Sales—shoes, other manufacturers

This detail will be carried all the way through your total sales categories. Each type of sale will have a subset number as well. You may want to be specific about any item that commands 5% or more of your total revenue. Find out where the majority of your revenue is coming from.

Adjusting for Discounts

Your sales categories will also provide for a line item to deduct discounts allowed. This may also be expanded into more detail so that you can determine which products typically sell for full price and which products need to be marked down to move the merchandise. To accomplish this, each category may carry a discount number. All types of businesses have some sort of discount or price adjustment to account for in their books. Make sure that yours reflects the specific information that you can use. Your future planning starts with a review of historic results; some areas may generate large gross revenue, yet have larger than normal set-offs as well.

Cost of Goods Sold

The category of Cost of Goods (COG) is where you account for what we have been referring to as the direct or variable costs. These are the actual costs of producing the product, purchasing materials for resale, or the labor and materials of doing a project. A simple, basic list may look like this:

- Materials or goods purchased
- Direct labor
- Union benefits
- Health insurance
- Subcontractors
- Freight incoming
- Purchase returns
- Discounts allowed

Knowing your cost of goods is a critical element of pricing and projecting the revenues you will require to break even. This number is directly related to each sale and goes up or down depending on revenue.

The Details Tell the Story

As in the expanded sales data, the amount of detail you include in your COG category will increase your insight into how well your company is operating. You need to be able to monitor any increase in these costs as soon as the trends begin. You can detail any one of the categories as follows:

5000   Goods purchased—clothing, designer
5010   Goods purchased—clothing, Ralph Lauren
5020   Goods purchased—clothing, Tommy Hilfiger
5030   Goods purchased—clothing, other

As you compare this to the sale category, you will see the link, and this will give you data on what your purchases are in comparison to your sales. When they are not in line, your inventory in those products is not turning well.

You can use the same strategy to define your labor as follows:

5100   Wages—warehouse employees
5110   Wages—delivery drivers
5120   Wages—shipping department

If you are involved in manufacturing, you can categorize each department. Or, if your business is in construction, each type of work (such as plumbing, electrical, painter, plasterer, etc.) can be listed individually. Make sure your detail is relevant, and the posting is done accurately. Comparing revenue to the direct cost required to generate that sale is the basis for cost analysis. And, if one department becomes less productive, here is where you will find the evidence. Personnel may have excuses, but numbers don't lie.

The Truth Is in the Percentages

What you are looking for, is how much (by percent) of your sales dollars you are spending to produce the product (or purchase it), and what percent of that same sale dollar you are spending to open the doors and keep them open. Your net sales dollars (gross revenue less any returns or allowances) will often be all the capital you have to spend. If you utilize more than 100% of it, you will be losing cash. This cannot go on very long. You want to be able to reduce each category to percentages because this gives you information to manage the company more effectively.

For example, if your net revenue is $100,000 and your direct costs (cost of goods sold) is $60,000, then you are spending 60% of each sale to produce or purchase your product. You will restate the labor and material and other costs in the same way, by percentage. This is how you begin to analyze your progress as you grow. Know what your costs are and how much you have left to operate the company.

Gross Profit Margins

Now you want to understand the margin, or difference you will have from every revenue dollar. This is the amount that you can use to pay operating expense. If, as in the previous example, your margin is 60%, as your sales expand you should retain 40% of all of your revenue to pay for operation. Sales of $100,000 bring you $40,000, and sales of $300,000 bring you $120,000. If you have set (or fixed) your operating expense at $80,000/year, your profits go up by 40% for every dollar you earn over $200,000. Your profit statement shows the following:

	Sales	200,000	
Less	Direct costs	120,000	(60%)
	Gross profit	80,000	(40%)
Less	Operating expense	80,000	
	Net before tax	0	

When the company grows to $300,000 in sales with the same gross profit margin, it looks like this:

	Sales	300,000	
Less	Direct costs	180,000	(60%)
	Gross profit	120,000	(40%)
Less	Operating expense	80,000	
	Net before tax	40,000	

Knowing your gross profit margin and keeping your percentages in check allows you to budget for profit. This assumes that you will control your overhead as you grow. Knowing the numbers will help you control them.

The Road to Profitability

Virtually all start-up businesses lose money in their initial phase, until the revenue grows enough to cover the overhead expense. The most important consideration in the early years is to maintain the gross profit margins you need to grow into profitability. The art of business is in providing something that customers will want or need. The science of business is in setting prices high enough to make those margins, and the fine art in business is to give customers sufficient value so that they are willing to pay your price.

Year-to-Year and Quarter-to-Quarter Comparisons

Many businesses are seasonal. If you are a landscape contractor, for example, your sales are up in the summer and down by late fall. Perhaps you are a printer, and your business is typically busy in the first part of the year and slows down toward the end. And there are always those who depend on holiday sales. For this reason, it may not be possible to see the trends in your own operation by comparing the results to the month before. What you need to do is make the comparisons to the same period the year before.

The most basic measure for any company is to use the results of the year before to describe the success of the current year. No doubt, it is important to see growth each year as you are building your business. But you also must look at other areas. Even if your sales growth is slowing, if your profit margins are growing, the trend is good. Raising margins and controlling costs are as important as growing revenues.

Are Your Direct Costs Stable as You Grow?

The cost of goods should remain at the same percentage of sales as the company goes forward. If this was 60% in year 2, it should be 60% in year 4. A percentage or two isn't a serious sign, but if costs are 3 to 4% higher, this is something to be checked. Your costs of material may be getting higher, and you need to pass them on to customers or find a lower cost source. Or, the productivity of your workforce may be going down and you need to motivate them, or employ better technology. Your job is to analyze where the problem areas are, and then to institute change when it is needed. Change is never easy, but it is the real measure of a leader.

Overhead (Indirect) Costs Should Be a Smaller Percentage

If you are controlling your overhead expenses, they should grow smaller, as a percentage, as your sales go up. Your rent remains the same (at least for the term of your lease), as will many of your other fixed costs. Insurance can be more difficult. In recent years, it has gone up annually. The real key here is managerial discipline. Set a budget for what you can spend and stick to it. If one cost goes up, check to see if you can make a cut somewhere else.

Compare with Industry Averages

There are statistics available within virtually every industry group about the typical profit margin and cost percentages as compared to sales. They are listed by business type, area of the country, and size of the company. You may be able to find them through your trade association or your local chamber of commerce. Look online for this type of information. The oldest and largest service that is available is RMA Associates.

Quarterly Comparisons

A month is often not a good snapshot of time in a business. An extra sale may be included to make the period look too good, or a third payroll in one month may show the expense as too high. So, looking at the same month from the previous year may not give you the best information.

Finding the Right Price

When I ran a manufacturing company, we produced leather safety gloves and clothing. Material costs were at least 30% of our total costs. Leather is a commodity, meaning that prices are reset frequently based on supply and demand (much like the current pricing of oil). Over the twenty years that I operated the company, I purchased leather as low as nineteen cents per square foot and as high as $1.15 per foot. With three square feet of leather in a pair of gloves, my direct material cost could be from sixty cents per pair to $3.45 per pair. This made pricing almost impossible, so we had to use cost averaging.

During a particularly volatile time, I found a workable solution. I set the cost at what had been the average over the year and, as material prices began to jump, I added a leather surcharge to every pair we made and sold. Customers were not thrilled by the price increases, but they were pleased that I was not making them permanent. We did reduce and eventually drop the surcharge completely, and we maintained our profit margins during a touchy time.

Better yet, you should look at the results of a quarter, which is a period long enough to smooth out any one-time-only events and give you some valid information about your progress. Again, compare the percentages of costs from period to period. Gross profit vs. gross profit as well as overhead line items from one quarterly period to the next should be compared. A small change may be easily corrected, but a large jump can seriously jeopardize the company's long-term success.

Little Things Add Up to Big Ones

The areas to watch sometimes are the ones that you know are necessary expenses and yet tend to pay little attention to, such as the telephone. Years ago, it was the control of long distance that had to be watched; these days, it is the cost of cell phones. As the technology refines and more capabilities are accessible, such as text messaging, the cost is increasing. Virtually everyone in the organization thinks they should be on the cell network, and the cost can double and triple to become a serious amount before you know it. Pay attention—is the cost that necessary, and are you still making the net profit you require?

Depreciation: A Non-Cash Item

One of the items that does not show up as a line item on your Profit and Loss Statement during the year is depreciation. For most companies, this is added at the end of the year by your accountant; it is included in your tax return as a tax deductible item. You will have depreciation on items ranging from the building you might own to automobiles. You'll encounter differing attitudes about the meaning of this deduction.

Business owners are usually happy that depreciation reduces their taxes. Bankers often write it up as non-cash and then adjust cash flow accordingly to support the loan they are making. Most people in business do not take the time to really consider that this deduction was established for a reason—to free cash flow to be put aside to replace items when they have worn out or to pay for repairs as they age. Think of your computers; they can become obsolete in just a few years and the value of used computers is virtually nothing. The really astute business owner will look at this item and consider saving and planning for replacements in advance. Don't allow old and nonproductive equipment to spell the end of your company.

Loan Principal: A Non-Expensed Item

If your company is paying back a big loan, you will not see the full monthly payment on your Profit and Loss Statement. What you will see is only the interest portion, listed under your Administrative Expense. The principal portion is booked directly off of the liability account and becomes a change in your Balance Sheet. In some companies, the total cost may be draining your cash flow while the business still appears to be operating profitably. If the dollars on your bottom line in profits is fewer dollars than your loan principal, this is likely what is happening.

A Sample Profit and Loss Statement

The following sample statement gives a good idea of the many elements that go into creating a Profit and Loss Statement. Your own statement will vary somewhat from this one, depending on what business you are in.

Kitchen Construction, Inc.
Profit and Loss Statement
January Through December 2005

	Jan - Dec 05	% of Income
Ordinary Income/Expense		
Income		
Revenues		
Additions	486,317.96	27.31%
Baths	97,285.50	5.46%
Countertop Remodel	5,080.00	0.29%
Discounts	5,010.86	0.28%
Kitchens	1,022,478.40	57.42%
Miscellaneous	164,682.43	9.25%
Total Revenues	1,780,855.15	100.0%
Total Income	1,780,855.15	100.0%
Cost of Goods Sold		
Cost of Goods Sold		
Direct Costs		
Direct Labor		
Direct Labor - Other	328,155.58	18.43%
Tax	37,041.79	2.08%
Total Direct Labor	365,182.79	20.51%
Material		
Sales Tax Paid	22,992.07	1.29%
Material - Other	735,991.18	41.33%
Total Material	758,983.25	42.62%
Subcontractors	84,829.68	4.76%
Direct Costs - Other	-17,914.65	-1.01%
Total Direct Costs	1,191,081.07	66.88%

	Jan - Dec 05	% of Income
Indirect Costs	1,646.65	0.09%
Total Cost of Goods Sold	1,192,727.72	66.98%
Total COGS	1,192,727.72	66.98%
Gross Profit	588,127.43	33.03%

Expense
  Administration
    Banking Services

	Jan - Dec 05	% of Income
Finance Charge (Finance Charge)	7,677.02	0.43%
Interest (Loan Interest Expense)		
Interest (Loan Interest Expense) - Other	97.50	0.001%
Total Interest (Loan Interest Expense)	97.50	0.01%
Line of Credit Interest	12,067.06	0.68%
VI/MC Fees	1,595.90	0.09%
Banking Services - Other	805.48	0.05%
Total Banking Services	22,242.96	1.25%
Insurance (Insurance)		
Liability & Auto Insurance (Liability Insurance)	16,062.00	0.9%
Workers Comp Insurance (Workman's Compensation)	27,427.00	1.54%
Total Insurance (Insurance)	43,489.00	2.44%
Miscellaneous (Miscellaneous)	-15.00	-0.0%
Occupancy Expense		
Rent Expense	15,119.15	0.85%
Showroom Displays	1,671.25	0.09%
Utilities (Utilities)	7,481.71	0.42%
Waste Removal (Dumpster)	3,270.00	0.18%

	Jan - Dec 05	% of Income
Occupancy Expense - Other	575.14	0.03%
Total Occupancy Expense	28,117.25	1.58%
Office Expense		
Cleaning	122.36	0.01%
Computer		
Computer Lease	1,996.69	0.11%
Software Lease	1,200.00	0.07%
Computer - Other	1,376.81	0.08%
Total Computer	4,573.50	0.26%
Equipment Maintenance	256.27	0.01%
Internet Service	913.78	0.05%
Postage (Postage and Delivery)	331.61	0.02%
Printing (Printing and Reproduction)	28.24	0.0%
Supplies (Office Supplies)	2,521.82	0.14%
Office Expense - Other	1,970.12	0.11%
Total Office Expense	10,717.70	0.6%
Office Payroll		
(Hourly & Salary Office Employ)		
Tax	23,187.37	1.3%
Office Payroll (Hourly & Salary Office Employ) - Other	179,634.38	10.09%
Total Office Payroll (Hourly & Salary Office Employ)	202,821.75	11.39%
Payroll Processing Fees	2,559.89	0.14%
Professional Fees (Professional Fees)		
Accounting (Accounting Fees)	6,850.00	0.39%
Consulting	11,843.99	0.67%
Legal Fees (Legal Fees)	2,859.75	0.16%

	Jan - Dec 05	% of Income
Professional Fees (Professional Fees) - Other	140.00	0.01%
Total Professional Fees (Professional Fees)	21,693.74	1.22%
Telephone (Telephone)		
Cell Phones	5,107.41	0.29%
Telephone (Telephone) - Other	6,037.39	0.34%
Total Telephone (Telephone)	11,144.80	0.63%
Administration - Other	151.99	0.01%
Total Administration	342,924.08	19.26%
Depreciation Expense (Depreciation Expense)	23,878.06	1.34%
Dues & Subscriptions	840.00	0.05%
Educational Expenses	219.00	0.01%
Gifts	243.38	0.01%
Reimbursements	-20.14	-0.0%
Sales & Design		
Advertising		
Web site	1,272.94	0.07%
Yellow Pages	638.25	0.04%
Advertising - Other	58,832.24	3.3%
Total Advertising	60,743.43	3.41%
Commissions	76,922.52	4.32%
Samples and Literature	1,605.17	0.09%
Travel & Ent (Travel and Entertainment)		
Meals (Meals)	4,809.81	0.27%
Travel & Ent) (Travel and Entertainment - Other	5,121.04	0.29%
Total Travel & Ent (Travel and Entertainment)	9,930.85	0.56%
Sales & Design - Other	55.40	0.0%

	Jan - Dec 05	% of Income
Total Sales & Design	149,257.37	8.38%
Taxes		
County/Twp/School	2,825.27	0.16%
Use Tax	17,736.29	1.0%
Taxes - Other	1.23	0.0%
Total Taxes	20,562.79	1.16%
Tools	854.26	0.05%
Vehicle Expense (Automobile Expense)		
Fuel	18,191.31	1.02%
Registration	465.00	0.03%
Repairs and Maintenance	8,327.00	0.47%
Vehicle Expense (Automobile Expense) - Other	7,324.23	0.41%
Total Vehicle Expense (Automobile Expense)	34,307.54	1.93%
Total Expense	573,066.34	32.18%
Net Ordinary Income	15,061.09	0.85%

▶▶ TEST DRIVE

Your Profit and Loss Statement contains a lot of valuable information; are you reviewing it closely enough? Ask yourself the following questions:

1. Do you know which category of sales is the most profitable?
2. Are your direct expenses remaining the same percentage as you grow?
3. Have you compared your current quarter to the same one from last year?
4. Are you preparing to replace equipment as it gets old and obsolete?
5. Is your banker working with you to keep loan payments reasonable?

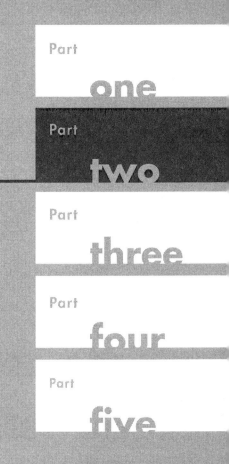

The Elements of a Balance Sheet

Second only to the Profit and Loss Statement as a barometer of the health of your business, is your Balance Sheet. This is a listing of your assets and liabilities, and the final number shows net equity of the company. The net equity is one of the factors of the company's ability to go forward into the future. When you are building worth, it is a good sign.

Typically, a Balance Sheet is arranged as follows:

Current Assets
    Cash and cash items
    Accounts receivable
    Notes payable—short-term
    Inventory
Fixed assets
    Land and buildings
    Machinery and equipment
    Autos and trucks
        Less depreciation (on all fixed assets)
    Long-term notes payable
        Total of all assets

Liabilities
    Current
        Accounts payable
        Payroll due
        Taxes payable
        Loans (current portion)
    Long-term
        Mortgage payable
        Loans payable—non-current portion
        Other long-term debt
        Retained earnings
            Total of all liabilities

Total assets less total liabilities = stockholder equity

Current and Long-Term Items

As you may remember, when we created the original Chart of Accounts we had one number for assets and another for liabilities. Within those categories, the first half of the numbers represented short-term items and the second half were listed as long term. The key element of the timing here is one year.

All assets that may be expected to convert to cash within twelve months are listed as current, and all liabilities that are due within the next twelve months are also referred to as current. The balance on both categories are considered long-term.

The theory behind this is simple: any account you do not collect, or any inventory you do not sell, within one year may not have all of the value that it once had (or maybe no value at all) and should not be considered liquid. A possible change of circumstance is considered for liabilities; those that are not due in the current year are not of serious concern as they very well may be restructured before they become due.

Things Can Change Rapidly

The circumstances (good or bad) of a company can change rapidly within a short period of time. A carefully developed start-up that is well managed may really take off and hit the revenue jackpot, and profits will be bountiful. An unattended, more mature company may hit a wall and get into serious cash flow problems. This is why you need to monitor current assets and liabilities, as they will tell you the story so that you can take quick actions if the circumstances call for it.

Fixed Assets

Fixed assets are items that are tangible and have long-term value. The ones that easily come to mind are land and buildings, furniture and fixtures, machinery and equipment, and automobiles and trucks. They are listed on your Balance Sheet (a general journal entry) with a beginning balance of what you paid for them, and the cost (debt) to pay for them is listed under short- or long-term liabilities. Each payment reduces the debt and, at the end of each year, the item is depreciated according to a fixed schedule set up by your accountant, estimating the life of the item. A 10-year life is expressed by a 10% annual deduction of worth.

Leasehold Improvements Are Fixed Assets

Regardless of whether you invested your own money to fix up your business location or your landlord did and is charging you for it over the term of the lease, this expense is listed under fixed assets. The theory is that, as you cannot remove what has been installed and it represents a long-term investment in your business, you receive value for it over a long period of time. This line item is also depreciated annually, as are all other fixed assets.

Long-Term Liabilities

The mortgage on your property is the most typical long-term liability you will have, although, for the purpose of accounting, you will list the non-current year's payment of all loans under the category of long term. A mortgage virtually never changes its terms, unless interest rates are going down and you are able to renegotiate the loan.

Most other business loans are for a multiple-year term with the exception of a line of credit, which normally must be paid down to zero once each year, so it is listed as a current item. On the typical term loan, the current twelve months payments are current and the balance of the debt is long term.

Where to Post Stockholder Notes

Often you will find an account number that is stored in most "box" software, listing Notes payable—stockholder under current liabilities. The theory behind this organization is that many business owners make temporary loans to their own companies. Perhaps the payroll needs to be covered, or an important vendor bill needs to be paid. The reality is, however, that money seldom gets paid back that quickly. But the stockholder controls when and if that will happen. On the other hand, if the company has any bank loans, it is very likely that these stockholder loans

Consider Replacement Costs

There are some fixed assets that are consumable, such as autos and computers. They last for three to four years and then must be replaced. The up-front cost of replacing is not usually that substantial. Car and truck down payments are small, and many computers are economical enough to almost be expensed rather than be depreciated. This tax benefit is meant to free up the cash to cover the cost of replacements, whenever they are needed.

The same cannot be said of actual production equipment, which may have a price tag in the six-figure range and may require a down payment in excess of what most companies have on hand. When one of my clients, a printing company, was forced to replace a big six-color press, the cost was in the five figures. They had not been able to put aside any excess cash over the previous years, and the $50,000 entry cost almost kept them out of the game. Not only was there a large down payment to be made, but the mechanical preparation and cost of installation was substantial. Preparing for situations like this one is the intended use of money not used to pay taxes.

All fixed assets will have a life cycle. Buildings, for example, may last a long time but they will require repair. A business owner hoping to be around for the long-term needs to prepare for making new investments. This is the reality of longevity. Don't take the benefit and consider it a gift.

will be subordinated to the bank, meaning that they cannot be paid back before the bank is paid. If this is your circumstance, it may, at times, be more accurate to put a loan from stockholders into the long-term liability category.

Short-Term Liquidity (Solvency)

Most business owners glance at their Balance Sheet occasionally, and many use a simple and often inaccurate test of liquidity. They check to see if the accounts receivable are larger than the payables—or, to put in another way, do you have more money due to you than you owe to others?

The more analytical determination of the solvency of a business (meaning, can it meet current obligations from cash flow of current assets) compares the value of all line items on the current asset side from all line items on the liability side.

You will total your cash, accounts receivable, inventory, and current notes due. Then compare them with the total of your accounts payable, taxes due, payroll owed, and current portions of loans due. This is assigned a ratio that is used often in banking decisions. Assets of $100,000 and liabilities of $50,000 gives you a liquidity ratio of 2 to 1—a good score. Some businesses that have higher fixed assets basis (like real estate investments) will have lower acceptable liquidity factors. You'll hear more about ratios later in this book.

Take a Serious Look at Your Balance Sheet

You need to do some further investigation of your line items to make a real meaningful analysis of your solvency. Cash is usually readily available, but it is not the same case with accounts receivable and inventory. All companies carry some customers who are seriously past due, with the hopes that they will be paid eventually. Is that realistic? Should you be writing off bad debts? Not all inventory is saleable for a variety of reasons—you know what is obsolete, so take this amount into consideration. Your own liquidity ratio may be lower than the numbers shown on your Balance Sheet. Whether you share this with lenders is your call, but don't hide from it yourself. This is management information, after all, and you are management.

Stockholder's Equity

The last line item of your Balance Sheet is called net worth or stockholders equity. This is the book value (your internal accounting records) of your company's tangible net worth. Each year, your earnings will be added to your Balance Sheet and they can grow the new net worth of the company, or if you have had losses, it will diminish the net value.

When determining the value of the business for a number of reasons, particularly in the case of a sale, you will want to look at a variety of methods in addition to the book value. But this is one of the major factors in a lender's decision.

Book Value vs. Real Value

There are many items that are carried in your books but may give a less-than-accurate view of the worth of the business. We've covered a few when discussing the solvency factor. You may have uncollected receivables or obsolete inventory that lowers the total value of your assets. Many companies write these down at the end of each year, but doing so also affects your Profit and Loss Statement. Bad debts are booked as a write down from sales, and inventory write-offs increase the overall material costs. So, making these adjustments will increase your overall losses.

There are other items that are actual increases to your net worth that are not covered by your Balance Sheet. Once you are an established company, you will be creating intangible assets such as a well-known business name, proprietary information, and (I hope) a well maintained customer list. These assets, known as goodwill, are valuable to another business if you go to sell, but they are not listed on your books.

And finally, your depreciation schedule is set up by general accounting standards mainly established to provide faster write-offs and more tax deferment. We all know that few buildings will have their value go to zero after they have been depreciated to that number. In fact, in the current real estate environment, chances are the property has increased in value. Your other hard assets such as machinery and equipment likely retain value past their book lives. If restating these values is important for any reason, hire a real estate appraiser or an industrial appraiser to get current values.

Review Year-to-Year Changes

Your Balance Sheet is a management tool and you need to use it to check the pulse of the company on a periodic basis. Don't just check the bottom line and see if your equity is growing. Verify on a quarterly or semiannually basis, whether the liquidity is still there. There are times of losses when long-term debts, those that must be paid down eventually, are decreasing, but short-term debt is getting higher as a replacement. You are paying loans instead of vendors or taxes. This can really threaten the solvency of the company. Collection actions could be forthcoming, from all of the short-term creditors you have been warding off.

Making Balance Sheet Improvements

There are some items you can shift internally that will help your Balance Sheet be balanced with your goals of growing a successful company. Look at any short-term liability you may owe to yourself either in the form of deferred income or short-term lending to the business. Are you willing to turn those investments into a more permanent or long-term financing? You can move balance from either one of those categories into Paid in Capital, which is equity. You can also agree that you will not redeem your loan for a period in excess of a year; in that case, it moves from current to long-term liability. The result is that your current ratios, or solvency, will improve and make the company far more attractive to any potential lender.

It is sometimes possible to make the same kind of adjustment with a vendor. Perhaps you owe them a lot of money in current invoices. They may be willing to work it out over a multi-year note, a negotiation that usually includes a personal guarantee and a promise to pay current invoices on a current basis. This will also move a liability from current to long term and improve the possible cash flow of the business.

Values Vary Greatly

A company can have a number of different values depending on the purpose for the valuation. At the point that a sale is being considered, having a professional valuation is a good idea. In the meantime, there are some issues to consider. A business in trouble has a distressed value—it is a pure asset sale. A business doing well can sell for a multiple of its earnings, which is far greater than the value of its assets. A business that is critical to another partner can have a substantial value above worth. If you keep growing and making reasonable profits, you will develop quite an asset.

Accounts Receivable and Accounts Payable Agings

These are bookkeeping documents that are not strictly accounting ones, but that are very important nevertheless. Easy to understand, these documents provide exactly what the names imply: listings of your accounts receivable and accounts payable by the age of each invoice that remains outstanding. The is a first step in determining when the money owed to you will come in, and strategizing what money you will need to pay out to vendors and how soon you will be able to do so.

An aging report (A/R or A/P) looks something like this:

	1–30	31–60	61–90	over 90	Total
ABC Co	1,000		1,000		2,000
Blue, Inc.	2,500	2,500		180	5,180
ZX Corp.		5,000		5,000	10,000
Joe's Store		500			500
XXY	1,000	1,000	1,000	500	3,500
Total	4,500	13,500	2,000	5,680	25,680

You can verify the accuracy by adding each column and making sure that it matches the final total listed. The final total should tie in with the number on the Balance Sheet. In this case, under assets there is a line item for accounts receivable. If this was your aging, that line should read $25,650. All numbers on the Balance Sheet tie in to numbers in the General Ledger.

The Aging Is a Tool

You need to review both your A/R and A/P report at least once a month. Have all of the details on all accounts that are overdue more than sixty days, and be sure to be involved in the collection of those accounts. Make sure the invoices were received, or that there aren't small matters holding up the payments. Sales aren't complete until payments are made, and your customer service skills are still in play here. Your effort may be the best collection tool you have.

Do not ignore the accounts payable. Just as you want to be paid, so do your vendors. If you're getting later in your payments, make a call and try to send a partial payment. When your suppliers know you are communicating and trying, they feel safer—just as you feel when your customers are communicating with you. Be proactive here, it will solidify your credit relationship.

A Sample Balance Sheet

The following Balance Sheet gives many examples of the categories you would consider adding to your own. Notice how it "balances" in that the total of the company assets equals the sum of its liabilities and equity.

Kitchen Construction, Inc.
Balance Sheet
December 31, 2005

	Dec 31, 2005
ASSETS	
Current Assets	
Checking/Savings	
Oak Tree Bank Checking	20,227.93
Customer Deposit act (business checking)	7,321.92
Total Checking and Savings	27,549.85
Accounts Receivable	
Accounts Receivable	221,970.04
Total Accounts Receivable	221,970.04
Total Current Assets	249,519.89
Fixed Assets	
Accumulated Depreciation	-209,916.00
Fixed Assets	
Computer costs	10,723.87
Showroom and Warehouse	
Improvements	31,293.20
Showroom and Warehouse	26,600.41
Total Showroom and Warehouse	57,893.61
Showroom Displays	124,983.22
Signs for Business	3,758.50
Vehicles	117,838.79

	Dec 31, 2005
Total Fixed Assets	315,197.99
Small Tools	19,528.00
Total Fixed Assets	
	124,809.99
Other Assets	
Note Receivable-Shareholders	149,637.76
Total Other Assets	149,637.76
TOTAL ASSETS	**523,967.64**
LIABILITIES & EQUITY	
Liabilities	
Current Liabilities	
Accounts Payable	279,923.80
Total Accounts Payable	279,923.80
Other Current Liabilities	
Customer Deposits (upfront deposits/unearned ret)	-10,090.59
Credit Line	169,000.00
Other Current Liability	
2002 Van	10,921.42
2003 Truck	19,798.04
2005 Truck	18,248.64
1997 Van	1,176.91
Other Current Liability - Other	-41.99
Total Other Current Liability	50,103.02
Sales Tax Payable	152.14
Use Tax Payable	2,588.80
Total Other Current Liabilities	211,753.37
Total Current Liabilities	491,677.17

	Dec 31, 2005
Total Liabilities	491,677.17
Equity	
Capital Stock	
Jane Smith-Equity	55,000.00
Capital Stock - Other	107,191.00
Total Capital Stock	162,191.00
Jane Smith	-20,746.33
Total Owner Draws	-20,746.33
Owner Equity	-57,071.11
Retained Earnings	-67,144.12
Net Income	15,061.09
Total Equity	32,290.47
TOTAL LIABILITIES & EQUITY	**523,967.64**

▶▶ TEST DRIVE

The Balance Sheet is the report card for your company. Can you determine (and understand) the important data found there? Try to answer questions such as:

1. Is your inventory a long-term asset?
2. How do you divide your bank loans into short-term as well as long-term liabilities?
3. What is the formula for determining liquidity?
4. Is the book value of your company a true determiner of its worth?
5. How can you build more equity in your business?

The Meaning and Importance of Cash Flow

Understanding the meaning of cash flow and how it is likely to occur in your company is a powerful knowledge. You can plan in advance, handle a cash crunch, or schedule expenses when you know the money is available. A Cash Flow Statement is formatted as follows:

Starting Cash
Plus collections (cash sales or loan proceeds)
Equals Total Available Cash

Less Direct Expense (labor, materials, etc.)
Operating Expense
Debt Service (principal and interest)

Balance is the ending cash, which becomes the starting cash for the next period. Cash Flow Statements are typically done on a month-by-month basis for a period of up to three years.

Understanding the Timing of Cash

While many businesses can predict sales revenue based on the time of year and current customer activity, determining when cash is coming in is a bit more difficult to predict unless all of your sales are in cash, which is not likely these days. Even credit card sales have a lag time in payment from thirty-six to seventy-two hours depending on your providers. Checks may be available as cash depending on the policy of your bank, when they are deposited if they are local, or if they are from out of town. You may set up an Electronic Fund Transfer System to speed the flow of cash. A credit sale presents even more of a challenge.

You start the process by setting your own terms on all credit sales. While many companies use a net 30 day basis, some will offer a discount for early pay, such as 2% for 10 days. This should be negotiated on a client-by-client basis. You want to determine how your customers typically pay their bills. After all, you will be counting on sales in one month to turn into cash the next. This is a good use of Receivable Turnover Ratio (discussed in Chapter 10), which is a predictor of incoming cash.

Credit and Collections

Regardless of the size of your company, good credit policies will increase your cash flow. Start out by knowing who your customers are and verifying any information they provide. Step two is to make sure you have valid purchase orders or agreements. Keep all the relevant paperwork and make efforts to collect anything that remains unpaid beyond the due date. An aggressive policy pays off in greater available cash.

Loans and Sales of Assets Are Cash Flow

Cash flow means exactly what it implies. It represents the available capital (cash) that flows through the company's accounts and is available for you to pay bills, purchase equipment, or payout dividends to owners. The primary source of cash for an ongoing company is from their sales, but a new business may be funding itself with loans. An older, less vibrant enterprise may resort to the sale of assets. Any of these proceeds will be recorded in a Cash Flow Statement as available capital.

Depreciation Is a Non-Cash Item

While this item appears on your Profit and Loss Statement, it does not appear on a Cash Flow Statement. That is the meaning of a non-cash item; it has profit and loss consequence, but does not lower your current capital. The impact may mean lower profits and lower asset values, but the effect frees up cash.

Keeping Your Business Afloat

In the view of most business owners, cash flow is the single most important issue to solving day-to-day problems. If payrolls are made easily, vendors are fairly satisfied with their payments, and cash is left to handle a repair or an emergency, then the company runs smoothly. A company making profits without cash flow is a hard one to run. A company may be losing money while, for a variety of reasons, cash continues to flow. The continual erosion of profits will still eventually shut the company down. It is the cash flow that has kept many airlines flying years after they are technically insolvent.

The Difference Between Cash Flow and Profits

Profit is the money you have earned from operating your company over a particular period of time. This is merely a financial calculation, and you may not see the actual cash from that profit for some time. You can be operating with positive cash and negative profits. This most often occurs with contractors when they get advance deposits, so they may operate for years on tomorrow's cash. The airlines can do it, as your money for a ticket is paid in advance. What follows is an example of how a contractor lost profit and maintained cash flow.

ABC Contracting	P&L
Sales Income	100,000
Less Labor and Material	73,000
Gross Profit from Operation	27,000
Less Overhead of Rent, Advertising, Office Expenses, Owner's Wages, etc.	36,000
Profit (loss) Before Tax	(-9,000)

Now look at the cash flow:

Beginning Cash	17,000
Plus revenue from Operations	37,000
Plus Deposit on New Jobs	68,000
Draw from Line of Credit	10,000
Total Available Cash	122,000

The fact is that a company losing $9,000 from operations can still have an extra $22,000 in cash during the same period. In this specific case, customers who represent future business have paid deposits, and a line of credit has been drawn on. At the time the line is drawn out and new business slows down, this company will be feeling the full effect of its operating losses. And quite a few customers will be left with half-completed jobs.

How to Avoid Falling Behind

After a three-decade-long career as a business owner and full-time consultant, I am convinced that there are many companies, primarily contractors, who are doing what I just described—running on fumes. They know it, and they even understand how this will eventually bring down the entire business. The line of credit that has been drawn on—not to fund ongoing work as it is meant to do, but to pay old bills—will have to be paid back, and net profit is the only way to retire debt. Any advance payments from customers are funds from which there has been no costs expensed, so when the jobs have to be started (and even more so, when they must be completed) there will be no cash or credit available to pay for supplies or labor. This is often the beginning of the end for businesses such as contractors. The day of reckoning comes when vendors' debts (and impatience) grows. When there is little remaining cash to spread around, the house of cards starts to fall. One way to prevent this is to segregate the deposit payments in a separate account and learn how to post this as a liability (customer's deposit) instead of an asset on your Balance Sheet—that is, do not treat this cash as a typical bank deposit based on revenue. It is revenue unearned.

Growth May Cause a Cash Strain

A company that is making profits, yet on a growing curve, will often find itself short of capital. Each month that has higher sales than the one before will have higher expenses as well. Material costs will increase, and more labor will be required, and this work isn't being paid for until at least thirty days after the work is complete.

This is the perfect situation for using a line of credit. A bank line of credit is meant to be used to smooth out the timing of business cash flow. A growth company with a profitable operation is the best candidate for this short-term financing instrument. As sales rise and cash is required to fund suppliers and employees, the business owner draws on her line of credit. As the expected cash comes in, the line of credit is paid down. This is the meaning of short-term—less than one year. Another version of a line of credit is *contract financing*, which is meant to fund one specific long-term contract.

The Cash Flow of a Growth Company

	January	February	March	April
Sales	100,000	130,000	150,000	100,000
Cost of Goods	60,000	78,000	90,000	96,000
Gross Profit	40,000	52,000	60,000	64,000
Less Overhead	42,000	42,000	42,000	42,000
Net Before Tax	-2,000	10,000	18,000	22,000
Beginning Cash	6,000	-11,000	-41,000	-48,000
And Receipts	85,000	90,000	125,000	138,000
	91,000	79,000	84,000	90,000
Less Direct Exp	60,000	78,000	90,000	96,000
Less Overhead Exp	42,000	42,000	42,000	42,000
Ending Cash	-11,000	-41,000	-48,000	-48,000

Remember, the depreciation is included in the profit and loss, but not in the cash flow. Loan principals are included in the cash flow, but not in a Profit and Loss Statement.

Managing Cash Flow

You will find that even in an average scenario, when you are making profits, cash flow management can be a problem. The amount of working capital the business raises from the beginning will be an issue for years to come. Few companies are able to begin with an adequate capital base, and unless there are years of profits that are actually retained rather than distributed, cash flow will remain an erratic force. Attention will always be required to its close management—that means keeping a watch on expenses and preparing for important payments so they are made in a timely fashion.

Growth Requires Capital

You will note that when the revenue grows along with the profits, cash can still become nonexistent. If the growth is funded by vendor debt, this may work for a while, but it will eventually become a problem. Vendors need their own cash flow. But, if the company has an asset base and some history of profitable business, this is the time to secure bank financing to get to the optimal business level.

The best lending program here would be a combination of a sufficient long-term loan with a line of credit. You take the long-term portion and pay down existing bills and use the line to fund the cost of your new sales. A reasonable business plan accompanied by believable pro-forma cash flow statements to substantiate your ability to manage debt service should be successful here. You should show how the company will grow and continue to have sufficient cash flow to retire debt.

A Sample Cash Flow Statement

Here's an example of a typical cash flow statement.

Kitchen Construction, Inc.
Statement of Cash Flows
January through December 2005

	Jan–Dec 2005
OPERATING ACTIVITIES	
Net Income	15,061.09
Adjustments to Reconcile Net Income	
to Net Cash Provided by Operations:	
Accounts Receivable	-160,047.04
Work in Progress	41,804.00
Accounts Payable	171,213.44
Customer Deposits	-60,621.90
Other Current Liability: 2002 Van	-4,775.06
Other Current Liability: 2003 Truck	-7,025.04
Other Current Liability: 2005 Truck	18,248.64

Sales Tax Payable	67.69
Use Tax Payable	416.84
Net cash provided by Operating Activities	14,342.66
INVESTING ACTIVITIES	
Accumulated Depreciation	23,878.06
Fixed Assets: Showroom and Warehouse	-21,403.70
Fixed Assets: Showroom Displays	-1,283.00
Fixed Assets: Vehicles	-21,559.29
Note Receivable-Shareholders	-500.00
Net Cash Provided by Investing Activities	-20,867.93
FINANCING ACTIVITIES	
Opening Bal Equity	0.00
Owner Draws	11,627.35
Owners Equity	-39,238.34
Net Cash Provided by Financing Activities	-27,610.99
Net Cash Increase for Period	-34,136.26
Cash at Beginning of Period	54,947.79
Cash at End of Period	**20,811.53**

Pro-Formas Are Predictions

There are a number of reasons that you will require a pro-forma statement—these are Profit and Loss and Cash Flow Statements that are projections for future performance. These should be part of your original business plan, as well as be included in virtually all loan applications. You will need to convince lenders or investors that the business strategy you have is a profitable one and will provide sufficient cash flow to manage your debt service. Lenders are concerned with the loan payment two years from now, not just today.

Typically, you will use spreadsheet software such as Excel to do this, although many higher-level box packages (QuickBooks and Peachtree) have these capabilities as well. What is critical here is the data you put in—do not just engage the mathematical calculations that are possible and let your computer make all of the predictions. This may look good, but it isn't likely to happen in reality. If there are seasonal issues, or a contract running out, include them .

Start on a Month-by-Month Basis

The first year is best done on a month-by-month basis. You can be expected to have enough market and cost data that the numbers you put in as sales and costs four months from now should be accurate. After one year, however, this ability to predict gets a bit less scientific, and so, in the out years, you can change it to quarterly projections. This works best when a company is not in the rapid growth mode, but in a time of slower growth. Rapid growth projections must have substantial backup explanation.

Start-ups Are Often Optimistic

No one goes into business unless he expects some level of success. The first measure of this is in your sales: how many people want to buy what you are selling? This is a challenge for a new company, and the predictions often fall on the high side. Sales seldom reach the levels desired when a business just starts out. The best technique to use is to predict the sales you would like and divide that number by three. Then use that new calculation as a base to insert all other numbers for expenses and profits. Better to be pleasantly surprised than to run out of cash. The lower number will likely be closer to reality—it takes time for your customers to find you and make you into a regular vendor.

The Pro-Forma Begins with a Profit and Loss

The first part of a pro-forma statement is a prediction of sales, expenses, and profits. You will need an accurate sales number because it will reflect how much cash will be available.

Next, both your direct expense (which is based on your sales) and your fixed overhead will be recorded, and you will determine what your projected profits will be.

Your cash flow pro-forma statement will be based on the profit and loss predictions you made. The elements of the pro-forma are:

	Beginning Cash	(you will start with a current number)
+	Receipts	(cash actually collected from previous sales)
+	Loan Proceeds	(These events may occur during the
+	Sale of Assets	term you are predicting)
=	Total Available Cash	
Less	Direct Expense	(no depreciation)
	Overhead Expense	
	Debt Service	(break this out to a separate category)
=	Total Ending Cash	(which becomes starting cash)

When you are creating pro-formas beyond one year, any footnotes you can add to substantiate a number is valuable. For example, a large event you will be supplying in fourteen months should increase sales. The need to replace a piece of equipment in eighteen months needs to be included as expenses, and the cash set aside for it. The more detailed you get, the more the reader will believe that you know your stuff.

Trying Out New Scenarios

The pro-forma statement is really an element of a strategic plan meant initially to plan for cash needs. But there are other uses for it as well. As you are researching to plug operating numbers in the out years, you will become more aware of some events that you still have time to change. Perhaps you have seen regular increases in your insurance and, if it continues on the pace it's going, this will be a back-breaking expense to cover two years from now. Now is the time to look at different coverages, and, if you haven't done so, start to share some of the cost burden with employees. Most larger companies do, and you cannot shoulder the entire burden.

What if you have a large sales contract that will run out in the next two years? Project what will happen if those sales are no longer yours. Your direct expense will go down, but have you allowed overhead to get so high that you are likely to be buried in it? Of course, you will be pursuing other sales, but it won't hurt to tighten the belt in case your sales drop.

Your pro-forma statement is not a fixed document. You will most likely design it on a spreadsheet program that will allow you to make many changes and run the numbers again to see what effect they will have. Take advantage—plug in higher sales and see where that takes your profit. Cut a single overhead line item and check out that effect. Before you decide to move to a better location, determine the effect of higher rent. This is called a *cost-benefit analysis*.

Plan two or three changes—you can make minor adjustments in several areas and see what the cumulative effect will be. Slightly higher sales, a two percent lower direct cost, and less overhead in one or two areas turns an average performer into a star.

▶▶ **TEST DRIVE**

The strategic planning of your company can be tried out in your pro-forma. Are you using one to its best advantage? Ask yourself the following questions:

1. Do you understand the format of a Cash Flow Statement vs. a Profit and Loss Statement?
2. Do you plan on the cost of principal payments even though they are not an expensed item?
3. Have you used a pro-forma cash flow to show how much debt service the company can retire easily?
4. Do you try changing management cost theories on a spreadsheet to see what happens?

Part

one

Part

two

Part

three

Part

four

Part

five

Covering Overhead Expense

Even before there was an accounting theory to describe the concept of "break even," there was a term to describe the circumstance. It was historically referred to as "making your nut," although few people know where this expression comes from. During the Wild West days of the old medicine shows, when the horses and wagons pulled into town to sell their potions and elixirs, the sheriff would remove the large wooden nut holding the wheel onto the wagon. This necessary piece of hardware would not be returned until the businessman running the show had paid all of the local tradesmen for food, lodging, and supplies. Only then was the nut and bolt put back in his wheel and his wagon was ready to go. This process may not have had a fancy accounting term, but it sure made the point. Not to break even means you are at risk.

For any business to progress, it must have sufficient profits from the sale of its goods or services in order to pay for the overhead of the business, to keep up with the ongoing debt service, and to make profit for the owner. In the early stages of business, this is a revenue growth-driven number. The direct cost increases with more sales volume and the fixed overhead stays the same, yet drops as a percentage of overall sales. You must get to a sufficient volume of revenue at an adequate profit margin so that you can easily cover your overhead expense. The bottom line will continue to grow at the rate of your gross profit margin if you hold your overhead even. For example, if you make thirty cents on each sale dollar, each $1,000 of sales over break even moves $300 to the profit column.

Overhead Is a Key Element

The break-even point requires the volume to grow high enough at the current gross profit to pay all overhead expense. This means that if your gross profit margin is 30% and your overhead is $100,000, your sales must be over $350,000 so that the operating profits are in excess of the $100,000 needed. Producing more than that level of sales at that margin is the key to moving into the profit zone. This is a number you should know from the start of operations.

Try Reverse Engineering

If you are a new business and are in the process of setting up operations, begin by determining how much operating profit you will generate. What percent of your sales are you spending as direct costs? Second, you will establish an operating budget—meaning how much it will cost you to keep the doors open and the company running. Keep that number within the operating profit (sales less direct costs) of year two's revenues and you will be in line with most new companies. Don't build fixed costs in excess of projected early sales.

Digging Out

It is easier not to fall into a hole than to try and dig out of one. One of my clients in the restaurant business was wooed into a new development with a terrific new concept for our city, a "town mall" shopping area. The problem was that his fixed overhead was far too high from day one. Rent was steep and the leasehold loan he was paying back was exceptionally high, even if the décor was spectacular. In the first two years of operation, he only went over his break-even point one month, and the constant losses used up all of his energy and all of his working capital. Great restaurant, but a bad plan, and not much of a future. The mall filled in after two years, but he is only now at break even and not able to pay back the loans he needed to cover early losses.

New Businesses Seldom Break Even

The early days of any start-up are usually at a loss, because a business must grow to reach its break-even point. Few companies start out with great sales, even when the idea and launch is good, but all start out with costs. For the purpose of a model break even, let's assume your fixed expenses look as follows:

Administrative Salaries	1,500
Rent	1,200
Utilities	400
Insurance	1,000

Taxes	400
Telephone	600
Auto Expense	800
Supplies	200
Sales and Marketing	1,200
Interest	250
Miscellaneous	300
Total	7,850

Remember, this is without any draw or salary for the officer (you). If your gross profit margin is 35%, then you have to gross $24,000 each month, or $288,000 in a year, to cover this "nut." That's not easy to do from a dead start. Then, you must also factor in your wages and assume you must sell three dollars of goods for every dollar you need to cover costs as well as draws. Determine when you will reach this point, and if you will have enough cash to get there. This is your equity capital; it will not be returned until you are operating at a profit.

Creating a Break-Even Budget

The goal of a business is to make a profit. This is the positive cash flow that provides a cushion and provides for the capital to continue to grow the company, or to perhaps make changes when they are needed. For a start-up or early stage operation, the goal is to arrive at the break-even point and then to stay there, and hopefully exceed your own projections. As we have seen from the pro-forma cash projections, funding growth is difficult when you are profitable, and it is almost impossible before you get there. The only way to fuel the business activity is through equity capital, not debt. Equity capital is an investment paid back when, and if, there are profits. Debt capital is loan money that must be paid back, out of cash flow, within the terms of the loan. Payments usually start immediately and the interest payment cost raises the break-even target, and principal payments uses up any cash. It's something of a counterproductive event.

To create the budget that will get you to break even, begin with the estimate of sales and gross profits you expect to be at by the end of the budget period. Then set your budget for realistic overhead expense based on that period and that goal of breaking even. You know in advance that all of the months leading up will be operated on a loss. As long as you can project when you will cross the profit line, you can create a long-term plan for success.

Fund Early Losses Sensibly

If you have done your start-up budget prior to securing your capital, you will know exactly how much equity capital you will need. Can you fund it with your own savings? How about sweat equity (work without taking a paycheck)? Another non-cash source might be barter—trading your product for one you need. A riskier source is money from family, and an undesirable one is cash draws from credit cards. The higher your credit card balances, particularly at a time when your income is low, the lower your credit score will go and the less likely your company will be to get permanent financing. Banks rely heavily on the credit score of the owner to make loan decisions, and a low score may be caused by the amount of total debt rather than by payment history.

Growth Begins to Cover the Break Even

In a business with rapid growth, the break-even point is reached quickly and quite often, painlessly. The assumption here is that the growth has a reasonable profit margin. It may be easy to see an explosion in revenue if your price is too low. Some new companies who launch a brand new concept in a product or service will see a healthy period of growth. Starbucks was an early example of this, and the Geek Squad is a current one. You may have started a business to meet an unfulfilled demand, and your increase in sales is surprising even to you. This is a terrific situation, but remember to temper it with a bit of caution as well.

Most companies should have some idea of where their set point is— what level of sales they can maintain given their existing infrastructure and resources (both financial and human). Once you get to that level, care must be given that the overhead doesn't begin to grow without any

Even today, with all of the classes on finance for small business, the theory of break even is seldom taught or stressed. I did not understand the break-even theory for at least the first ten years that I operated my own manufacturing company. I took over the company at a good time, when sales were growing, and I managed a lower overhead than my father had. My own salary was lower, and we had several fewer cars along with lower insurance. I did not entertain nearly as much. We were quite profitable.

Then I ran into the double whammy. I allowed overhead costs to grow by paying little attention to areas such as office expense and travel, something I had begun as a learning tool and continued to maintain customer relationships. We came to a time when sales were dropping because the industry we served was going through a cyclical contraction. We fell below the break even and lost money for over a year before someone (an accountant, but not ours) sat me down and taught me what I needed to know.

Costs were tightened and many were cut out completely. We made extensive additional sales efforts, as I realized that we could not just wait for our business to come back. We even developed some higher profit items to produce and to sell. I learned how to increase the gross margins, which lowers the break-even point. I was able to make the save, but I was running out of time when I did. It was a painful lesson.

controls. People who contributed to the success, including you, want to have a chance to enjoy the fruits of their labor. They have waited patiently and worked hard for this moment.

Before you know it, small cars are traded in for SUVs, salaries are raised, and insurance coverage becomes more comprehensive. Perks are given to everyone who worked hard to get to this point, and all of a sudden, you are losing money, not making it. The break-even level has just risen to cover the costs that were assumed.

Higher Prices and Cost Controls Have an Effect

Perhaps the break-even number at your business is one million dollars a year and, at this moment, your sales are at $850,000. All of your efforts go toward getting that extra growth. That will work, but so will another, more balanced approach. If you can raise prices just a few percentages, cut costs across the board just a few percentages, and also grow sales (it will take less than you think), you will change that set point.

As someone running a business, you can get fixed on a sales number when you think of your direct costs as an absolute, and of overhead as at its best control. That is seldom the case. Try a multiple approach; it is easier to achieve.

Suppose your loss is $25,000, and your gross profit is 25%. The pure mathematical calculation is that you need another $100,000 in sales to neutralize that loss. Depending on what you sell, that may be a tall order. What if you raised prices by 2%, worked on a 2% increase in sales, and a 2% decrease in costs? All of those numbers fall into a doable range and, depending on your gross revenue when you started, this may be enough. Determine what your own overall strategy would have to be, and don't just dump the responsibility into the sales category.

▶▶ TEST DRIVE

If you don't get to break even, you don't get to profit. This is a number you must understand. How familiar are you with it?

1. Do you understand your direct expense and how it generates operating profit?
2. Have your gross profits been stable at the same percentage?
3. Do you know what sales volume you require to break even?
4. Can you make several small changes to affect your break even?

3

Strategic
Planning by the
Numbers

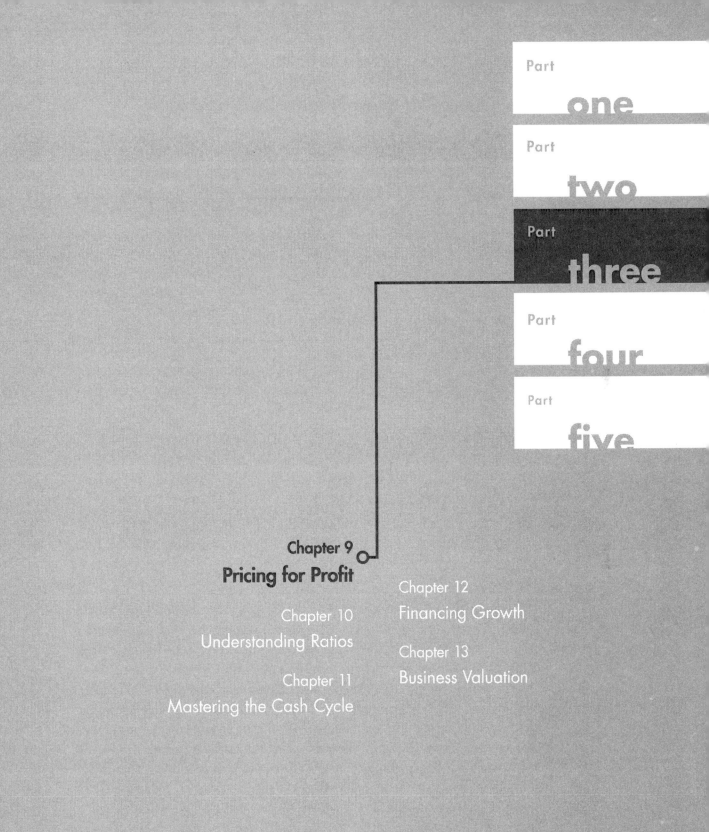

The Theory of Supply and Demand

A number of different elements are involved in creating and sustaining a profitable business. One of the most important is setting prices that will generate adequate volume and still provide healthy profits.

There are two considerations when pricing your product or service. The first, and most important, is knowing what the real costs are. The second consideration is your awareness of current market competition. If you price substantially higher than your competition, you will have trouble attracting new customers. But, on the other hand, it never makes sense to leave money on the table by pricing below what the market is willing to pay.

Over the past few years, we as customers have had a lesson in how the theory of supply and demand works in practice. The major teacher has been in the price of oil (although there is a political component to this as well as a market one). When the suppliers hold back supply, the price of oil goes up. When demand rises—whether it's due to the time of year or the growing economy of China or other factors—the price goes up. If the world economy is slumping and demand for oil goes down, so, too, does the price of a barrel of oil.

There is one theory that speculates that prices can get high enough to dampen demand, resulting in the leveling or lowering of prices. This has happened in many commodities, although in recent times oil has not quite responded in this way. For the purposes of most businesses, there is a general trend in the area of supply and demand.

Starting a business in a field where the demand is growing will allow you to set prices at a healthy level. As other players get into the game and choices expand, you will find pricing pressures. This will force pricing down. When a new product becomes a commodity, prices drop.

The recent experience of the airline industry is another good example. In markets like the Far East and the Caribbean where demand is growing, low prices are less frequent. Short hauls and point-to-point flights in the United States have become little more than a commodity with low-cost, low-fare airlines controlling the market. As your own industry matures, you may experience the same trend.

Niche Products/Services Produce Higher Margins

Niche products are those products that fill a fairly small but fairly defined market. Those products can include manufactured products still in use but no longer made by a larger company, vegetarian restaurants, specialty clothing stores, or pet-sitting services. Wherever there is some demand, a business can grow. If the total market is small, you are not likely to have a large number of competitors, and pricing pressure should not be great.

Inventing a Better Mousetrap

One of my clients worked for a fairly large manufacturing company. Among their products was a flexible hinge that was an integral part of a larger piece of equipment. The company closed its Pennsylvania operation and moved the production to Texas. My client and his partner worked on improving the design and materials on the hinge and started their own company. This product is a pure niche play, one with fewer suppliers and a new, eager market-driven one on board. They have made substantial inroads in less than four years. Their gross profit margins are healthy and, while they are not likely to grow to be a large company, they have proven to be very profitable.

Added Value for Added Price

The most efficient way to justify above-average pricing is to differentiate your company from the competition by adding something to your product or service that makes it stand out. Examples include: a clothing store offering free alterations (especially for women); a food store with online shopping and home delivery; a furniture store with decorator service; or an auto repair service with evening and weekend hours. These are all examples of special value-added extras that will support premium prices. Busy consumers are looking for ways to make their lives easier. These days, even banks and post offices are expanding their hours.

Before setting your prices on the low end of the range, look around and see how you can enhance your existing offerings to come in at a higher level. Your business will be easier to run from the very first day.

Many Online Stores Are Profitable

The perceived value of online shopping is that it is faster and easier than shopping in a store. A few clicks of the mouse and your product is on its way. Although the prices seem reasonable, when you realize that the company you are buying from has very little overhead costs—no rent and few employees—their margins are very healthy. Everyone wins here. The story of eBay's success is one of the major business events of our times. Buyers and sellers set the price. Your company can get into this type of play as well. Be different, and then charge a premium for it.

Account for All of Your Costs

As a business owner, you absolutely must know all of the direct costs that are involved in creating or selling your product, including the materials, labor, and incoming freight. If you are providing a service, know what direct elements go into that service. Selling anything below the actual cost of production is the kiss of death for a smaller company. Your gross margins are set to take you to the break-even point where you make a profit. Lower your margins, and the more you sell, the more you will lose. Raise your prices and you lower that point. A higher price generates a higher gross profit margin, which lowers the break-even number.

Do Not Forget Your Hidden Costs

The less-obvious cost in most businesses, but one that must always be taken into consideration, is the cost of "shrinkage." Shrinkage is the amount of product that goes unsold or unused. Virtually every business has this cost—a commercial printer spoils paper or has some left over; a restaurant has spoiled food or some food just disappears; industrial suppliers have returned products that can't be resold; and retailers have product that just won't sell. You will not see enough shrinkage in the first days of business to know how extensive the shrinkage will be, but you can eventually determine how much of a problem it is in your operation. Account for this expenditure in your direct expense.

Set Goals for Gross Profit Margins

Once you know exactly what it costs to purchase, produce, or provide the product or service of your company, you can calculate the mark-up that will give you the gross margin you need for profit. If you are a start-up, you will need to rely on the pro-formas you did as a part of your business plan. If you have been in business for a while, you will already have some track record of your overhead expense. There are some costs that are not included, such as the normal start-up fees such as printing, initial marketing, and any on-site preparation. These are classified as *non-recurring costs*.

How to Establish Mark-Ups

Determine what your ongoing overhead costs will be for the year and what level of sales you expect to achieve. For example, if you are expecting sales of $600,000 and you have fixed costs of $300,000, your products will have to be marked up 100% so that your profit is 50%. Your anticipated sales of $600,000 will give you a gross profit of $300,000. Remember to factor shrinkage into your pricing. Get to break even and the next step is profitability. Growing revenue and holding expenses steady is the winning formula.

Volume Is the Key—Be Realistic

If you set a gross margin that requires an unrealistically high sales volume, you will not meet your goals. It is most likely you will run out of money before you get to that level of revenue. Always remember that capital lost as a company grows is hard to replace. The longer it takes to get to break even, the less likely you will be able to sustain the effort. This is the principal reason that some businesses close in the first few years. Keep your initial overhead in check so that the gross profits you need to break even are at an attainable level. You will sell more if the customers believe they are getting a good deal for their money.

Understanding Competitive Pricing

There are some businesses that allow for little or no pricing decisions by the owner. A franchise operation where product line and pricing are established by the franchisor fall into this category. In the case of retail operations that sell branded merchandise, the customer already has a good idea of the price point. On the other hand, there are a variety of businesses that require different pricing strategies. Here are some strategies franchises need to think about:

- Is your product a commodity sold in high volume?
- Are there many other businesses in your area doing the same work?
- Are your hours convenient for the customers?
- Do you customize your product in any way that makes it distinctive?
- Do you offer free delivery or a liberal return policy?
- How do you compare in terms of quality and service to your competition?

Remember why you are trying to determine where your company fits in the general marketplace. There is a reason one beauty salon charges $60 for a haircut, while a nearby salon charges $40. Creating the perception of high value will offer you the opportunity to charge more and still attract loyal customers. Know what your possibilities are before you open the doors of your business.

Creating Volume with Price Cuts . . . A Good Idea?

This is a far riskier strategy for a small or medium-sized company than it is for a larger one. First, as a small business, it is unlikely you will be able to handle major volume, and the reality is that you will need to have a substantial increase in sales to make any money. It is very easy to fall

For the Service Provider or Consultant

Inside Track

When I first started my consulting career, I had no idea what to charge my new clients. I surveyed other consultants working with smaller businesses and found the hourly rates ranged from $35/hour to $200/hour. There seemed to be very little substantive reason for the pricing, as the services were not that different. I knew, from my own research, that I would likely average 25 billable hours per week. I needed to divide that by my desired weekly (or monthly) income to get to where I wanted to be. But then my workload increased to be more than I could handle. At that point, I put into place another costing strategy I had learned. Heavy demand signifies market acceptance and usually means you are charging too little. I raised my hourly rate and the balance came back. As my expertise grew, I have raised prices a few times since. When you are selling an intangible service, the marketplace will tell that when your pricing is accurate. The value is there by the demand that you create. It's also important to know what the norm is in your community.

Be careful that you do not undervalue your services in order to keep busy. You may take on too many projects, not meet expectations, and then find business falls off regardless of your prices. A good goal is to deliver more than is expected.

into the lost profit column and never be able to get back to where you need to be.

If you haven't done the math on price cuts, I will give you an example to follow. Let's assume you sell widgets, and your direct cost for each is $6.00. Your business is currently selling about 1,000 widgets per month. For this product, your results are as follows:

1,000 units @ $10.00

Sales Income	$10,000
Less Direct Cost	$ 6,000
Gross Profit	$ 4,000

This means that you have $4,000 to cover your overhead, as well as any revenue from other products.

If you discount the price by 10%, the result would look like this:

1,000 units @ $9.00

Sales Income	$9,000
Less Direct Cost	$6,000
Gross Profit	$3,000

Now you have $1,000 less to cover overhead. But what if your volume grew by 20%? That's a great showing.

1,200 units @ $9.00

Sales Income	$10,800
Less Direct Costs	$9,200
Gross Profit	$3,600

Most companies are happy for a 20% jump in sales, but with this price cut, you would have to grow by more than one-third. Here's what a 35% increase will bring to the company:

1,350 units @ $9.00

Sales Income	$12,150
Direct Costs	$8,000
Gross Profit	$4,150

This is a very aggressive jump in sales, and that is very unlikely to happen without some real effort. Also, any higher revenue is going to have some additional costs associated with it. Perhaps the sales effort without the price cut would be more valuable. Be careful before you lower prices as a knee-jerk reaction to a soft sale time. Try marketing and a temporary, smaller cut first. A short-term sale may do the trick.

When the Merchandise Is Stale

Holding a sale for the purpose of moving obsolete merchandise is far different from a sale to boost volume. Old inventory, sitting on the back of shelves or in the basement of the building, has little value to the company. You need to turn it into cash. If you have already written off these products from your Balance Sheet, all of the revenue will be profit. If you have not taken this inventory write-down already and are carrying the material at full price, you will show a loss when you sell it at a low price. However, you will have money in the bank instead of inventory on the shelves. Putting this capital to work for you instead of remaining illiquid is always a constructive step.

Price Reductions That Are Temporary

The Grand Opening Sale—it's a business tradition, as are sales for special holidays and events. To lessen the expectations that prices are being permanently lowered, give out discount coupons, perhaps ones that say "for use on specially-marked items." The coupons should have an expiration date, and when the sale is over, the prices go back to where you want them to be. Don't train your customers to wait for the next markdown before shopping again. You need the full-price customer, because that's where you can find the most profit.

If you are selling intangible professional services, a special offer for a discount on the first hour or first treatment may be in order. Let your customers know what the regular price will be, but attract them with incentives to try out your services. Also, quoting a lower price for a series of services instead of pricing each service individually may generate more business. A new customer will cost you in terms of marketing; repeat customers are more profitable.

The Psychology of Pricing

Why is one seat on an airplane more valuable than the one right next to it? Because the airline company has used their best technology and experience to price it higher, and the passenger has expectations that it is worth the cost. There is a large element of psychology in the process that goes along with the knowledge of finance.

For large publicly traded companies, the game may be over revenue and cash flow, and the airline industry is a prime example of this. Any incentive they can use to get passengers to book and pay for future flights works, at least in part, to their advantage. A ticket purchased six months in advance is cash in without any cash having been spent. The game is to fill the plane in waves and then sell the remaining seats at a price high enough for the flight to be profitable. Are you ready to price under these rules?

| Inside Track | How Much Is a Photo Worth? |

Several years ago, I was attending the Maui Writers Conference, which teaches about the skills, as well as the business, of writing. I attended a session about how to charge customers when you are a freelancer. One of the panelists was a freelance photojournalist who had been approached by a major airline because they wanted to purchase the rights to his photos for use in their advertising campaign for trip to Hawaii. He called a colleague in New York City to get some advice. The following conversation was reported to the class:

"How much do you think I can charge for one photo?"

"Whatever you can say, you can charge," was the response.

"You don't think I could get $8,000, do you?"

"Apparently not, because you can't say it."

"I believe they are worth at least $5,000 each."

"You seem comfortable with that; sounds like that's the price."

And it was for the initial charge—the first five pictures. By the time he was teaching this class, his price was up to $85,000 per photo.

Can you say out loud that you are asking top dollar? Don't think you are worth it? If you believe that the value of your works deserves a premium price, your job is to create that image for your customers. Perceived value is one of the basic drivers in the market today. Many products are actually quite similar in quality, but the one with the extra service or name cache will cost more, and that is where most small businesses should strive to be.

Not likely. Few smaller companies have the sophistication to track patterns well enough to take advantage of opportunistic pricing. You must begin with your costs and then determine the highest value of your product/service that will cover them and be profitable. Here is the interesting question: Are you confident enough about the quality and desirability of what you do to set a premium price and then hold to it? There are vast examples of companies that undercharge their services because they are not sure what customers would be willing to pay. Consider how many people purchase a three-dollar cup of coffee that has twenty cents of costs. Or a real estate market that goes up 30% per year. Any good explanations for these examples? It is mostly just the interesting psychology of pricing.

The Fine Art of Price Increases

Establish your pricing strategy the minute you open your business. Do some research about where you are positioned in the competitive market; then it is up to you to meet the expectations of your customer. If your quality and service goes down or remains flat, customers will resent any price increases, even if prices on the other items around them are going up. Clients will become hypersensitive after years of little price hikes.

If you make it a practice to give people more than they expect, they will accept most of the new cost you set. You can always identify frequent customers by offering a program that gives them extra discounts. Loyal customers are worth keeping, as their volume has bottom line value.

If you are fearful of losing business with a price increase, the same exercise we just did with price cuts may surprise you as well. Using the same widget, we can raise the price 10% to $11.00 and sell 20% less and still have the same gross profit. You are not likely to lose 20% of your sales over a price increase.

For example:

    1,000 units @ $10.00
    Sales income $10,000
    Direct cost   6,000
    Gross profit   4,000

10% price increase gives you:
    1,000 units @ $11.00
    Sales income $11,000
    Direct cost   6,000
    Gross profit   5,000

20% sales decline:
    800 units @ $11.00
    Sales income $ 8,800
    Direct cost   4,800
    Gross profit   4,000

Know your market and know your customer enough to predict the effect of a change in pricing. Do some secret shopping in your area in your type of business and get a sense of what others are charging.

One Restaurant's Strategy

While I was consulting for a restaurant, we decided that the restaurant's pricing was too low compared to other fine dining choices in the area. We knew that if we kept the costs in check, the profit improvement would be substantial. Every increase in revenue less the direct costs would drop to the bottom line. As we did an overall menu price increase, we also removed some of the older items, added new items and did not raise the cost of the highest price item. It still remained under $26.00. This was almost a 5% increase and no one ever noticed or, if they did, they did not complain. Business actually increased and so did profits. The only cost was the printing and the effort involved in the menu updating.

▶▶ TEST DRIVE

When you set your prices, you are setting expectations of customers and profits for your business. Are you considering all aspects of these choices?

1. Is your product in great supply or great demand?
2. Can your business be considered a niche market?
3. Are you adding special value for your customers?
4. Have you considered all of your costs?
5. Are you being cautious before having a sale or cutting prices?

Analyzing Progress with Ratios

Ratios are mathematical comparisons that can be used to provide a very effective indicator of the financial progress of a company at any particular time. They may be measured against a standard of similar businesses, or you may compare your own trends to see the progress of the company.

These ratios do not have to be difficult, and even though a financial analyst can utilize a vast number of them, you will only need to look at about six on a regular basis. ▶▶ **You are primarily looking for trends, and you will want to compare same periods (third quarter to third quarter) from one year to the next.** Consider any seasonal elements of your business so that you can account for times when inventory is very high comparable to sales, or when allowed payment terms are more liberal and payable turnovers are slower and out of whack. To successfully manage your business, you need to be able to understand and interpret these ratios. Your bank will watch them closely to make decisions about your existing loans or providing new ones.

Receivable Turnover—Cash Collections

This ratio is calculated by dividing annual sales by the dollars of your outstanding receivables. For example, if you have $300,000 of annual sales and $50,000 of receivables, you will divide this sales number by $50,000, which gives you a turnover of 6 times per year. Turning this number into days can be done by dividing 6 into 365 (the days in the year) and you come up with 61 days. That tells you that, on average, a credit sale that you make will take 61 days to turn to cash.

Determining this number gives you a guideline with reference to your cash flow projections. For example, a sale of $20,000 made in January is not likely to show up in your cash until March. Particularly, if you are in a growth mode, you will determine in your pro-forma that you need more capital to reach your goal than you would if you had a 30-day cycle. A turnover ratio of more than 48 days needs attention, as most companies set their terms at 30 days, and your customers are exceeding your terms.

Aggressive Collections May Improve the Timing

Unless you are in an industry where it is traditional to give 60-day payment plans, you should work to improve this ratio by setting very clear credit terms and holding your customers to those terms. Statements, phone calls, and reminders should be standard; and you should possibly start to charge interest on unpaid invoices. (Be sure that you state this policy on the original invoice.) Many big companies and banks do charge interest this way. Look at all of the fees on your credit card bills. Charging fees, however, does not mean you will collect. An incentive for prompt payment also may be effective, such as a 2% discount for payment in 10 days.

By checking this ratio on a quarterly basis, you will know how your collection policy is working. The standard for most sales on credit terms is 45 to 48 days. This means that most of your customers are paying on time and a few are taking a bit longer. This is sometimes a result of a missed bill or a disputed charge. Follow up on unpaid invoices and find out if there are any problems. A good paper trail aids in collections.

Payable Turnover—
A Cash Management System

Just as the receivable turnover ratio gives you an indication of how your customers are paying their obligations, the payable turnover ratio is a measure of how you are meeting yours. The math, again, is fairly straightforward: you take your total purchases of goods and divide them by your current accounts payable.

For example, if your total purchases are $500,000 and your payables are $100,000, then your turnover ratio is 5 times. Divide that number into 365 days and you get 73, which is the number of days it takes your company to pay a bill, on average. If you are using cash flow adequately, the time it takes for you to get paid should be fairly close to the time it takes you to pay others. Be careful with the trend in this area. While vendor credit is a good source of short-term cash, if you do not meet your obligations, you may find yourself the object of costly lawsuits. And you'll be without a reliable source of income.

Vendors Are Important

Reliable vendors are a big part of the success of your company. Being able to get what you need on a timely basis is very important, and being offered an occasional discount or special purchase can help your bottom line. These deals are often saved for the best customers, those who meet their obligations.

They are also a source of low-cost financing, as you are getting 30 days free use of their capital. If you stretch that too far, however, it might be withdrawn and you will be paying cash up-front, if they will deal with you at all. Watch this ratio carefully, as it is a sign of working capital problems.

Dealing with Suppliers

Some business owners who are too busy selling to their customers and making sure product is delivered, as well as all the other day-to-day tasks, will simply ignore the financial side of the business, including the accounts payable. Earlier, it was suggested that you produce an accounts payable aging monthly and review it. If there are bills you cannot pay in full, send a partial payment. Let your supplier know what you are doing and, by all means, answer their calls. If someone owed you money and wouldn't take your call, you would get nervous. Your vendors will have the same reaction, and this is how a collection action or a lawsuit starts. However, do not make promises that you know you can't keep. Offering partial payments may help to buy you some time.

Inventory Turnover—Managing Material and POS Information

This is the formula to show you how well you are managing your inventory. You may be carrying too little, which can result in lost sales and more frequent shipment from your suppliers, and at an increased overall cost for freight. Or, you may be holding too much; in that case, you have your capital tied up in slow-moving product and may risk loss of value as time passes, as goods will be eventually sold at a loss.

The calculation starts with the annual material cost of goods. You find this number on your Profit and Loss Statement under direct expense. Do not use all of your direct cost, only the material (take out labor, for example). Now, divide this number by the value of the current inventory.

For example, if your material costs for the year were $300,000 and you currently have $50,000 of material in stock, then your inventory turn is 6 times a year. Divide the number into 365 and you are turning inventory in 61 days. The more frequently you turn inventory, the less of your money is tied up in material costs.

Turning Inventory into Cash

Since your vendors want to be paid in 30 days, turning your inventory into cash while the inventory isn't selling isn't going to be easy. It may mean that a portion of what you are buying isn't selling at all, and the goods are carried from month to month. The time may come when you need to take the profit hit; write down the value of your existing obsolete inventory and sell it for whatever you can get. Move it to your regular customers or sell it to a surplus dealer. Clean out the items that fall into this category and set up systems to prevent a repeat. Find suppliers that can ship quickly and try to order on a "just in time" basis.

Virtually all of the "box" accounting software systems have an inventory component in their specialized versions for retail, distribution, and manufacturing. Enter your inventory when you begin; added purchases, and any sale, will reduce the stock by what product you sell. You can then monitor what is moving and how quickly. If your company has too many items or a complicated manufacturing build, this is reason enough to move up to a more customized software package. Knowing the real cost of material, including what portion has to be written off as unusable, is an important cost factor. All retail companies must know their shrinkage number, or the percent of your inventory that does not turn unless it is sold at a loss.

> ## Quantity vs. Cost
>
> There are times when your suppliers offer special deals to push their own slow-moving merchandise. This may include lower prices on larger quantities plus some freight concessions. The good news is that when you sell the goods, your profit will be higher; the trickier question is whether you can afford it. If you have good information on your typical inventory turnover, you can make this decision more easily. How long will it take you to use what you are buying, and will the tie-up of cash pinch your other needs? Not all bargains are good bargains. Don't let a vendor turn their problem into your problem.

POS Information

For many companies that use a cash register to take money, their systems are connected to Point of Sale software. Not all of the databases will interface with your accounting software, but valuable information can be available, particularly for restaurants and most retail companies. These businesses can see exactly what they are selling on a daily basis and plan purchases accordingly. This can be very important whenever inventory is perishable, such as in restaurants, or seasonal, such as in apparel stores and children's stores.

Quick Ratio Determines Liquidity

In Chapter 6 on the Balance Sheet, we covered liquidity, or solvency, ratio. These were described as current ratios. There is another version of this measure called quick ratios. This calculation drops the inventory from the mix.

Take all of your cash and near cash items (accounts receivable and current loans due) and divide them by current liabilities (accounts payable and current loans and obligations). The reason to drop inventory is that, depending on your turnover, it may not be that liquid.

The expected ratio here is different from what you would expect in the current category. A company that may be a 2 to 1 in current ratios may now have a 1.4 to 1, meaning $140 in assets for every $100 of liabilities. Measure your results with the standards in your industry. Your banker

Bad Debts and Old Inventory Can Spell Disaster

I worked for a very long time at a plumbing contracting company in New York City. Their lack of cash flow was so critical that every payroll was an adventure. I did some of my work via phone and online, so it took me some time to see where they were hiding the problems. A visit to the office for a look at their internal documents was an eye opener.

Customers would complain about the work and refuse to pay, or they would demand a credit. No one would deal with the problems, so invoices went unpaid and were never likely to be paid in full. However, the invoices were still on the books. Over 50% of the accounts receivable listing was over 90 days old, and a third of that would never be collected.

Inventory was primarily materials left over from jobs and not likely to be used again soon, if at all. Each truck carried its own basic material, but, again, less than half had any real value.

The Balance Sheet they received from their accountant, and the one I reviewed, indicated that the company was borderline solvent. Once we made tough adjustments, it turned out they were not even close. If the owner had not ignored this situation, corrections could have been made. Here, the only choice was a Chapter 11.

All business owners are better off with the truth—there are turnaround strategies that can be employed, if you find a problem early in the game. Denial or the lack of information never cures anything. If you know some of the items on your Balance Sheet are questionable, bring it up with the your accountant.

may be able to give these to you or direct you to where you can find them. The norms in quick ratio are very industry specific; some businesses generally carry little or no inventory.

Compare Yourself to Industry Standards

Virtually all of the financial ratios and profit percentages you develop for your business can be compared to similar companies in your industry. A group called RMA Associates maintains these numbers. They are sorted by specific type of business, as well as size of business. You can find the information online for a fee. It is worth the price.

Debt to Worth Ratio Signals Leverage

Divide the total debt (current and long term) by total equity (called stock-holders equity on the Balance Sheet). In other words, if your debt is $300,000 and your equity is $100,000, then your debt to equity ratio is 3 to 1. This is the upward limit in the eyes of most lenders.

This ratio is a sign of leverage; it shows how you are able to generate additional capital to invest in ongoing operations. In the early years of any business, growth is financed primarily through debt. The ratio will be highest at this time. Once growth level is achieved, the ratio should stabilize and go down. A trend of rising debt to equity ratio may be dangerous, because if new loans are not forthcoming, a cash crunch could follow. The business is surviving on borrowed money. This can only go on for a limited period of time.

The more stable the assets are (cash instruments or real estate), the higher the debt to worth ratio can be. More consumable assets, such as inventory, lower the tolerance for debt. Real estate, in particular, can be leveraged because there is appreciation that is not shown on the books.

Return on Equity: Is the Business a Good Investment?

The method to determining this ratio is to divide net equity by the net profit. For example, if you have $200,000 in equity and earn a net profit of $20,000, your return is 10%. The reason to review this number is to determine how your investment in your business is working for you. Could you earn a higher rate of return in another type of investment, such as stocks or money market funds? Remember, this is your money at risk. Or, it is the money you have convinced others to invest, or money you hope to attract.

When considering the return on your investment, think also in terms of your salary (could you earn as much elsewhere?) and other benefits and perks you receive from the business. Being in business is not always a pure investment play; it is often a lifestyle choice. But you should always know the difference between a business and a hobby. If your return is quite low or nonexistent, you need some professional advice on how to generate a positive return. If you are taking all of the profit out in personal pay and expense, you may be risking your own future. Consider what the cost of a professional manager would be and don't exceed that number by more than 10%–20%. Doing so is short-term thinking.

▶▶ TEST DRIVE

There are many ways to measure the performance of your company. How many of the following do you check?

1. How long does it take for you to collect your money?
2. Are you paying vendors within acceptable terms?
3. Are you managing inventory to increase profits?
4. Is your business a good place for you to invest your money?

Sources of Capital

Capital is the lifeblood of any business. Beginning with equity capital to get the business started, continual cash flow is needed to grow, to prosper, and to reward those who have worked hard to get the company to that level. ▸▸ **Successful business owners plan for cash needs and develop strategies to handle times when cash is short.** This is one of the most critical skills to develop.

Basically, there are four sources of capital available to any business:

1. Equity Investment

This is the capital initially invested by the founder or other interested parties. The form of this investment may be either a casual transaction, one that comes from family or associates with assumption of return when the company turns profitable, or a more formal investment of outside investors. They will require more detailed information and projection of profitability of return.

Some equity investment is quite sophisticated, requiring the company to earn a substantial rate of return and to develop a pre-planned exit strategy, most often in the form of an IPO. The investor holds a percentage of interest that allows for shares of stock that are traded after a certain date. Few start-ups can secure this type of funding. Some individual investors may also be willing to make a loan that can be converted to equity if the company exceeds expectation. The principal is set, interest is paid, and profits are distributed.

2. Debt

Small businesses just starting out tend to fund much of their beginning expense with debt, usually through bank loans. Various loans funding growth (contract financing and lines of credit) are often available to a company meeting its goals. The critical factor for a new business to consider is not to leverage your company too early in the game. Debt growth should be highest during times of rapid increase of revenue.

3. Operating Revenue

The best source of ongoing capital is positive operating income—in short, profits. When your company has positive cash flow, all vital signs are healthy. Simply put, this is cash coming in that exceeds cash going out. Break even will not feed cash reserves; only profit will do that.

4. Sale of Assets

For a mature company looking to raise money, one way is to sell off older and unneeded assets. There may be both income statement and Balance Sheet implications if these assets are fully depreciated. Check values listed on your books. If what you are selling has little or no book value left, you will show a gain from the sale; and you'll have more space! This is not a profit from revenue, but will add to your total bottom line.

On the other hand, if any asset is sold below its book value, it will be booked as a loss on your Income Statement, although you can list it as a separate line item. The exception is when you liquidate inventory below cost, which will reflect in current loss from sales.

Need for Capital

Interestingly, just as there are four sources of capital in a business, there are also four needs for capital. These fall into the following categories:

1. **The purchase of assets**—The need to buy machinery, equipment, vehicles, and other tangible assets is the most primary need for cash. The purchase of land and buildings would also be covered by this capital need. Payback from these purchases will likely be over the mid-term or long term (meaning at least three years or more), and that is one of the features you need to consider when looking for the right type of capital to fund these purchases. Do not use short-term capital sources to fund long-term needs.

2. **Repayment of debt**—The internal cash flow pays the cost of debt (interest), but it is outside of this flow (excess profits or

external investment) that pays the principal debt down. The repayment shows as increased equity on the Balance Sheet; as debt decreases, stockholder equity increases.

3. Repurchase or redemption of equity—This may include a redemption or payback for the original investment in the business or a buyback from an outside stockholder. You may have invested a good bit of your own capital in the business to get the company started and now is the right time to redeem it. You may be able to replace it with debt from an outside lending institution to be retired from future profits. Some loan agreements, however, may prevent you from doing this. Make sure to read the small print. The loan agreement may require a subordination of owner's debt.

4. Funding losses—This is the most difficult need for cash because it is not as optional as the first three. Few businesses plan to lose money, yet most do early on. Unfortunately, there are times when this trend begins and is left uncorrected. If the trend goes on for long enough, it threatens the company's future as well. Few sources of capital are truly appropriate for replenishing loss of cash from operations. The most typical source is creating debt by not being able to pay ongoing expenses.

Do Not Jeopardize Liquidity

There are times when a company is operating at a profitable level, but the money is not sufficient to pay off the principal of its debt to its lending institutions. This is the time to renegotiate these payments with the creditor, not simply make payments that strain your cash flow. If this drain goes on for very long, it will jeopardize the liquidity of the company. You will replace long-term debt with short term, by sending money to your bank and not paying your vendors.

Being Financially Astute

The best lesson I have learned from fifteen years of consulting with small businesses is how to master the four sources and four needs of capital, and funding them to meet the appropriate use. Short-term cash needs were acquired on a temporary basis, but longer term capital required investment that required no immediate payback. This was not a skill I had when I was in my own manufacturing business. I made the most common mistake: we were losing money and I went to the bank to get a loan. They turned me down and I was surprised, as I had more than sufficient collateral. However, I did not have the cash flow to pay them back.

Later, I realized that bank money was for purchasing assets that would show a profitable return. Asset sales and perhaps equity investment may be able to fund temporary losses, but not for very long, depending on where the equity comes from. The risk will be calculated by the investor, and they will expect a return comparable with that risk. The higher the risk, the higher the interest rate. This is a good way to take the temperature of your own business; determine how an objective outsider sees it.

A business owner who has knowledge of capital issues (or hires someone who does) is more likely to have access to capital in most business situations. A company with good prospects can get funded. A company with potential and a good advisor can open the door to the capital market.

Funding a Start-up

Here you are, with a great idea, one that will produce dozens of potential new customers, but you don't have enough capital to get it off the ground. That never stopped a dedicated entrepreneur before, and it shouldn't stop you. But you do need a plan to secure a sufficient level of funding. The following are eight different sources of capital for a start-up:

1. Personal Savings

In these days of low interest rates, the return on regular savings is very minimal, hardly above inflation. If you have some money put aside, money that you won't need for living expenses, using a portion of that money to fund your start-up may be a very good idea. In addition to lowering the immediate pressure you may be under for payback, this is a good sign for any potential lender. After all, if you're willing to invest your own money, the lender knows that you have both the confidence and the commitment to the venture. Do not use all of your savings; you don't want to leave yourself too vulnerable and feeling anxious. And you may need it to pay personal bills as well. Your early income could be limited.

2. Family and Friends

Start out by determining whether those who are close to you are lending you the money or investing it in the business. These are very different situations—a loan is expected to be paid back, and an investment is money at risk. Do not ask anyone who doesn't have the cash as discretionary income to become an investor. Do not take a loan either, unless you are fairly certain that you can pay it back.

Only you can really understand how the people you approach will react over the long term about their involvement in your company. Some may be very casual and happy to help or participate. Others may continually badger you for information and assurance. This can create personal pressure that may be very distracting and negative.

Individuals React Differently

It is my experience that the response of family or friends has little to do with their own personal financial situations. I have had clients that were harassed by wealthy relations and others who were encouraged by those who really needed the money back. You need to be honest with yourself about who you are dealing with. Risking family peace over money is never a good idea—even when a brother or college friend tries to encourage you to let them "in on the action." If you are really experienced at finance and know that you will be able to make the return when promised, that is the time to take in a few real "insiders."

3. Outside Investors

If you have formed an open corporation and choose a Sub S tax status (that is, chose to be taxed as a Sub S Corp with a pass-through for initial losses, instead of as a Sub C Corporation), you may be able to look for a limited number of outside investors without having to deal with the security laws. Check with your company attorney on this. You will need a complete business plan. It is best to approach only sophisticated investors who understand the risk and can well afford the loss. Be sure to add a caveat to your plan, acknowledging the speculative nature of an investment in any new business venture. Investors expect their money to be returned on a timely basis. The benefit to some may be that they can deduct their losses from their personal income tax.

4. Personal Lines of Credit (Home Equity and Credit Cards)

This is a frequently used source of raising cash, and it is often a very risky one. When you draw against the equity in your home, you put the very roof over your head in jeopardy, unless you have a good bit of collateral available. It is, however, at a much lower interest rate than most credit cards will be over the long term and, with the continuing rise in property values, it is a more desirable loan than drawing out cash advances on your credit cards. Be particularly careful of the credit cards with a low introductory rate that jumps up after six months.

There are two problems here. One is that repayment is required from the start. The other is that you will lower your credit score with any excess personal borrowing, as your debt to income ratio will go up. This will impact future business loans. Be cautious. Take only what you need and pay it down as soon as you can.

5. Sweat Equity

In your original Business Plan, you will have a pro-forma that should record your own salary as an administrative cost of doing business. If you can go without that salary for a while, this is start-up capital you will not have to raise. Continue to accrue the cost, however, because if you don't, your entire overhead structure will seem too low and give you a false projection of profit. Show it as a "deferred" debt to stockholders, one you want to try to pay down as cash flow becomes better. Once you get a bank loan, however, your lender may require you to subordinate it to their loan. This is an issue that can be negotiated. As you pay down the bank, you may pay yourself as well.

6. Vendor Credit

There are several ways to use vendor credit in your start-up. One is to lease the tangible assets (machinery, autos, trucks, computers, etc.) directly from the manufacturers. You have immediate use of what you need, and they have made a new sale. Their credit terms may be very liberal because there will be profit in the sale as well as in the financing. Some companies produce a healthy return from their financial subsidiaries.

Merchandise suppliers may be a bit more reticent to sell to a new company on credit. They have no security in their goods and do not have a lot of leverage to get paid. Try out some early negotiations with vendors, such as 50% in advance and the balance in 10 days, until you work yourself up to a net 30-day account. It often takes 7 to 10 days for the shipper of COD packages to get your check. Then there is the time for them to clear your check. Needless to say, you are getting extra time to cover the amount in the bank, right? Do not float checks on this basis, however! Know the money will be there when it is needed.

7. Bank Loans

Recently, several banks have been marketing business loans that are actually home equity loans. How can you tell the difference? You will not be asked for a business plan and as long as there is equity in your home (which will be used as collateral), the loan will be approved. As long as you understand this is basically personal funding, and not based on your business, this can be a good source to use.

It isn't easy to get a bank loan for a start-up, but it is possible. If you have a good business plan and good personal credit, find out which banks in your area are SBA lenders and are aggressively marketing new business loans. You may have some success this way, although usually you may not get as much money as you want. Don't settle for a portion of what you need, as you'll be tying up all of your collateral and it's almost impossible to go back for a second round. Few banks will rewrite a first loan with a new one unless it is almost paid off. Also, the SBA does not like new loans that involve more refinance than anything else.

8. Customer Deposits

Some businesses charge an upfront fee for their work. The construction industry is one that comes to mind, as the company gets a deposit to purchase materials. Lawyers and consultants will often charge a retainer fee. If you are a new company, this may provide the needed capital with which to get started, but it also comes with a caution. If you haven't done the work, you haven't earned the money. Be careful. This will be discussed more fully at the end of this chapter.

Funding Growth from Internally-Generated Cash

Earlier, we identified four sources of capital: two are external (investment and debt) and two are internal (asset sale and profits, also referred to as retained earnings). The latter is an excellent way to fund growth because it has no cost to the business in terms of interest and dividends. There is also a self-governing aspect, in terms that you can't grow faster than your cash flow will permit. Many times this is good because you are less likely to chase down high-risk paths when you are on a "pay as you go" basis. However, there are times when the potential for growth exceeds the funding.

Leverage Your Profits

The easiest loan you will ever get is the one you apply for when the company is making positive cash and there is a plan in place to grow to the next level. Most banks covet this type of lending, so shop around for the best deal. When the positive cash flow is there to cover debt service, it's an easy loan to make. You are likely to be given a break on terms; enjoy it, you earned it. Be reasonable when you create your pro-formas and spend the money wisely, and your profits will grow even higher. Too much available capital can be a trap to unreasonable spending.

Depreciation Frees Up Cash

As you are reviewing your past few years of Profit and Loss Statements, you will notice the line item expense for depreciation. Remember that this is not actually a cash expense, so that the actual cash is still flowing in to the business. In fact, in most software you can generate a cash flow report that shows you two important items:

- Cash flow from operations
- Net change in cash from last year

These are good numbers to use as you budget your growth with the excess cash on hand. Be aware that the tax laws allow for this deduction for a reason; assets need to be repaired and replaced. You want to keep a reserve to cover these eventualities.

Customer Deposits Are Not an Asset

In the very early chapters of this book, we described the difference between a cash and an accrual system. I hope most of you have chosen an accrual system. But there is an anomaly in that as well. What do you do when you get a customer deposit? Is it a sale? Have you earned the money?

The answer is a resounding NO! A deposit is actually a liability, and the amount gets posted in the bank on the asset side and the second entry is in short-term liabilities—an account called *customer deposit*. As you begin to complete the work you have been paid for, the number gets moved out of that liability account and into revenue. If this is a major factor in your business, learn how to set up a system that gives you an accurate picture.

The Big Trap

If your business constantly generates 50% deposits on new jobs and uses that cash to finish old ones, it won't take long before you are in some real trouble. You are feeding off new and unearned money, and if sales slow down, there may not be enough cash to finish the work that you have. There is no discipline here unless you take the initiative and put it into place. Keep cash in reserve to cover work paid for and not completed. Not doing this can be a serious mistake. I know of at least one contractor who faced criminal charges for failing to complete work that was paid for in advance. His customers charged him with theft, saying that he took their money without intention to do the work he contracted for. This really wasn't the case, as his lack of business sophistication was the real culprit. However, all the angry customers knew was that they paid for products and services they did not receive.

Understanding the cash cycle in your business is the key to planning success. Answer the following questions:

1. How many sources are there for capital, and what are they?
2. What primary capital needs does your company have?
3. Are there strategic ways to fund a start-up?
4. Why is retained earnings a good way to fund growth?
5. What is the actual category of a customer deposit?

Sources of Outside Growth Capital

The early days of a new business venture are described as the start-up phase. This can last for a few months or even a few years, and it represents the initial trial run of the concept. In most cases, some tweaking is likely to be done during this maiden voyage. If the venture is enjoying success, the time may also have come to grow the company. This is Stage II in the life cycle of a business, the time of growth.

The need to fund higher and higher levels of current assets and capital equipment will outstrip, sometimes by a wide margin, the current cash flow. You are funding future capacity. The gap does not usually begin to close until growth slows and the bulk of the marketing expenses have been made as well. Here are three basic strategies to secure enough outside capital to take the company to the next level: traditional bank lending, joint ventures and strategic alliances, and investment capital.

1. Traditional Bank Lending

The first steps in securing an adequate and advantageous bank loan do not involve the lender. It is internal planning, so that when you go out to shop for a loan package, you are asking for only what you need, not what the lenders are offering. By reviewing your historic results (the past year Profit and Loss) and converting the numbers into a pro-forma, you should be able to determine how much capital you will need. Your monthly cash deficit will have to be covered, and you will need some cushion as well.

2. Joint Ventures and Strategic Alliances

How does a small company find a way to conduct its business as if it was a larger one? It joins forces with another business and pools resources. The most recent case of this has been in the airline industry. U.S. Airways and United, after failing to merge, formed a strategic alliance that gave them shared flights around the world. Although the model is a good one, the industry was too damaged to execute this one successfully. But, every day you see other examples that are so seamless that you don't even notice them.

Imagine that you are an electrical contractor and a very big job is currently up for bid. Your prices are too high to bid as a subcontractor and cover the cost of profit for the general contractor, so you join forces with a plumbing contractor and other specialties and bid the job as one. You have formed a joint venture to compete with a general contractor who takes a 20% plus markup. Your group needs to organize and govern itself, but the results are usually in higher profits with newer and bigger opportunities.

Fund the Whole Growth Period, Not Just the Beginning

The most serious mistake that most new businesses make is securing any loan they can get and then tying up all of their collateral, even though the amount of capital is insufficient to get them to the next level. If your three-year pro-forma shows you will require $250,000, that's what you must borrow. Don't accept the first offer of $150,000 just to get you started. You will get stalled in a very vulnerable place. Banks sometimes think they can lower their risk with a smaller amount, but the reality is they raise it by making the company more vulnerable.

The Difference Between a Joint Venture and a Strategic Alliance

A joint venture is a partnership normally set up for a specific amount of time and limited to a specific project. The agreement often has a termination date that is specific, so the end of the venture ceases at the end of the work. Both parties have an out.

A strategic alliance is an open-ended, understanding agreement between you (your company) and another person or business. This type of relationship should be a mutual benefit. The time is open-ended and the areas of collaboration could be many. The agreement will include a mechanism for cancellation, but it will not be date-specific.

Financial Benefits of a Strategic Alliance

There are numerous benefits to using this type of growth strategy. While you are learning and utilizing another company's resources, your own business will continue to grow. Here are a few of the benefits:

- Access to new customers, without the cost of new marketing
- Evens out the workload—you won't have to pay for employee downtime
- Undertaking larger projects
- Sharing space and equipment for shared customers
- Learning more about the general industry
- Sharing marketing costs

Put Your Agreements in Writing

All of the details of either a joint venture or strategic alliance need to be in writing. The contract or agreement should not be thought of as a document that you would use if there is conflict or litigation, but, rather, as a document that helps to identify all of the issues and how you plan to deal with them. Start with who the formers of the venture or alliance (exact legal names) are, and specify what you are doing; include where (the physical location) the finances will be kept and how you will share revenue and profits. Make it as specific as you can and let an attorney review it for accuracy. Keeping organized is a good skill for success. The written agreement will allow you to consider all the issues that may come up and have plans in place to deal with them. As a last resort, it will also be used to settle any disputes.

Know Your Partner

A business partnership has a lot in common with a marriage. You will spend a great deal of time together and not all of it will be great. There will be differences of opinions, and you will enjoy success as well. Choose the individuals you will be working with carefully—personal conflicts can destroy even a great deal. Make sure you share a vision and both of you have similar expectations. Mutual trust and respect are important to ensure that all decisions are made fairly. The synergy of good partners can't be beat. The sum total will be greater than the parts.

3. Investment Capital

Perhaps you aren't quite eligible for a bank loan, or you need more money than the bank is willing to lend. Your project may be longer and more speculative than a bank is comfortable with. This may be the time to consider an equity partner.

You will sell off an interest in the business for cash that you will infuse back into the operation, causing growth and continued profitability. You increase the overall worth of the business, which will mean that your equity may be more valuable even if you do hold less of the ownership.

The tough thing is not necessarily finding investors, but putting a value on the interest they want to control. Professional investors are likely to ask for a lot, often operating control, while family and friends might be more reasonable. Most business owners think they can sell off 10-20% of their interest for a large dollar investment, and most investors want half of the business and sometimes even more. They understand that, without control, they have no real influence. The challenge for you is to access the investment dollars while still keeping ownership of the business. Perhaps a loan that may convert to equity at a later time will work for you.

The Basics of a Loan Proposal

Many companies believe they can drop off their business plan along with a loan application at the bank and come back later to pick up the money. A business plan is not the same thing as a loan proposal, and you will need to learn the difference. Ask the bank what they require, and provide all of the documentation. Receiving a bank loan starts with a loan application but that is only the beginning.

Most smaller loans (under $250,000) are based on collateral and credit score (your personal score) because they are not large enough to go beyond a centralized loan center. Write up a few pages about what you need and attach current financials. The manager should be able to walk you through the rest. For larger or more complicated loans, you will need a full-blown proposal. Here are the elements of a loan proposal:

Purpose

Why do you need the money? Here, you need to be specific. A lender will approve of loans to buy equipment, expand inventory, pay for marketing and sales to open new product lines or increase your territory, and hire new people to meet growing demand. They will not lend money to pay off old debt, fund losses, or make speculative moves into new and unfamiliar fields.

You must identify how this new capital will be used to increase revenues and profits. Your continued growth and positive cash flow is what the lender needs to know and expects. The loan will only be paid back if the company is profitable. Your job is to convince your lender that the new profits will be there when there is capital to fund it.

Payment

You must demonstrate how and when the loan will be paid off. A term loan will have a monthly payment and your pro-forma needs to show that you will have sufficient monthly cash flow to make that payment. A line of credit is to fund receivables, and when they are paid, the bank should be paid as well. Show the payment in your cash flow projections. The funds will come in to retire debt and then when you need them, you can draw on the line to fund new orders. This credit instrument is normally issued for one year, but it can be renewed indefinitely.

Protection

What assets will you use to secure the loan? This is what the lender considers as protection, where they will look to find secondary payment. Remember that your equipment and inventory will be discounted because the bank would not be able to liquidate them at the value you may believe they are worth. The best collateral (other than a cash equivalent) are good receivables, and the bank will accept most of what is 60 days old or less. Invoices over that age will be considered questionable as to whether they will actually be paid or not, unless there are special circumstances that are disclosed.

Personal guarantees and other programs such as a Small Business Admistration (SBA) Guarantee would also be security for a loan. If the business cannot pay, the guarantor will be expected to do so. In the case of the SBA, they insure a portion of the loan.

People

Always point out the experience, special talent, and expertise of your management team. Toot your own horn and those of your associates. Your credibility and your track record will increase the bank's comfort level that you can and will do what you say. If there have been previous difficulties, disclose them and explain the circumstances. Bankers do not like surprises; you have the chance to put a positive spin on what has happened when you are the one who brings it up. In the small business world, credit is a very personal issue, and it comes down to you.

Make Sure This Is the Right Bank

Spend time researching banks before approaching one to request a loan. Depending on your location, you may have some smaller independent banks that are easier to approach. A savings and loan may not be the best place to go to for a commercial loan, even when they advertise this as a service. The larger, national banks always market their small business loans, but their response varies with the manager who will assist you in getting through the channels. Not all banks are created equal, so shop around. Remember, it isn't just about interest rates, it's about availability. Access to capital when you need it is a valuable tool; find a bank and a banker who understands this.

Loan Guarantee Programs

The most widely known loan guarantee program is the one run by the SBA. They allow the banks to do most of the underwriting, but will guarantee up to 75% of the loan. This means that if you default, 75% of the outstanding balance will be covered by the SBA. It's somewhat like an insurance program. They do charge a fee for this service, which may be up to 3% of the loan.

State and local governments have their own loan programs that also provide guarantees to the banks, as well as some agencies that do direct lending. Development departments or authorities are often the ones who administrate these programs. A good commercial banker can tap into what's available, as can your state representative or senator. Call around and investigate. Call the Small Business Development Center at your local university and talk to a consultant. They know most of the sources of capital.

Over the past few years, the Federal Home Loan Bank became involved in backing up business loans. This program is not available in every district throughout the United States, but it does exist in a number of their regions. The interest rates are lower and the underwriting criteria is more liberal. They are reinvesting their profit.

There are community development centers and nonprofit organizations that have revolving loan funds. The amounts are likely to be smaller and the time from application to acceptance can sometimes be painfully long, but interest rates are lower and requirements are also less stringent. Ask tough questions about the timing issue, and don't let it blindside you so that the money won't be there when you need it.

Timing Repayment with Use

Once you know how much you need, you'll want to choose the type of payback that best meets your needs. Financing may be short term (less than one year), mid term (two to five years) or long term (more than five years). Work with your lender to find the right loan with the term that you need. A large equipment purchase is not a short-term investment. A building has the longest term you can secure. Finance a contract or a single job that can pay you back when the work is complete.

Short-Term Loans

Normally established as a line of credit, you may draw on available funds as you need them until the maturation of the note, likely within one year. This is meant to meet short-term cash flow needs such as funding a large order. A line of credit is *not* permanent financing. Some companies begin with a line and then draw on it when money is short because business is slow. Doing this can make it very hard to pay the money back.

A Loan That Made the Difference

There are loans available for even the most extreme conditions. A Chapter 11 reorganization is never an easy experience, but there are times and circumstances that make it the only real alternative. One of my clients is a printing company that went through the entire court proceedings very successfully, with one exception. At the end, the company was left without a large printing press. Part of the settlement was to return the one they had been purchasing to the supplier. It was time to secure a new press, but who would lend money to a company that just filed bankruptcy? The numbers made sense: the sales were there and they were running smaller presses 24/7 and outsourcing a good bit of work. And not having a large printing press was not a profitable way to go on.

We found a bank interested in helping, and we worked hard to put together an SBA loan package. After a long face-to-face meeting with local SBA managers, the loan was approved, and the new press was purchased and installed. The ordeal took a toll on everyone, but the company now has a future, thanks to an SBA Guarantee. In such cases, the Small Business Administration agrees to underwrite a portion of the loan in case the borrower defaults. This lessens the risk of the bank. In addition, the company had a payment that was affordable.

If you do not need to make capital purchases (such as equipment), but you need to advance material and labor cost for new orders, this may work for you. The line is usually given for one year, but may be renewed if it is handled well.

Intermediate Term Loans

Normally, these loans have terms from three to five years. You may have one funded as a cross between a line of credit and a long-term loan. You can draw on the funds as you are completing your project. Once the draw is complete, the loan terms out to one with regular payments over the agreed-to period. This works well for a building or expansion project, one that takes time to complete and pays off in profits over a few years.

Long-Term Loans

If you know that it will take some time to generate a return on the investment you are making with your borrowed funds, you need a payback of more than five years. The use is likely for a major expansion, including real estate and the purchase of major equipment. Terms longer than five years almost always require an SBA Guarantee, because the longer the payback is, the more things can happen to sidetrack the project. This is a general belief in the lending community—the plan you have now for five years down the road is merely an educated guess. To be more convincing, use actual data to support your request.

Know What You Need

One of the things that impresses bankers is a borrower who knows exactly how much he needs and for how long. This is an indication that the owner has made an effort to learn and master the financial aspect of his business—a necessary tool for success. You may get help from a consultant in putting together a loan package, but be prepared to answer questions. If you think it would help to take your accountant along, do so, but make sure you know everything that's in your loan package.

Special Purpose Loans

There are a number of specific loan programs that might meet your needs. They are offered by both traditional and nontraditional lenders. Check out the benefits (earlier closing date) and the challenges (higher costs), but this may be what you need.

1. Contract Financing

Offered by most traditional banks and secured by the SBA, this loan is exactly what it says. You have a large contract and the bank will finance it for you.

The loan is very specific and you must submit the original contract as well as all changes along the way. The loan is secured by the payments made by your customers and they are likely to be asked to jointly issue checks to you and the lender. As you complete work, the bank advances money. As bills are paid, the advance is paid back. This is a simple concept that works in specific circumstances.

2. Factoring

This is receivable based lending where you actually sell your accounts to a factor (a type of lender) and they will collect the money. You get only a percentage of the invoice until the principal is paid and interest rates are higher than normal. The credit decisions are often made on the basis of your customer's credit rating, not yours. This loan can be the way to go if you have a less-than-perfect history. One drawback is that the factor's credit policy may be more stringent than yours, or it has serious collection procedures. This may offend some long-time customers.

3. Inventory Financing

Often described as floor planning, this is available from larger banks and commercial financers and is used for a company that sells large ticket items like appliances and autos. This type of loan requires the close supervision of inventory, so only an institution willing to work a little more would be a logical candidate. The bank lender finances everything on your floor, and each sale requires a payback to the lender.

4. Export Assistance Financing

Most states are anxious to have their local businesses begin or continue to export goods. The federal government supports this effort as well. To that end, there are special loans to help companies with potential international business. You can use the proceeds for marketing, traveling and attending shows, and modifying your product for a global market. Interest is usually at market prices, but funds are more readily available.

5. Asset Based Lending

One of the lenders considered to be the last resort is a finance company (even some banks who lend against 100% collateral). The value of the security is more important than the potential cash flow to the lender, and costs may be high. These lenders are quick to foreclose to maintain their security interests.

> ### Find the Right Fit in a Loan
>
> There is also consignment, more general receivable lendings, and some programs specific to your area or your industry. There are programs that are directed at minorities, women, and veterans. Find a way, or find someone who will review options with you, to get into the program that fits your needs. You can hire a loan packager, but check references before choosing one. She may charge a percentage of the loan if she is successful.

Collateral and Personal Guarantees

In addition to business collateral, many banks will ask new owners to add personal collateral to the mix. It may be a second mortgage on your house or a savings account or a Certificate of Deposit. These items will be liened by the bank until your loan is paid off, or you may be able to negotiate their release as the loan is paid down. And then there are personal guarantees that require you to sign with a co-signer on the loan. Many entrepreneurs resent this, but the banks are fairly strict on this. Owners who are married usually both sign the loan. If your spouse has valid reasons not to, such as he has other businesses of his own, it may be waived. You can ask.

The Care and Feeding of Your Local Banker

Securing a loan is not the end of a good banking relationship, it should be the beginning of one. You want the right source of financing to be in place throughout the life of your business.

Here is the advice of a very experienced and small business friendly banker. Tom Nunnally started with the Bank of America and eventually moved to Pittsburgh, where he worked with PNC Bank and became CEO of Iron and Glass Bank. He retired after helping to found a business-only bank, Enterprise Bank, and serving as its senior loan officer. Here are his Four Rules for Working with a Bank Successfully:

> **Rule # 1**—Win over the local person (branch manager, relationship manager, etc.), but always provide the documentation that will

pass scrutiny at all levels of the bank. A phone call is only the first part of the process; provide the written material that your local connection requests and do so accurately and completely.

Rule #2—Local proposals should be specific, well-documented, and realistic. If there is some problem that you feel might be an impediment to approval, you need to cover this issue up front and not leave the discovery as a surprise for the loan officer who is trying to support you.

Rule #3—Understand your responsibilities, before and at the closing. Furnish everything that is required, such as insurance certificates and material receipts. The bank adds time and cost into this phase of the process; you should understand that this is their investment in your working relationship.

Rule #4—Good, honest communication can prevent or even rectify many problems. The absence of information will usually result in a negative impression. If your business conditions deteriorate, don't try to hide that fact from the bank hoping to make a change before it is noticed. Discuss the problems and possible solutions before the situation gets worse.

Why Wouldn't You?

The thinking of the bank on a personal guarantee is this: If you don't have enough faith to sign and personally assume part of the risk, why should they take it all? When the loan is satisfied, you are released. In addition, there may be a side benefit to you, as the lien on your assets will protect them from the actions of anyone else. This could be valuable when the company goes through some rough times. A creditor with no easy recourse will often settle, so you might be litigation–proof for a while. The bank will seldom take your home precipitously, but they want you to understand the seriousness of your commitment.

▶▶ TEST DRIVE

Growth financing from outside sources presents a number of choices for the business owner. Do you know what to look for?

1. Are banks the only source of growth capital?
2. Can a partnership bring new resources, including cash?
3. What is the difference between a business plan and a loan proposal?
4. What is a loan guarantee?
5. Should you be willing to sign a personal guarantee?

The Current Value Is Equal to Present Worth of Future Benefits

There are a number of necessary reasons to have a business valued even when a sale or transfer is not imminent. Once you have acquired some assets and built a reputation and a customer base, you are likely to want to know the value of your company. This is a tool for future planning. One of your goals should be to build a company of greater value. Many accounting firms have partners or associates who are skilled in business valuation; their services are comprehensive as well as expensive. There is a lower level of study called a "compilation of value" that may be what you need for now. Do you know what your business is worth? Find an expert and let him or her evaluate what you have.

The statement above—"The current value is equal to present worth of future benefits"—may sound very complicated. What it means is that the current value to the owner in today's dollars is restated by the future value of the business that will pass on to the new owner over a fixed number of years. You determine your value on the basis of future earnings. Let's assume you have a good, positive cash flow; if you do not sell your business, the cash is in your control. A buyer would be willing to pay a certain multiple of that cash flow now, so that they will control it. That begins to set value. When you use earnings as a benchmark for value, you also use a formula to determine exact cash flow—it is known as EBITDA.

Restating Earnings or EBITDA

EBITDA is *Earnings Before Interest, Taxes, Depreciation, and Amortization.* You take the net earning number and back out all taxes paid on it, as well as interest on borrowings and depreciation (again, a non-cash expense). This number gives you the actual free cash flow, which a new owner will start out with. They pay you for the value of this positive cash flow with a multiple based on other industry or business considerations. There may be further adjustments based on the owner's excess draw or benefits.

Fair Market Value

This standard is required by the IRS when a business is being valued for tax purposes. The rule is defined as the cash, or equivalent price, at which property would change hands between a hypothetical willing buyer and a hypothetical willing seller, neither being under compulsion to buy or sell and both parties having reasonable knowledge of relevant facts. As with many tax rulings, the language may be confusing to some business owners and buyers. However, they are required for estate purposes.

The closely held company is fairly difficult to evaluate under these rules. Most valuation analysts (a specialty within accounting denoted by the initials CVA) will be able to issue a report that has standing in tax matters. Although entrepreneurs seldom use this as a basis for selling their companies, it may be a starting point. You will have strengths and weaknesses that add or subtract from this fair market value.

Valuations Are Often Used in Litigation

If there is a lawsuit between partners, between a couple over marital assets, or when a business has been damaged by the outside action of an individual or business, the formal valuation of fair market value will be the most commonly used basis by the court. This method will be an advantage to some businesses and a disadvantage to others. While you do not have to take action or make decisions because you expect trouble, knowing what an objective valuation expert sees as the worth of your business can give you a good baseline to work from. Know the factors so you can modify them if required.

Factors Involved in Valuations

The income approach to a valuation is the one most frequently used. Regardless of the method, there are several internal and external factors that are considered in the determination.

External

One of the external factors is the general economic condition at the time of the appraisal and the near future expectations. Good general outlook increases the demand for business purchases, which adds value to all businesses.

Another factor is the current interest rates and rates of return from other investments such as common stock and money market investments. The cost of capital has an effect on the price of an ongoing business and when other assets such as stocks, etc. are undervalued, the price of businesses trend upward.

Market conditions in a specific industry will drive valuations as well. Newer and growing industries bring a premium, while maturing ones have less value. A company employing cutting-edge technology can improve their standing.

Internal

The internal strengths and weaknesses of the specific company in question are a major factor. Quality and depth of the current management is considered. Market position and competitive strategy are evaluated. Will the key personnel be retained? Is there an opportunity for continued growth? Is the customer base solid and will they be retained?

Are the conditions conducive to continued profitability? Is the labor force stable? Are the tools of production modernized, and internal controls in place and working? How does this business compare to others in its field? A company that is poorly run in a good industry has value, but it is discounted by the inefficiencies of the specifics of the business being evaluated.

Income Approach to Value

The EBITDA is capitalized by expected growth, then multiplied by a valuation factor. For example, if you have pre-tax earnings of $50,000 and interest payments of $30,000 and depreciation of $20,000—your EBIDTA is $100,000. Interest is a return on capitalization; the new owner can see this return on his investment.

If your business is in the middle range and has a stable present and future, the multiple may well be 5 times, so the value is $500,000. This means that any new owners should see their initial investment returned in less than 5 years, assuming some growth.

Asset Sale vs. Stock Sale

When you are setting the value of your company in anticipation of selling it, you will need to determine exactly what is for sale. Are you selling the going concern (a stock sale) including all assets and liabilities? Or will you sell the assets only, providing the new owner with the tools to carry on the business in the future, but not being responsible for its past obligations?

Small closely held companies are more difficult to value and sell as a stock sale. There are several concerns to new owners, the primary one being any lingering liability that may come back to haunt them years later. Products sold years ago might fail and litigation could be filed. A workers' compensation case keeps rates up for years. Pension liabilities may grow to unacceptable levels. These costs that have crippled major airlines, auto, and steel companies recently are the same issues that impair stock sales of smaller entities.

The benefits of a stock sale to the seller is that a price is set on the going concern and the entire package is sold, with the risk and the entire liability passing on to the buyer. And the tax basis is on a capital gains, not a multiple including personal tax, unless you are selling stock in a C Corp when the tax is paid corporately, as well as again when the dividend is paid to equity holders. Talk to your accountant about these implications.

Due Diligence May Lower the Price

Later in this book, we will cover the final process of a business sale, known as due diligence. That is the verification of all financial records and any adjustments that need to be made for variances from the original financial documents that were submitted and reviewed. If there are a lot of unsettled issues, the sale price may drop dramatically and the seller will receive far less than they ever expected. When I am involved in a business sale, I prepare my client (the seller) for the possibility of walking away from the deal rather than taking far less than the business is worth. A savvy business buyer will use last minute techniques to drive the price lower.

Valuing by Assets

Setting a value and then a price by selling all (or most) of the assets at their current market value is another way to go about the process. Regardless of current book value, each piece of equipment is valued by an industrial appraiser to set its current worth. A piece of equipment no longer available as a stock purchase from any manufacturer may be worth more now than when it was purchased.

Receivables under 60 days old are priced at face value, and older ones are discounted—marketing material and signage, or inventory with some adjustments of what might be out-of-date or out of style. You may be surprised that there is more value in the parts than in the entire package. You may or may not add the receivables to this total as well. The buyer will pay for your assets and you will settle your liabilities. Many buyers prefer this method, but the result may be almost taxing the seller twice. Gains will be taxed, as will be redemption. This conclusion assumes that we are discussing a corporate entity.

Setting Value on Goodwill

The value of a business is increased by the value of intangible assets, a majority of which is often termed "goodwill." This is a general concept that covers the good reputation, the name, the customer awareness, customer data, and the tools and inventory that may be unique to a special market. Some companies spend years sourcing special materials. This information falls under this category as well. When you are valuing a business as an asset sale, you add a premium to the price of tangible goods that covers these elements.

Book Value or Liquidation Value

Take a look at your Balance Sheet and you can easily see the book value of your company. It is the net stockholders equity; the bottom line number on your balance sheet will give you that figure. Your total assets include receivables that are in question, inventory that may be obsolete, and equipment that is depreciated. These items are added together, all liabilities are deducted, and the difference is the book value of the company. But is this

Looking for Hidden Value

My own business was once sold as an "asset sale," and much of the equipment was fairly old but in excellent working condition. What we did have was specialized dies crafted to make "to order" product for a number of good, steady customers. When we purchased these dies, we expensed rather than capitalized them so they were not listed on our Balance Sheet. When we sold them off, they were valued separately, which added substantial value to our assets and accounted for the "customer goodwill" that attached to our ability to provide specialized service. I also arranged a payout based on future business that was attractive to the buyer and cost effective to me. The buyer was buying a new market along with the tools to serve it.

Having learned from these negotiations, a few years later I sold a printing company for an owner who had felt for some time that there may not be much real value in the company. Some years they barely broke even, and when there was profit, it was slim. However, the depreciation from the big presses did provide adequate cash flow, and debt service was shrinking.

I realized that they did have a substantial amount of value that did not show on the Balance Sheet, as had happened in my own case. The presses were sought after by new owners. Years of business and scores of satisfied customers had ordered and reordered numerous printed pieces. This company had all of the pre-press on these pieces complete and most of the work was ready to go back on press as soon as it was released. Printing customers are fairly loyal and enjoy going back to a current supplier. This was over a million dollars worth of sales just waiting for the new owner, and he knew it. We marketed the value of this "almost" captive audience, and we received a premium price. It was not a typical line item on a valuation.

accurate? You can take the time and make your own adjustments to these line items and determine the actual book value. The most frequent adjustments come from writing down receivables and inventory and, perhaps, valuing up machinery and equipment that actually has a higher market value than book value. It is highly likely that items that have been completely "depreciated off" the books still have a good market price.

What Is Liquidation Value?

Think of what would happen if you had to turn your entire business into cash in a hurry. This would not be an orderly liquidation. You may not be able to collect all of your receivables, as some customers will not be willing to pay. Perhaps you haven't completed a contract, or maybe they know you won't be around to finish any serious collection. Some will think of the strangest reasons for not paying you, because they no longer need to maintain their business relationship with your company.

Inventory will have to be discounted to be sold quickly. Equipment is used and may need updating. Most of it will have to be sold at auction and often will be purchased in bulk at a bargain price. In all, you may realize less than 25% of what you listed as value on your books.

An orderly liquidation conducted by you may bring in 50% of the value of your assets. You will participate in collections, and have an opportunity to finish outstanding work or deliver a completed order. You may be able to hold a slower sale of goods and inventory that will carry a lower markdown, and you can sell off assets to a buyer who is willing to pay a higher price. This process can take six months and is sometimes done by an owner who cannot, or does not, wish to sell the business, but perhaps wishes to retire.

Liquidation value is a good way to understand how the bank views your assets. And this is a reality check for you. If you are losing money (or barely breaking even) *and* losing real value as assets deteriorate, you cannot afford to go on any further without making some changes.

A Single Asset With Strong Value

You own equipment that is no longer made but the products you manufacture still have a market. You own a building in a great location that has always contributed to your business success. You have developed software that is an innovation in your industry. Your head designer is under exclusive contract to you and is known throughout the industry. These are some of the unique features that make a business more valuable than others. Do not underestimate the premium these assets add to the overall value. Make sure that you promote this extra strength and quantify how this adds to the bottom line.

One Asset That Is Worth More Than the Company

I had one client that owned a large building in a light industrial area. They used less than half for their own business operation. Their Balance Sheet did not look bad because the value of the building gave the entire business a net worth. The truth was, when we analyzed it, the building would be worth more as a total rental property than as their business location. They ended up selling the building, retiring debt, and moving to a smaller location.

The Intangibles

Intangibles include intellectual property, a well-known name, proprietary software, or the rights to a lease. For the most part, small companies don't book these things on their Balance Sheet, although the value may be substantial. Consider all of the additions to tangible assets that you bring to the table and place a reasonable value on them.

There are some intangible values that few notice but can come into play if a company is sold. Some types of businesses are very appealing to wannabe owners. They will try hard to find a business to purchase. If you run a bookstore or a restaurant that is doing well, the business will have value that is almost unexplainable. Call it Dream Value.

▶▶ TEST DRIVE

You need to know what your company is worth so you can build value and determine how to eventually exit. These are some of the considerations:

1. Do you quantify the current value of the company?
2. Do you understand EBITDA?
3. What multiples of income are common in your industry?
4. Does your book value reflect the real value of the business?
5. Do you have a unique asset that goes with the company?

Budgets and Cost Controls

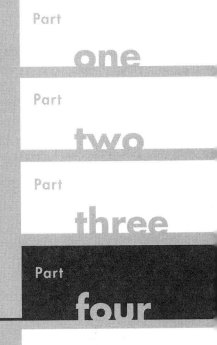

Getting Started

An adequate and complete start-up budget is an unavoidable and necessary first step when creating a successful business. Underestimating what these costs will be is almost sure to be a serious impairment in the early stage of growth, because working cash flow (the money you generate from operating) will have to be used to meet additional debt service on start-up expenses. There are several key issues to consider:

1. Start-up expenses are one-time costs primarily for organizational expenses (lawyers, accountants, etc.), space preparations, and required equipment and inventory that may not see an immediate return. Use long-term money or equity to finance.

2. Make sure you include the expense of initial marketing, utility deposits, and insurance coverage. There may also be industry-specific costs such as licenses.

3. The reserves you keep for working capital must be sufficient, because your borrowing ability will be severely limited without a track record. Businesses that are just starting out are the most vulnerable to running out of cash, even when they are meeting targets and beginning to turn the corner.

The Cost of Forming a Company

You've been thinking about it for months, you have a great idea, and you are absolutely sure it will make money. Now is the time to rent a spot, hang a sign, and open up the doors and your dream will be a reality. Not so fast!

▸▸ **Starting a business is a major undertaking on many levels, and the more bases you cover in the beginning, the higher your chance for success.** Begin by taking some basic business classes, which will cost you time rather than money. The Small Business Development Centers, located at over 1,000 university campuses in every state, often offer free or low cost seminars, as does SCORE (Service Corps of Retired Executives), sponsored by the SBA. Take one or more of these classes and pay attention to all of the presenters, particularly the ones who speak about business planning. Make the effort to write a comprehensive business plan and take your time when working on any required financial projections. These projections will tell you when and if your cash flow will turn positive.

Find a good attorney who will you give solid advice on business formation. Of course, you can save all the start-up professional fees and simply be a sole proprietor; you simply register under a fictitious name and use it without incorporating. Or you and a partner can do much the same thing. There are risks involved here. In the end, this may still be the choice you make. However, before you begin, learn enough to know the pros and cons of all the different types of legal entities.

Ongoing Costs to Consider

The quickest and cheapest way to start a business is as a sole proprietor or a partnership without any corporate formation. Register the fictitious name you will be using and print some letterhead and cards and YOU are in business. Each year you will attach a separate schedule to your tax return that specifies your business income and expense. You will pay tax on the profit you make. From a recordkeeping standpoint, this is a low-cost way to operate. But does it offer you enough protection and adequate tax advantages?

On the other hand, if you decide to form a corporation, you will have the legal expense of writing and filing all of the necessary paperwork. There are forms to send to your state to register, and bylaws and agreements to be drawn. Minimally, you are looking at an expense of about $1,000. Don't forget the visit to your accountant. You need to decide which corporate entities will work best for the type of business you plan on starting, and you need to immediately set up a reporting system so you can file the proper reports on a timely basis. You will have ongoing accounting fees that will keep the corporation in good standing. Is it worth the expense?

An Overview of Choices

Here are some business structures that you may want to consider:

Proprietorship

A proprietorship has one owner, although there is no limit to the total number of employees. The recordkeeping will be somewhat easier, as you do not need to file separate corporate returns on the business operation. However, remember that this does not negate the need for information on the financial progress of the company.

The two major disadvantages here are in raising capital and the risk of personal liability leading to financial distress. A business that is not a separate legal entity cannot sell off an interest of itself to attract an outside investor. Money will have to be raised personally by the owner. That limits your sources of capital to lending institutions or friends and family. Personal loans are just that—personal. Any lending institution will factor all of your personal financial obligations, and not just those related to your business.

Perhaps the more important disadvantage is the risk of personal liability for all company debts and claims. Any lawsuit that is filed as a result of business activities will be against you personally, and if there is no insurance coverage, you may find yourself in deep personal debt.

Partnerships

This is another noncorporate business entity. The main difference is that each owner has a share of the partnership, rather than ownership of any specific business assets, and the partnership is the actual owner of the assets. Taxes are normally filed on a partnership return and each owner pays tax on their share of any earned income. The share is based on percentage of ownership, not on the time or work involved in earning the profit. You may also share in losses as well, which could shelter any other earned income, including that of your spouse. This can be a bonus to a start-up business, as it frees up personal cash.

There are some serious downsides to a nonincorporated partnership. The liability, while the responsibility of all partners, can fall on the shoulders of only one. Without any prior agreements, one partner can create obligation for the partnership entity. And any creditor looking to be paid can look to the partner with the most personal assets to grab, even if they were not the one who incurred the debt. And if the partnership is dissolved, it is important to make sure your name is removed from any partnership obligations, or you may find yourself being sued years later.

Shared Vision Is Critical

Whenever more than one entity joins forces with another in an alliance, a venture, or a partnership, everyone must be on the same page with regard to goals and obligations. In the shorter-term relationships, there is less at risk, and often a term certain. If it doesn't work, there is an end. A partnership is a marriage in many senses, and the dissolution is a complicated and often painful experience. As long as there are shared liabilities, you are both obligated to each other. One cannot just quit and leave without the full legal release of the other. Two heads and two sets of hands are often better than one, but they seldom share a workload equally. Know what you and any partner expect before you take the plunge. And make sure you have comprehensive agreements with regard to financial responsibilities.

A Corporate Entity

Any type of formed corporation is similar to a partnership in that the owners (called shareholders) control the entity and the entity owns the assets. And in most cases, the entity also assumes the liabilities, unless there are personal guarantees.

This is the basic advantage of forming a corporate structure; you will protect yourself, in most cases, from shouldering business liability personally. The primary exceptions to this protection are taxes and fraud.

There are different types of corporate structures; some are "close corporations" which allow shareholders direct management of the company without having cumbersome governing boards. There is also a form called an LLC, which means a Limited Liability Company. This has most of the protections of a corporation with many of the simplicities of a proprietorship, even down to the simplicity of tax forms. Smaller LLCs file only income/expense schedules to their personal tax returns. They are treated, for tax purposes, the same as a proprietorship or a partnership.

Corporate Status and Tax Status Are Not the Same Thing

Any business owner with intentions of being successful over the long haul should know they need a good accountant on their team. And from the beginning! An accountant will help you form a start-up tax strategy. The first thing to decide is what is the best tax status for your company to achieve your goals. Even standard corporations have a choice on tax status—Sub S or C Corp. In one case, losses (and then profits) are passed directly to the shareholders. In the other, they remain in the corporate structure. Losses are carried forward in the corporation books to offset future profits. Your choices may depend on whether you or your investors have other income to shelter. The simplified LLC also has choices that can make a real difference. The business can be a single member and file on a Schedule C, or a partnership that files a 1065 return, or elect to be a Sub S Corporation and file a full corporate 1120 return. Find out what will work best for your business. You need to make your tax decision within 90 days of your start date, and then file the proper forms for the IRS. Any changes after the initial startup may be costly in terms of professional fees.

Other One-Time Start-Up Expenses

Once you have determined your legal structure and officially become a company, you need to consider a list of other expenses that will be specific to the start-up phase. The following will cover what most businesses require, but you may have some specific additions.

Site Preparation

It is not likely that you will rent a building that is ready to move into and open the doors. Whether you are using an office, a retail operation, or a fabrication (manufacturing) site, the required changes could run from putting on a coat of paint or building walls and adding storage to developing an attractive décor. You may be making structural changes such as building in a load bearing floor or heavier HVAC. Some of these costs may be included in the lease, and some may be completed by recruiting your friends or doing it yourself. Determine the cost and what portion of it you will need to raise. Keep in mind what you will need in the next year or two as well and include this in your startup expense.

Don't Be Doomed from the Start

I have worked with more than one company whose fate was sealed before they started. In each case, the problem was easy to identify and almost impossible to cure. They had spent far too much on their business location and the money they borrowed to do the work, as well as the increased rent from the work the landlord added, buried them from day one.

Several of these clients were restaurants, and this is a known occupational hazard in the industry. The expense of the kitchen and the HVAC is major already, and additional elaborate décor tips the scales. What to do? Try to phase in the expense; keep some of the touches for a later round of remodeling, when the revenue flow is already there. And by all means, put in as much sweat equity as you can. Menu creation is critical to the success of a restaurant, but if your overhead expense is too high your chance to make a go of it will be lower, regardless of how good the food is. Make a budget and stick to it.

Another type of business I consulted with that fell into this trap was a shoe store that spent money that should have gone into inventory on decorating touches. The store was beautiful and everyone loved it, but it was the product they were coming to buy, and stocking the shelves was a critical issue. The one-time cost should be conservative, and when profits flow, then reinvest some of it into your space. It is all about choices.

Deposits, Fees, and Licenses

There are other deposits beyond those required by a landlord. The phone company (land line and cellular) and most other utilities will require a payment to activate service. The amount will depend on the size of service you require, and often your credit history. Usually the charge is equal to the projection of two months of service.

You will need to put a variety of insurance policies into place to protect your tangible assets as well as any liability from injuries, etc. A new business is difficult to underwrite without a track record, and you are likely to be required to put down 25% of the first year's premium as an initial deposit to activate the coverage. Don't open the doors if the proper insurance isn't in place.

You may also have professional licenses, occupancy permits, registrations of vehicles, etc. These are all cash costs you will be required to fund.

Marketing Material

Any new business requires an identity package (letterhead, cards, bro-chures, etc.) as well as other marketing and promotional material. You do not have to go to the most expensive graphic designer in town; desktop capabilities mean that you may be able to do your own logo and graphics, and small instant type printers can help as well. This is another case of starting out slow and spending more as the revenue funds are coming in.

Other Start-Up Costs May be Leveraged

You will need your space and the equipment to fill it, as well as inventory or products to sell. These may not all have to be paid up front, which lowers the requirement for extensive start-up capital. As we have covered, raising that money won't be easy, so a strict budget is necessary. In case you aren't aware of it, there is even a cost for a business loan. Banks have preparation and document fees, and if there is a SBA guarantee, that fee can be up to 3% of the loan.

Try securing at least some credit from your future vendors, which you can pay off as you sell their products and generate your operating capital.

Negotiating the Best Lease

If you have never negotiated a commercial lease, my advice is to hire a professional to help you. You may use your own real estate agent or an attorney, but don't just look at the rent figure and then sign the document. What you are signing is a contract, and quite often, a new business owner will be required to sign personal guarantees. This means if the business fails and closes, you are personally on the hook for the unpaid rent, even if you are no longer using the space.

Commercial leases are written for the benefit of landlords, and many have provisions that are added so they can be "thrown away" in negotia-tions. Read each clause and strike out the ones that will impede your pro-ductive business operation, such as limited access for delivery or forced hours of operation. You know what you want, and here you are the cus-tomer. Remember that.

Make Your Business a Desired Destination   Inside Track

One of the most popular appliance dealers in my city is in a town so small that most people have never heard of it, even though many people are aware of the company. I usually can't find my way without a map. Yet they are always busy, I see their trucks all over the area, and a contractor I used fifty miles away recommended them. They use their money to advertise and promote, not to have a high-priced, centrally located storefront, and their bottom line must show it, although I have never seen their financials. I would be willing to bet that the cost of their location is less than a fourth of most stores doing that volume.

Have enough confidence in what you are doing to expect people to come to you—pass on the savings in rent as discounts or higher level of service. And then let potential customers know of the value you provide. This is a winning formula.

And the business does not have to be a retail store; it can be a restaurant or a spa. Create a demand for your product or service that makes you a destination, and you will not have to pay high rent for traffic which, at times, does not work to your benefit. This is the reason that you see mostly chain stores in the mall—their formula is to drive high volume through the store to meet required sales numbers. Your formula should be to develop well-served and loyal customers.

Weigh Your Negotiating Power

Some locations are very popular and the available space is filled most of the time. Some areas are on the fringe of the activity and filled only part of the time. There are also stretches of empty space with very motivated landlords.

What do you really need? If foot traffic is important, you want to be where the action is and you are probably not going to be given many incentives. If YOU are the attraction, you can go where the bargains are. And if you can operate out of anywhere, consider the money before the prestige. Although it is always pleasant to walk into beautiful surroundings each day, it is also a pleasant feeling to be able to pay your bills and put the rest of the money in your pocket.

Money Terms Associated with Leases

Here is a list of terms that you need to familiarize yourself with so that you will understand the full cost of renting space.

1. **Triple net lease**—This lease includes payment for rent plus real estate taxes and structure insurance. These costs will be spelled out and you will make a single payment to your landlord each month.

2. **Plus lease**—Your rent will change with any rise in taxes and structure insurance. This can be a serious issue in new construction where there has been short-term tax abatement. Your lease has a built-in mechanism to pass this cost on to you.

3. **Common area maintenance (CAM)**—Here is where the landlord allocates (as a separate charge) the cost of maintenance and upkeep on the building on a pro-rata basis to all of the tenants. The decisions for what work has to be done remain with the property owner (i.e., resurfacing the parking lot or landscaping), but the cost will be passed on to you. Careful of this add-on—perhaps you can set a ceiling. And ask other tenants what their experience has been.

4. **Escalation clause**—Should you default on your rental payments, many leases have a clause that makes the entire value of the balance of the lease become payable immediately. It's similar to calling in a loan. If you have a 5-year lease at $1,000 per month and you do not pay the 12th month's rent, the entire amount for the final 4 years is due. This can be the basis for a lawsuit to evict you even if you catch up with the past due rent. And a personal guarantee will make it a personal debt.

5. **Renewal options**—After the first term of the lease is over, you have an option for a second, and perhaps a third, lease period at a new price not to exceed a percentage of the current cost. It is a good idea to negotiate such options, if long-term stability in one place is important to you. Being forced to move after you have developed a customer base can be costly. Also, see if this option can be passed on to successor ownership, in case you decide to sell the business.

There are other terms and conditions that will have a financial implication for your business, so it is best to read even the smallest print. And ask questions of your attorney—don't try to save legal fees with such an important business document.

Buying the Equipment You Need to Begin

Here's where a start-up budget is really needed, and not one that is created after you have made a wish list and called around to get prices. This is the time for discipline. Remember two words—productivity and payback—and try to keep them both in balance.

▸▸ **You want equipment that will allow you to be as productive as you can, because that is a real source of profits.** There are some features on virtually every piece of equipment you will need and use that will make it easier to operate, but not necessarily more productive. Try to get what you require to do the work, no more and no less. Perhaps the answer is to purchase equipment that can be upgraded when more funds are available.

Payback is determining how long the equipment will be in use before it pays back its cost and becomes even more of a profit center. Any type of equipment that becomes outdated in a matter of years falls in to the area of caution. If, by the time you get it paid off, your system is obsolete, is it worth it to get the top of the line now?

Consider Buying Used Equipment

A three-year-old computer has almost no value, but some industrial equipment can be used almost forever. And when you buy from a reputable equipment broker, you will often be getting new parts and a new guarantee.

One of my clients replaced a printing press they were forced to return, that had cost the company over a million dollars originally, with a rebuilt model, a bit older but with more features and a price tag of $380,000. The payments were cut by two-thirds, and the end product coming from the cheaper press is actually better. Don't feed your ego, feed your bottom line.

Lease vs. Purchase: What Makes Sense?

Another alternative to raising the capital to purchase equipment is to lease it. You may be able to do this directly from the equipment manufacturer (although these days they are likely to use a separate financing division), or you can do it through the bank or an independent third party. Here are some pros and cons to consider:

The Benefits of Leasing

1. Lower down payment, usually a few months of fees, set up as first and last month, and a security deposit.
2. Leasing is a secondary source of financing and does not show up on your Balance Sheet as debt. Therefore, you will still have other collateral to borrow against.
3. Credit may be easier to secure as a lessee because the title to the property stays in the hands of the lessor. The process of collection becomes less cumbersome and costly.
4. There may be some additional maintenance agreements included, but don't buy one if you don't think you'll need it.
5. You may only want the use of the equipment and not the ownership, so when the lease is over, you can turn it in.
6. There are tax advantages, since the entire lease payment is an expense, but on a purchase, only the interest payment on the loan is deductible.

The Drawbacks of Leasing

1. The ownership of the property stays in the name of the leasing company, and you cannot treat it as if it were your own. Normally, you cannot alter the equipment without permission, and any upgrades or changes you make may become the property of the leasing company.
2. You may pay more for the lease without gaining any equity in the equipment. Leases are not long term so you are paying the equivalent of rent.

3. If the equipment increases in value due to market conditions or upgrades you have made, they belong to the leasing company.

4. At the end of the agreed-to payment period, you will not have a piece of equipment free and clear of loans that you can then use without charge for the balance of the life of that piece of equipment.

Not All Leases Are Created Equal

There are two basic types of leases, and each has its own particular characteristics:

1. The operating lease—The ownership of the item being leased never passes from the lessor to the lessee. The total monthly charges are fully expensed and deductible. The asset will not appear on your Balance Sheet and the cost of your lease payments will not appear as a liability. You will not have to charge off depreciation as an expense. It may be possible to purchase the item at the end of the lease for its "fair market value." This value will not be established at the inception of the lease. Sometimes this is a negotiable amount; never hurts to make an offer.

2. The capital lease—This type of lease is virtually a lease-purchase agreement throughout the term of the lease, covering the full cost of the equipment. At the end, there is a nominal buyout, normally of $1.00. This type of lease does have Balance Sheet implications. The value of the equipment will be listed as an asset and depreciated under normal schedules. The current (12 month) portion of the lease will become a current liability, as will the balance over the long term. From purely financial record-keeping purposes, this will be treated the same as a purchase.

The Need for Adequate Working Capital

There are a number of times in this book that you will read about the need for working capital. The reason is simple: this is one of the single most critical elements in operating a business and you must plan, in the start-up phase, where you will find the capital. A start-up or early stage business does not usually generate positive working capital. Your proforma will show you where the gaps will be. Plan to fill them long before you get there.

There are two basic solutions. One is to raise the extra cash and set it aside for when it is needed. The other is to negotiate a working capital line of credit with the bank that will be made available once the business has reached certain benchmarks. Starting a company, getting it halfway to success, and then running out of money is a very frustrating situation and an all too frequent one. That's why the early years are the riskiest.

▶▶ TEST DRIVE

You need to plan for the cost of starting a new business. Ask the following questions to see how far you have gone with your budget.

1. Do you know what type of legal entity you should be?
2. Have you located an accountant and discussed your profit expectations and tax needs?
3. Are you considering the cost of your location, as well as its desirability?
4. Have you explored leasing some equipment?
5. Is working capital one of your line items?

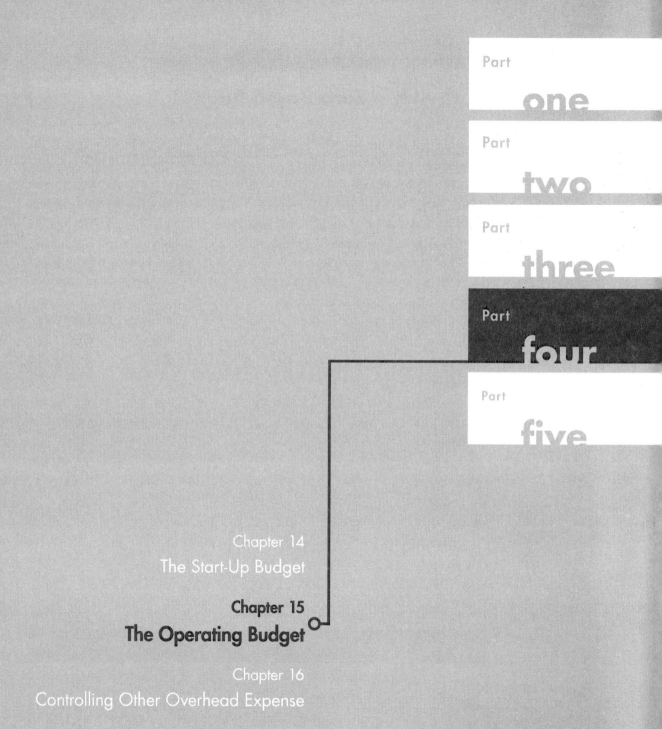

Start with a Zero-Based Budget

Before the current year ends and all of the results are in and accounting adjustments are made, you need to be thinking ahead to the upcoming year. If you have done well, you want to sustain that momentum; if you haven't achieved all that you expected, plan to make some changes. The operative word here is plan. A budget gives you a heads-up to get in the right direction.

What does it mean to have a zero-based budget? The first time I heard this concept was from my corporate friends. I knew that large companies always had a lot of money to spend and they often did so lavishly. Raising money from an equity market is always less painful than creating debt that has to be paid off. There are some small companies that run a low cost operation and others who seem not to care at all about the expenses. The more cautious the approach, the more likely of success.

Zero-based budgeting is a theory that you begin with a zero rather than the number you stopped with last time around. If your 2006 cost of machinery repair was $25,000, do not start 2007 with that number plus an add-on for inflation and growth. This assumes that all of the equipment breakdowns will happen again plus some. That is not necessarily true, and it's not a good idea to plan for it, because someone will find the way to spend the available money whether you need to or not.

Instead, start 2007 with a conservative number, building it from the zero base and not from the previous year. Perhaps you have newer equipment that has a warranty period and needs less work because it is new. Don't allocate money to spend based on anything but actual need.

Use It or Lose It

Most government entities work with a use it or lose it budget allocation. Anything left at the end of the fiscal year goes back and everyone knows they are likely to get a smaller budget next year. This becomes a psychological drive for agencies, because the amount of budget you control says a lot about your relative power. Here's where the $300 toilet seat came from. You never want your business to get into this mode. Perhaps a bonus for coming in under budget would encourage alternative behavior.

Give Managers Budget Authority

A critical element in delegation of work and authority is assigning responsibility for expenditures and the bottom line outcomes. At the beginning of each period, identify the amount of money budgeted for each department and ask the manager to identify priorities. At the end of the reporting period, compare the requested budget to the actual expenditures. Perhaps you can include an incentive program for those who come in under budget. Whether you are in the corporate world or in a small business environment, it is human nature to spend the entire budget because there is always a piece of equipment to buy or upgrade or extra inventory that would make the process the more manageable. In some organizations, the more money a manager spends, the more important he is considered to be. Make sure that is not your company's culture.

Keep Equipment Productive

I know a company that hasn't bought a new piece of production equipment in five years and, for the most part, they have cannibalized parts from older models to keep the newer ones working. Their bottom line looks very good right now. But the future is cloudy. With so much equipment down at any one time, the only way to get out excess work when they are busy is to work overtime, at a premium cost that cannot be passed on to customers.

You need to take care of the tools of your trade, whatever that trade is. Keeping track of when it was purchased and what maintenance is required is a good idea. Knowing good service companies in advance and developing a business relationship with them is important. You want to be in the front of the line when you need something fixed.

The advice here is that there is a combination of factors that lead to a profitable business. What you produce, and how quickly you produce it, will serve to earn you loyal customers. You want to be cost effective as well. Make sure that your equipment is as current and productive as you can afford. This is a good motivator for your employees. With technology changing as rapidly as it does these days, you need an edge of your own. Being able to meet expectations of customers is certainly a great start.

> ## Old Airplanes, Low Profits
>
> The airline industry has been set on its ear over the past few years for a variety of reasons. High labor cost structure is certainly one, but another of great importance is the age and condition of the equipment. A plane not operating because of maintenance is earning no revenue at all. One of the not-so-secret reasons for the success of Southwest Airlines is that they fly a single type of aircraft. Having a fleet of Boeing 737s means that all mechanics can handle all planes, and all parts are basically interchangeable. This makes cycling in regular maintenance checks much easier, and it keeps more planes flying more hours and making more money. In addition, all of the crews are trained to fly the same plane, so moving one crew to another flight is almost seamless.

Direct Labor Must Be a Constant

By now you understand the theory of direct and indirect costs, and you should realize that direct costs are variable. They are directly related to the volume of the business. For every dollar you make, you will have a certain percent allocated to direct labor. Assume you have a restaurant; the labor factor is usually around 33%. In a manufacturing setting, it can run around 20–30%. All of this depends on the type of business and the subset within the business.

A fine dining restaurant would be at the top of the cost; good service is critical. Fast food would be considerably less. A service business would have a much higher labor component. Whatever your type of business is, it *must* be consistent. When sales are soft either due to the season or the general economy, the cost of your direct labor force has to go down accordingly. Don't wait around hoping the next big order will come in. Take action as soon as the evidence of lower revenues is evident.

Layoffs Are Painful

The first time a business owner has to lay off staff is a very tough experience. And frankly, it almost never gets any easier. In the first place, you feel as if the failure was yours for not having enough work to keep employees busy. These are not strangers with a number, these are people that you know.

Taking the Difficult Steps

There have been a number of announcements recently that several auto plants are closing throughout the United States in the next few years. This restructuring has been a long time in coming and has caused serious losses for the major auto companies. I once operated a manufacturing company whose main customers were steel, auto, and other heavy industrial manufacturing businesses. They are all cyclical. We had a few great years, some slow times, and some times so quiet that the work was almost nonexistent. In a slow year for auto sales, plants shut down for sixty days or more to "adjust inventory." That meant orders from that customer were nonexistent. If we had gone into the slow period with back orders, we could at least have kept employees working for a while. But, eventually we had to lower our own workforce. I still remember the first time I laid employees off, and that was decades ago. I did not sleep a wink the night before, and I walked around in a funk for weeks afterward.

So, when I talk about taking action to cut labor costs, I do not say this as a frivolous recommendation. I know it is difficult and very personal, but I also know that if you want to have a company to thrive to provide future employment, there are times you must take action quickly and decisively. That's what good leadership is about. Be as open and honest with your employees as you can, and try to balance fairness with good business practice.

Additionally, you will be asked questions for which you are not likely to know the answers. "How long will it go on?" is the primary one. And in many companies, some employees you want to keep on will offer to take time off voluntarily. To them, collecting unemployment compensation for a few weeks can seem like another paid vacation, and they may feel secure they will be getting their job back. However, this is not a good idea.

What may work best for the company is to cut hours from 40 to 35 and have all staff in at least most of the time. This is hardly ever greeted with approval because it represents a pay cut with no benefits to offset the financial loss. You know what your own employees are willing to do in order to help the company. Use careful judgment when deciding on a strategy.

Take Action Sooner Rather Than Later

You need to react to any changes in projected labor costs when revenue goes down. Every extra percentage is dropped to the profit line and can quickly turn a stable operation into a losing one. Use the numbers you generate to project what you can afford in the slower months, and make thoughtful decisions. But make them quickly.

Cross Training Staff Helps

Having someone stand around with nothing to do, while work remains undone because there is no one there to do it, is poor business management. In industries where there are labor agreements, this behavior is sometimes forced by the contract. But in your small business, the cost can be high. And this is a cost to the employee as well as to the company. ▸▸ **Rather than having a layoff, perhaps you can move some people to necessary slots and keep them employed.**

Ask for interested volunteers, but don't just show them a new task and assume they could move into that slot when needed. Take the time to train, allow for some work experience to get them up to speed, and keep them informed. You will end up with a more secure, and likely more productive, workforce.

Try Outsourcing

You have a small department doing work that is not constant, and the cost of their labor is far too high. Maybe this work is best done on the outside, and not in-house. Many small companies outsource their payroll; just one call to a data processing company, and the work comes back complete with tax returns.

Few small companies have enough work to start an offshore operation but you might be able to share some elements. One caveat here is about customer service. The expectations of a small business are far more personal than a larger one, and your customers expect to know whom they are talking to.

Some domestic manufacturers outsource many of the assembly components to outside labor, and perhaps do only the final steps at a local facility. Fulfillment centers that house and ship products can replace both space and people in your organization.

Consider Sheltered Workshops

Many local charities run in-house programs where they do work for private companies as a way to raise funds as well as train their clients. If you have simple, repetitive tasks, this may be somewhere to look. Prices are reasonable because they are not looking to take jobs away from others. In addition, they often stand behind their work.

Rent Your Own Employees

There are employee-leasing companies that will hire your employees and then lease them back to you. Why would you want to do that? Interestingly, even though they charge you a fee, it is possible that the leasing company can give your employees more benefits, and the overall cost to you might be less. The main reason is that the rates they pay for everything from workers' compensation to health insurance are lower because they are based on a larger population sampling.

Control Shrinkage

Sometimes you buy product or materials and, at the end of the day, they don't turn into revenue. There are several reasons why this happens. Few businesses plan for this reality, though, and if it gets out of control, you can really find your company in a tough position. Here are some things to consider about shrinkage:

1. **Loss from theft**—Depending on what you sell, a small amount or a substantial amount of inventory may vanish. This can be a serious problem in a restaurant where unrecorded drinks are served and premium food is consumed. You may require a running inventory that you can check frequently, and you may even require surveillance cameras. In one particular troublesome restaurant, the bank hired me and I hired private detectives. This business was going under with a lot of thievery and an absent owner.

2. **Makeover products**—You've produced an order and the customer refused to accept it because it had too many flaws. All the material (let alone the time) is wasted. A few of these are the expected. if you have more of these situations, you damage the bottom line. Make sure everyone understands the costs of sloppy work.

3. **Unsold inventory**—At the end of the season and the end of the sale, you have leftover product that didn't move. The value of this material has gone to almost zero; many companies actually donate it. This is likely a buying problem, and a costly one at that. Use better information from the previous sales before restocking the shelves.

Doing the Same Job More Than Once

I have worked with a variety of contractors over the years, and the major unplanned operating costs (perhaps second to insurance) come from the times they go back to fix a job they've already completed. They may have to replace something that was considered substantial, or they have to freshen up the finished work. These are costs not in the original estimate, and can only hurt profitability. Too often all the profits disappear. The best solution: monitor what is going on in your company, and minimize such situations.

The Cost of Administrative Personnel

There is a category in your accounting systems under your General and Administrative Costs that is titled Salaries—office. Often, when a company is establishing a start-up budget or even a cost projection to lower overhead, the assumption will be that the number in this category is the total expense of an office staff. What you must remember is that the fully weighted cost of any employee is likely to be 28–34% over the actual cost of their salary. This takes into account payment for time off (holiday and vacation) as well as unemployment compensation, workers compensation, the cost of the employer's contribution to FICA (which is 7.65%), and social security and Medicare portions. So, when you hire an office assistant at $30,000 per year, the real cost to your company is more than $40,000. Keep that in mind as you build your budget.

Set Specific Benchmarks and Measure Progress

Once you have determined what the year ahead should produce in terms of sales, and the expense and profits and pro-forma are done, break everything into quarterly bites. Let each manager or associate understand what the goals are for him in terms of budgets. Explain why you have established the numbers and listen to the reactions. The number everyone comes up with is a benchmark, and as soon as the quarter is closed, report how the actual number came out compared to expected budget. Discuss what went right and how to sustain it, or what did not work as well and how you can improve.

Be a Motivator

There are many elements in a successful business: a great idea, sufficient capital, the right timing and at the end of each day, a leader who believes what he is doing is worthwhile and valuable. Most costs are controlled by people other than you, and your job is to explain the program for budgets and accountability, and to motivate your associates to participate fully. One disgruntled employee can do a good bit of damage to your company.

Try Incentives

Forget the cash bonus for making budget numbers—your employees may love it, but you've just given away the advantage earned. Find a method of recognition, an extra day off and/or a special meal paid for by the company. Show the appreciation of the organization in a public way. For those who reach the annual benchmark, bonus cash is appropriate, along with your recognition of how much they have contributed to the goals.

When Goals Are Not Met, Try Plan B

Don't give up or accuse someone else of failure. You want them to get better, not frustrated. Work together to find problems and correct them. A good, motivated leader gets 100% or more from the team. That is your challenge.

▶▶ TEST DRIVE

Each year starts with a clean slate on your **Profit and Loss Statement.** Budgeting the cost side is the way to store the profits. Make sure you work on this aspect, and ask yourself the following questions.

1. Do budget numbers start at zero and then cover what is necessary?
2. Is your equipment as productive as it should be?
3. Are you aware of ways to outsource or lease employees to save you money?
4. Do you monitor mistakes, do-overs and material disappearances?
5. Do you spend time working on your role as a motivator?

Downsize from Unnecessary Space

Overhead costs are made up of so many different items, and come in such small increments, that it is easy for costs to grow almost unnoticed. Even an item like office supplies can get out of control when the products are stored in one area while orders for new items are being placed. When you started out, you probably did not fill out all of the space you rented, but you were sure you would need the rest, if not more space, soon. Over the years, the area may not have been needed, but you spread out by keeping excess inventory, equipment, or storage. In my own factory, we had 5,000 square feet of space that was virtually unneeded. The space was in the basement, and I didn't think about it. When the rent kept increasing (based on total square footage) and the utilities continued to climb, it finally got my attention.

Look around, are you wasting space and barely covering the cost because you have been at this location for a while and cannot take the time to make a plan to downsize or move? This may well be your highest single overhead cost each month, and your profits suffer from paying the expense. You want to spend your money wisely, so you need to take the time to find a solution.

Can You Sublease Some of Your Space?

If you are considering doing this, first talk to your landlord and have your lease reviewed by your attorney. Taking in a subtenant may be prohibited by your agreement, but if not, this may be one way to cover some of your rent as well as the utilities that come along with it. You may be able to rent out storage space to another company that has outgrown theirs, or share your office with a compatible operation. Find someone with a compatible business and you may develop synergy that benefits both companies.

Think About a Co-op with Another Company

You might also think about a co-op with another company. Few people realize that many department stores and grocery stores actually rent departments out to independent operators. These operators pay for the space and share a portion of their revenue for the built-in traffic. Is there a business compatible with yours that might make you consider this type of relationship? You can share costs and customers, yet sell different products or services.

Can You Share Resources with a Strategic Partner?

Whether you are working on a joint project or not, you may know of other companies with equipment or capabilities that you do not have. You may need them only infrequently, and it doesn't make sense to spend the money to incorporate the service with your existing business. The best advice is don't—share the resource and save the money.

Use these outside companies as subcontractors; hire their equipment and personnel when they are needed, and don't carry the burden of debt service and employment costs full time. Twenty years ago, the general advice was to expand in any area as you see the need. Given current concerns about overhead costs, it is more astute to keep your core business lean and ready to change focus quickly. Newer players in many industries are agile because they drag less weight. Outsource what you don't do to any experts who do it all of the time.

Become Important to Your Vendor

If you are a frequent buyer of outside services, you should develop a smooth and mutually beneficial relationship with the companies that you use. Be the type of customer that you want to have. That is, be one who shows loyalty, pays as promptly as possible, and communicates well. You want to be an important client whose needs are moved to the front of the line and handled quickly. If the situation arises that a bill cannot be paid right away, don't avoid the situation, go out and hire a new company. When and if you come back, you won't find a warm reception. Work with your contractors to make sure that your mutual self-interest is being served.

More Chiefs Than Indians

In a competitive world that is frequently downsizing to cut costs, take care that you don't build such a large management structure that you are out of balance. When your company is growing, attract talented people who will get the business to the next level. Bringing too many on board too quickly may turn out to be a problem, and sooner rather than later. Any new hire needs time to learn the system and become a profit center. Integrating new hires on a staggered, as needed, basis is the best policy for any company.

Any form of fixed overhead—whether it is rent, debt service, or administrative salaries—creates the set point for you to break even. The higher that bar, the longer to get over it. You want to keep the set point from becoming an overwhelming amount.

An energetic and competent sales and marketing team is a critical element in any business success, but this team does not pay for itself, as many sales professionals claim. Even a commissioned sales force has costs such as marketing materials and administrative support, and many companies allow for a draw against future commissions. It will take anyone time to get up to speed, and that means out-of-pocket costs (not to mention the time and effort required of you or other personnel to support the sales effort).

The most difficult aspect of growing a structure with a large number of chiefs is that these are the first-team folks, the ones you get closest to. When business is soft, it is very hard to make cutbacks in these ranks in any way, such as cutting time or reducing benefits or jobs. You may understand the flaws in wearing too many hats and not delegating enough authority to others, but there is a cost flaw in having a large and expensive management team. It may become a long-term cost burden that your company cannot afford.

Plan for Target Marketing

New business owners know they have to get the message out even if they aren't quite sure how to do this in the most effective way. There are so many marketing tools and gimmicks to use, how do you control the costs?

The first step is to set a budget and stick to it. This is not easy, because possibly the most charming and persuasive vendors who will call on you will be marketing and communication firms. They have creative ideas and you are likely to be attracted to many of them. Many of their strategies are very good; the question for you is, how many can you afford?

Start by Determining the Value of Your Customer

Each customer who walks through your doors, calls you on the phone, or writes an inquiry to you is important to your company. Some customers will be more frequent and major buyers, and others will be only occasional; cumulatively, though, they will all have an average economic benefit to your company. You can determine this benefit by finding out the average revenue per customer and the average profit per customer.

Existing companies can find this information in their financials. Divide your gross volume by the number of customers and you will find an average dollar of sales for each. If you have one client who spends a lot, and a few customers who spend less, take the extremes and their total revenue out of the mix. Let's say, then, for example, you have 30 customers remaining, and your volume for them is $600,000. This means that each customer is worth an average of $20,000 in sales. Now look at your gross profits on sales and that will tell you what each new customer is worth in profits. At 30% of gross, a new customer adds $6,000 to your operating profits. Over 3 years, this number may grow close to $20,000. Ask yourself how much you can afford in order to attract a few new customers. Look at your average sales expense as a percentage to calculate this number.

A new business must go through this same exercise, except it will do so on a pro-forma basis. What is your expectation of annual sales to each client, and what is your projected percentage of gross profit? Now you know what a new customer is worth.

Don't Spend More to Get Customers Than They Are Worth

No matter what type of a marketing program you use, your response will be in the single digit return. Direct mail brings 2–5%; other strategies may be a bit higher. Many marketing programs project several passes before you get any serious response. So, if your customers are worth $100 each to you, don't spend $10,000 to find 20 new customers. Flashy campaigns are ego boosters for the business owner, but they need to be cost effective as well.

Identify the Target, and Use a Rifle (Not a Machine Gun)

The first task in any marketing plan is identifying who your likeliest customer will be. Don't let an enthusiastic marketing firm try to convince you that you can sell to everyone—you just can't. You can see, on a daily basis, where you find the most receptive audiences. What do they have in common? Age? Income level? Location? Education? Be honest about what you are selling and where you can find new customers similar to the ones you already have. If you are a business-to-business (B2B) business, answer the same demographic questions.

Start with limited plans: a small direct-mail piece, telemarketing, e-mail blasts, advertising, or gimmicks. Test the results and put the most vibrant program in place on a more continual and aggressive basis. If you get little or no results, move on to a new concept. You won't succeed jumping from program to program, but you need to know when to cut your losses as well.

A Well-Thought-Out Communication Plan

Do all of the employees in your organization have cell phones, including the cleaning crew? At the time you put the phones in service, the cell phone company gave you an offer you could not refuse—10 phones for the price of 5. A year later, your cell phone bills alone are $2,000 per month. Oh, you know that people use them occasionally for personal calls, but it costs more to monitor them than the cost of it, right? Wrong. These are costs that can dramatically climb as text messaging is added and other upgrades come along as well. Do a complete review of how many lines are in service and consider whether they are needed, then cut the number to a manageable figure. Decide by looking at your Profit and Loss Statement to determine how many is reasonable. Set a budget number and stick to it; each month that the bill is higher than the projected budget, have the bill reviewed and make an effort to get it back down.

Land phones, Internet access, and other forms of communication have made doing business easier and more interesting. But technology has costs, and it must be controlled. Not only do the bills add up, but they may encourage your employees to use company time for private communication. As a result, your costs increase at the same time you lose productivity.

I have worked with companies in a wide variety of industries and fields. In several cases, unplanned big jumps in costs had almost blindsided them. A New York plumbing contractor sold his building on the upper West Side for a nice profit and relocated to a rental garage and office in Long Island City, resulting in a much lower cost for his facility. Being just across the 59th Street Bridge from Manhattan seemed to be a fine new location. But after 9/11, the cost of crossing a bridge grew dramatically. Security checks and traffic jams cost thousands of dollars for gasoline and unbillable hours. His workmen were out for hours trying to get from job to job. Every bit of the savings from the cost of the building was consumed by this unexpected increase, and profits soon disappeared. There were not enough other cost savings available and even price increases barely brought their revenue to break even. In a few years, they were operating back in Manhattan and making money again. If this second move had not been made, they would not have survived. Another company I worked with had a "secret" supplier, from whom they bought the cheapest fabric around. The price advantage was phenomenal and when it went away, because the supplier closed, their whole price structure had to change. If your cost advantages are temporary, do not treat them as if they are permanent.

The Rising Cost of Energy

Whether it is the price of heating your premises, running machines to produce goods, or fueling automobiles for delivery, energy is a source of continually rising costs that has virtually destroyed some businesses. The airlines are one example. Old-guard manufacturing is another—natural gas prices decimated the foundry industry a few years ago.

The cost pressures of rising energy are coming at you from all sides. The companies that manufacture what you buy pass their costs on—the trucks that bring the goods raise the freight, and the cost of a sales or service call goes up as well. A few percentage points from three or four different areas will add up to be enough to destroy your bottom line.

The answer isn't just to try to pass it on to your customer. You must first monitor what the costs are and how they are going up. Can you make your building more energy efficient? Can you ship products in larger quantities to lower the freight rate? Can you spend more time effectively scheduling car trips so you aren't just running around town without a planned route? Can you develop a computer model for your deliveries to save time and gas? Put internal controls in place and then pass them on with your own price increase to cover the rest. A sharp rise in any prices, yours or your vendors, gets the attention of customers—and almost always negatively. Keep your increases to what you really need and keep the frequency of price changes down as well. That takes study of the trends as well as vigilance.

Use Outside Professionals to Keep an Eye on Costs

Every company needs to have an accountant and an attorney and at times, some consulting help—a computer wizard, perhaps—on the ready. Don't wait until a lawsuit is filed or a tax deadline has passed to find the one you want to use. From the time you are a start-up, these professionals should be identified and on board. In most business situations, prevention is more cost effective than trying to fight back. And don't just dump a problem on your professionals and then not find out how much it will cost to solve. Perhaps you can do some of the backup work to save hourly billing.

Tax Planning

The time to look at how you are doing from a tax standpoint is not after the year has ended. You may want to do quarterly reviews with your accountant, but you should certainly go over your financials with her at the end of the third quarter. Make sure that your internal recordkeeping is in balance at that time as well. Having to go back and recreate some transactions after the fact can be time consuming and very expensive. It is easier to find a mistake when you are making regular reviews, and then to make changes you need to prevent the problem from continuing.

You need to pay the taxes, but you don't want to overpay beyond what is required. Finding the best strategies to pay taxes is the job of your CPA—seek her advice and take her recommendations. You or someone in your organization needs to know the basics in order to provide the information required. End of the year decision-making is often done with taxes in mind. Learn what that entails and how to take advantage of any opportunities.

Legal Self-Defense

The time to find out that there is a flaw in your service contracts is not after a customer refuses to pay. If you are forced to go into a collection action, any language you may have used to give a customer a built-in defense will be turned on you. Be sure that the documents you use in all of your transactions are reviewed by your legal advisor prior to using them. When there are unique circumstances, write them in the service agreements.

➤➤ **Learn that you must identify your company as a corporation to get the legal protection, and, that if you sign anything with your name and not your title, you are leaving yourself open to personal liability.** Have your lawyer look over the documents *before* you sign them. This may cost a few hours of his time, but the cost of litigation is very high in dollars as well as aggravation. An ounce of legal prevention is worth hours worth of legal cure. The same goes with employment contracts, if you have them. They must be reviewed by your lawyer to make sure you are adhering to current law.

Choosing the Professionals

Small companies, as a general rule, do not need the services of large, national legal or accounting firms. These firms are more expensive and tend to give less attention to the smaller companies. There are some exceptions of course, but this has been my experience. An exception to this rule would be if you are doing a very sophisticated deal that requires special expertise.

Medium size local or regional firms are often a good choice. Fees are in the mid range and a variety of expertise is available. Single practitioners may also be a valuable asset, because they can give extra time and energy to help out a new company. The only downside is that with a limited workforce resource, tax time could provide a crunch for you. Also, a lawyer involved in a consuming case for someone else may not return phone calls as soon as you would like. Check it out for a while, and don't feel stressed if you decide to switch. Your professional advisors are there to serve your needs, so make sure that they do.

Learn to Be a Good Customer

Be prepared whenever you call or meet with your lawyer or accountant. If there is a contract under question or review, locate all of the paperwork before you make the call. Be prepared to go over all of the details at one time. To do this, you may want to create a series of questions in advance.

If you have a tax question, generate copies of your returns and the backup internal statements and send them to your accountant before you call. Taking excess time from any professional will cost you. You can't expect them to teach you how to be brief and keep costs down, as their business is to sell their services. Remember that. You need to control the contact as well as the costs. That way you won't be blindsided by a large bill.

Cars, Clubs, and Travel

The reasonable purchase and use of an automobile is an understandable and legal business expense. And if you can get one, why not two? Then the insurance and gasoline bills for all of the vehicles goes under the name of the company. You have just dumped an expense that had been costing you $8,000 to $10,000 out of your pocket. Being in business is great. Second car goes to your wife and the third to an uncle who works for you part time as a way of saying thanks. Under the category of cars and trucks, you now have expense equal to 10% of your overhead. That is a reasonable perk, isn't it? Let's forget whether it meets tax requirements or not.

This all depends on how well the company is doing, how necessary the transportation is, and how reasonable the type of transportation you choose. A CEO does not need to drive a Lexus or a luxury SUV. Keep in mind, it is much easier to move up than move back, so when you begin to build your fleet, begin on the low side in luxury and numbers. If profits warrant it, you can trade up. I once suggested that a business owner's father return a Mercedes, because it was both unnecessary and in default. It was a difficult moment and it took time to repair hurt feelings.

The company got over it, and the business had a chance to get healthier. Remember, it is easier to be generous in small ways than to have to pull back from unreasonable largesse.

For example, is there ever any real business reason to go to Maui? I think so because I often attend a writer's conference on that beautiful island. But, I certainly would not head down there if I had unpaid debts or pending business issues to settle. My clients have a right to expect me to be on duty when they need me.

No one ever holds trade shows in Boise, Idaho, or Tulsa, Oklahoma (not any I know of); however, Vegas, Orlando, and San Francisco are desirable locations. You may have every reason to attend these trade shows, but some years it is easier to justify than others. Don't expect much sympathy for the grueling travel from staff or others. Everyone is likely to be envious. Go if you have to, but not because you just want to get away. Take vacations to your own spots with your own money.

Much of your overhead expense is optional and based on your judgment. Consider all of the implications when making these decisions. And consider how it looks and whether it passes the tax "smell test."

A Round of Golf at Oakmont

For those who don't know, this is Arnold Palmer's home course, and it is located not far from me in Pittsburgh. I am sure that going there with clients would be a lovely outing, but if there isn't a real business reason, it may not be a prudent move. When you spend the company's money on luxuries, you may be under more scrutiny from vendors when cash flow is soft. How embarrassing to meet someone you owe money to on the 14th hole! Are your customers aware they are paying for this lifestyle? And would they still think of paying you as a good value if they were? In light of recent corporate excess, err on the conservative side.

▶▶ TEST DRIVE

What kinds of controls do you have to monitor the cost of overhead? Consider the following:

1. Do you need all of the space you rent?
2. Are you creating an infrastructure that doesn't have a high level of usage?
3. Do you target your marketing expense to your most receptive potential client?
4. Are there more phones than people to answer them?
5. Are you driving a big car and entertaining lavishly when it's straining the budget?

What Types of Coverage Do You Need?

For many business owners, the very thought of insurance conjures up images of long, boring, and unintelligible contracts that are delivered after continual, sometimes annoying, sales calls. And who hasn't experienced that uncomfortable feeling that you are paying for coverage you don't understand, and may never receive, even if you file a claim. Let's face it, the only way you're going to benefit from insurance is when a disaster strikes and, as an entrepreneur who is always the optimist, you don't think this is going to happen. Despite this fact, insurance is an important aspect of business planning, and in some cases it is a legal requirement.

Insurance will protect a number of different areas of your business: the tangible property, the individuals, and liability you may have. Here is a rundown of the types of policies you will want to review:

1. **The package policy**—This covers your business assets from fire, damage, and theft. It also protects you from most types of liability, such as the unexpected failure of a product, etc. Depending on your industry, product liability coverage may have limits. But you will get the services of an attorney to defend you.

2. **Auto and casualty**—This is the policy that covers property from accidents and incidents.

3. **Business interruption**—Often an add-on to your other coverage, this provides revenue for the company to use to pay expenses when the business shuts down due to accidents or other insurable events such as fires or floods. It doesn't matter if your building can be repaired, or if the business was failing during the time it was operating.

4. **Workers' compensation**—This insurance is mandatory in most states to protect your workers from any industrial accident or work-related activity that prevents them from working—even for a short period of time. This cost should be added to your labor cost. It is based on your payroll.

5. **Key employee insurance**—This is coverage of life or disability insurance on the key employees of the company (including

you) so that there are extra funds to compensate the business for the loss of their services.

6. **Life insurance**—This includes policies payable to personal beneficiaries. Life insurance is often offered to employees as an extra benefit of employment. Disability may also be offered to employees. These policies are a part of an employee compensation package and should be considered under general employment costs.

7. **Health insurance**—This may be the most difficult type of insurance to offer while you attempt to control costs in a reasonable way. The coverage can range from simple coverage of catastrophic health incidents, to a much more comprehensive program which includes eye and dental coverage.

When Flood Insurance Wasn't Enough

In August 2005, Hurricane Katrina came charging up from the Gulf of Mexico, leaving torrential wind, rain, and a storm surge along its path. As with most catastrophic weather events, it left destruction in vast areas of Louisiana and Mississippi. Many businesses that were beyond the normal flood plane had no coverage at all, but some had property coverage without the business interruption add-on. Water takes a while to subside, and cleanup is a time-consuming task. That is before any replacement can even begin. For these devastated areas, it will take years to rehabilitate. Think of being without revenue for weeks or even months. How would you pay bills, retain important employees, pay bank debt, and have any money for a reopening? Without this specific coverage added on to your overall business insurance policy, your loss will be covered, but your days in business will be over.

Bidding Out Insurance Premiums

The days of active and competitive bidding on insurance coverage have mostly passed. In the past, the large insurers made as much or more money on their investments as they did on premiums. This phenomenon ended a few years back and, as a result, premiums began to rise. This is the revenue they require to cover losses. This does not mean that you should keep all policies you have in place and never look for more competitive bids.

Your package policy and casualty, including business interruption, are the insurance types to most likely have multiple candidates. If your record is clean on workers' compensation, it may be an area for multiple candidates as well. Be sure that all the coverage you are comparing is comparable—the old apples for apples theory. It is too easy for one company to quote lower coverage in order to look competitive.

Key employee and life insurance have very differing types of underwriting for you to choose from. Some may be term policies and others whole life, which builds cash value over the years. The carriers who write these insurances are often aggressively looking for new clients in the hope that the insurance packages will grow as the company does.

Workers' Compensation Coverage

Some workers' compensation is sold through your state on a pooled basis, although you need an agent of record to administrate the policies. However, if your previous record is good, you may be able to find a dividend paying policy.

The fact is that you need to find competitive sources of your various insurance, and the deciding factor may be finding a good agent who will source the best coverage for you. Agents who can use a number of different carriers are often the most competitive.

A Good Insurance Agent Is an Asset and Your Advocate

I have used the same insurance agency for more than twenty years. It will shop around for all of my coverage, almost always finding the best price with the most appropriate coverage. It always recommends that I get complete coverage where there are risks and back off when it isn't so critical. I consider this agency as a part of my business team. And, my claims are handled promptly and always settled. Perhaps I could have bought a cheaper policy here or there, but my overall expense has been very competitive. I am secure in knowing that I won't ever be left without the coverage I need. When it comes to any dispute with my carrier, I feel sure that my agent will go to bat for me. There is nothing worse than having a claim refused and perhaps even having to litigate over it.

Watch Out for Inadequate Coverage

Determine all of the situations that might befall the company and make sure those concerns are all covered by adequate insurance. You can't imagine anyone getting hurt by the potholders you make, but what if one catches on fire? Your food is organic, but there is always someone with a food allergy. The entrance to your building is completely flat, but what if someone leaves an open umbrella for someone to trip on? Don't think it won't happen, because it just might.

On the liability subject, you would be amazed by what an aggressive lawyer can drum up. I have recently seen the copy of a lawsuit asking for no specific damage except embarrassment and humiliation. We all feel that from time to time, but few of us sue saying someone else was the cause. Each case requires a response, and that is where the legal services of your insurance company comes into play.

One of the reasons to have a good agent is that few lay people can actually read the language in an insurance policy, and the agent will review what he sells you to make sure you have all the coverage you must have. Few people have flood insurance, but if you are where major storms happen from time to time, you should. Few companies have a mine subsidence problem, but that also happens in places. Count on your vendor to sell you all that you will need, not more or less.

Control Costs by Controlling Claims

Do you have a loss prevention plan in place in your business? Do you even know what that is? Often you can get a representative from the insurance company to visit your site and tell you where the trouble areas might be. Are your facilities dangerous for the public? Do you accidentally create hazards and do nothing about them? Where are your vulnerable areas that may create a claim? Learn them, and you may avoid a claim.

Having a Safety Committee

You can make your employees safer on the job, and possibly keep accidents down and generate a credit against your insurance premium, by

Know How to Handle Claims Before They Happen

One of my clients is a small contractor and designer who uses highly skilled and well-paid workers. Their work is high-end and they use craftspeople to do it. One of their employees had a small fall from a ladder, and his personal physician wrote a report to the insurance company that he would not be back to work for ninety days. While was on leave, the worker decided to pursue another type of work, and was gone from his previous employment for more than a year. The doctor continues to certify this need, based mostly on the physical complaint of the patient. The insurance company has been fighting it, but it continues to lose round after round.

This business has a current cost of workers' compensation that is making the company uncompetitive for many new contracts, and now the owner is looking for ways to solve this serious problem. Had the company sent its employee to a physician of the company's choice, this might not have happened. Check with your current agent to see how you can handle these claims proactively so you don't find yourself with higher rates that can't be reduced for years. The insurance company believes this is abuse, but there is only so much it can do.

forming a safety committee and having regular meetings. Talk about the use of protective gear and the ways to report any hazards. Have a formal way to report any incidents (recordkeeping is critical), and make sure your employees know that you have an official Physician Panel for them to see if they get hurt. These are doctors you have employed. Unfortunately, there are some medical personnel who do not consider the economic implications of making a general diagnosis of a work-related injury and certifying time off. This is a costly problem for a small company because the increase in rates is substantial. Companies have been forced to close when their insurance rates exceeded their ability to generate profit. Construction businesses are particularly susceptible to this.

Preparing for Audits

Each year, the insurance carrier will send an auditor out to review your internal records. You will have estimated your total sales and your payroll expense before the year began, and now is the time to compare those numbers to the actuals. You want to work with your agent prior to any visit. Have the sales and payroll records printed and set aside so they can be reviewed. Check to see whether you have any anomalies in your system, like sales to internal organizations which should not be counted; these should be identified with any backup documentation. All returns and credits should be calculated.

With regard to workers' compensation insurance, the critical issue is the category your employees are insured under. Secretaries are low cost and welders are higher, and construction workers even higher. If one employee does more than one job, document their primary work when you pay them (perhaps it is at two different rates). You want to pay their compensation at the lowest levels as well, if at all possible.

You will get an adjusted premium bill after the audit. Don't be surprised and don't fool yourself that you can underestimate your levels of insurance and never have to pay the difference for the increase in sales and payroll. If you see a big jump in hiring, you may want to call your agent and have the level of your coverage increased. By the same token, you can lower coverage if times get slow, and your numbers will be less. Pay as you go is always the best strategy.

You Can Time Payments But Not Avoid Them

A company undergoing a period of substantial growth will have many expenses that are related to this stage, including growing costs of inventory and payroll. Most of these costs will be due on an ongoing basis. Insurance premiums usually do not have to be prepaid. You may know what the expected growth might be, but you do not have to disclose the increase in sales and payroll to your carrier. The carrier audits at the end of the year and charges the difference. This is usually an interest-free advance that you may want to take advantage of at some time. However, the bill at the end of the year can be substantial, and you are unlikely to have planned for it. Phase this increase in by upping the numbers midyear and paying the new charge; the shock when the audit premium comes in won't be that bad. If you are delinquent in paying your insurance bills, word gets around fast. These days, there aren't that many carriers, and if you have been dropped for nonpayment, other companies may not quote your coverage. No insurance, in some cases, means no business. You cannot operate without insurance.

The Right Healthcare Plan

The most challenging insurance issue for all companies, large and small, is in their healthcare plan. You have to consider how extensive it should be, as well as whether you can still provide the side benefits of dental and eye care coverage. You may be able to include your plan in a large one that covers an industry or a geographically larger sampling of people, which would give you a more varied sample to set fees. A larger group may lower the age and lower the rate. This is a good strategy if your workforce is more mature.

Deductibles and Co-Pays

There is absolutely no way to provide complete coverage to all of your employees these days. The cost of the policies have gone up in each period until they are not within a feasible range. If your company is providing this benefit for a substantial number of people, the bill can be staggering. It may be the largest, or close to the largest, single cost you have.

The only answer is to modify what you are providing by adding a deductible or co-pay amount to be covered by the policy holder. Each visit and service will require a co-pay of perhaps $20.00, and coverage will only kick in when the paid deductible has reached $500, $1,000, or more. No doubt this is a painful charge, but is one that absolutely must be made. You may need to phase it in, but you will have to make this change. A new Health Savings Plan is available that may be used to lessen the effect on individuals. Money is paid into an account and used when there are uncovered charges.

▶▶ **TEST DRIVE**

Insurance is no longer a casual expense for any company, but one that must be attended to and controlled. Are you actively working on this cost center? Ask yourself the following:

1. Do you have more than one bidder for the coverage?
2. Have you made sure that your coverage is adequate?
3. Do you have the proper documents prepared for an audit?
4. Are you actively controlling the potential for claims?
5. Have you instituted a co-pay program on your health coverage?

Problem Solving
by the Numbers

No Growth; Margin Creep

All businesses have ebbs and flows; there are times when sales and profits have an easy rhythm, and times when one or both of them are scarce. Responding with the right action is critical, and the response must be timely. There are a number of problems that should send up red flags; these are the times action must be immediate and major in scope. The following are critical issues that must be addressed quickly and with structural change, not just small moves along the margins.

Starting a business is like starting a car—you begin at a dead stop. The early stage of business life is when sales begin and then, for most companies, there is a period of fairly rapid growth. The second stage is often a plateau where revenues hit a comfortable level and little growth is forthcoming. General economic activity acts like this as well. The concerns are for how long, and how to adjust. Growth is required for any business to retain its success. Continued increases in revenue requires ongoing focus from your marketing and sales efforts. Surely, over the years you are likely to do more business with some existing customers. However, some customers will leave as well. They must be replaced, in addition to acquiring new clients. Even if you think you have reached a very busy level, you can't stop there. A year, or even two, of flat growth will not jeopardize your business if you keep a watchful eye on gross profit margins as well as overhead costs.

Flat growth in terms of revenue is actually lost volume in realistic terms. Either you are selling fewer units, or billing a smaller number of clients, or you are deriving less gross profit. Direct costs are bound to go up, and your revenue must meet or exceed these increases.

Periods of no growth that go beyond two years (sometimes sooner) are likely to become critical because there are fewer dollars to pay overhead expense. Even if you have been able to hold down direct costs and keep somewhat of the same gross profit margin, the higher overhead will dissolve any available cash. With no cash to pay down a loan principal, to make unexpected repairs, to invest in ideas, or to market for the future, the company will inevitably begin to suffer.

A no growth or margin creep mode that destroys profitability immobilizes a business. There will be no cash flow to move forward, and the only alternative is to begin to shrink further. Worse yet, this is not likely to be the time when the bank will loan you any money. As always, capital remains the major fuel for growth.

Overhead Grows Even with Controls

On a year-to-year basis, it would be unrealistic to think that costs such as insurance, energy, rent, and taxes will not continue to grow, or that the same usage will cost the same amount. These items will become a larger percentage of your general overhead, and in short, these costs will absorb all of your bottom line. This depletes your cash and causes that dreaded cash crunch! A company with little or no cash on hand is one that can no longer continue.

Not the Time to Cut Prices to Generate Demand

No-growth periods are a part of every business cycle, but when this trend has gone on for a long time, most likely the aggressive sales and marketing are no longer priorities in the company. Old customers are in place, and as they leave or change their buying habits, they are not replaced. This must be changed with real action.

Many companies kick start a new sales campaign with a price cut. Larger companies with larger capital bases can do that (airline price wars; auto discounting), but, as we all have seen at times, these steps are catastrophic for even the biggest players. They are always sure to be damaging to a smaller firm. In a previous chapter, we reviewed actual numbers and how much volume you would need at a lower price to keep your profit at the same level. When you are trying to make a profit again, take the time and make the effort to do so at the margins you need. This requires effort at servicing customers and providing perceived value. This is the major issue that supports pricing levels.

Low Productivity: Technology or Attitude?

It isn't easy for a small operation to benchmark productivity and remain at, or exceed, the levels it requires. A manufacturing operation usually understands how many units it should produce per shift or per day. But what about a sales or service business? How many calls or how many customers should it contact? How many service jobs should it complete? How many repairs or installs should it make? These numbers may be far more esoteric.

You need to take the time, and have the information, to decide what you must yield to remain productive and profitable. There are new technology tools on the market regularly—are you using them to your advantage? Some are found in the job-costing module of your accounting system, and others in contact management software and time-slip recordkeeping. Find out what is used in your type of business and become familiar with it.

The Productive Contractor

Many small contractors use little in the way of technology or proven organizational methods to remain productive. They work as hard as they can, and then push themselves and their workforce a little bit more. In the end, this hardly ever succeeds. Organization falls in the midst of a disorganized rush, and jobs completed in haste require callbacks that lower the productivity because workers are inevitably unpaid. There are available tools for a company to use (PDAs and Blackberrys) that allow the users to set and change schedules in the most productive way. Smaller contractors can also hire a "virtual office"—a professional who will schedule jobs and appointments, create and retain estimates, do billing, and collect and pay bills. Remember, your time can, and should, be spent where it is most effective. Models of productive work are available in every industry.

Look Around—Are You Overstaffed?

As a business grows, it is natural to increase staff to provide administrative or service support. These people become an integral part of the company, but sometimes this may not be true of their functions. Much of the administrative work such as answering phones and accounting now can be done with automated systems. The secretarial or administrative assistant position has virtually vanished. If you really do care about the person who does the job, perhaps he can be retrained. There are many other time-saving and staff-limiting automations in place: are you using what's available? Or, are you too loyal to make the changes that will save all of the jobs for the long run?

Don't Cut Out Your Fallback Plan

I was in the manufacturing business for twenty-one years, and I learned many lessons about productivity and controlling direct costs. We produced a line of safety clothing and gloves, and our process was essentially what is described as "cut and sew," although we also had some finishing operations to seal seams or add additional safety features.

When I took over the operation of the business, the company had quite a few excess cutting machines as well as sewing machines. A few were taken out of service for parts, to save space. For a few years, I was willing to sell off the equipment not being used on the line—until, that is, we lost our full-time mechanic and had to rely on outside service people. Then I had far too many days watching work stop because of failures; half of them occurring with orders almost completed laying around, costing us money and making none.

My response was to have as much serviceable backup as I could afford. I sent machines out to be rebuilt, and when they came back they could be reinstalled to replace nonworking ones in a matter of minutes. You cannot operate efficiently without some fallback plans in terms of your tools. Don't be one machine short of the job.

Equipment Failure Has a Cost

Perhaps you cannot afford to have backup equipment in all of the phases of your operation, but you need to support the critical areas, along with extra parts, and some contingency plan. If the entire operation has to shut down because of a bottleneck, you will quickly learn how costly that is in terms of revenue. Be careful when you cut budgets that you don't cut too deep.

Don't Underestimate Poor Morale

Whether it is poor customer service, wasted time, or sloppy work, the effects of bad morale are corrosive. All of these problems add up to lost business dollars and threaten a business's ongoing operation. Poor quality and service can both drive customers away and raise costs in terms of real dollars. Taking too much time raises costs and encourages poor workmanship, and it may bounce an entire job or create the necessity for all or part of it to be redone. That costs money in many ways—non-billable labor hours, time lost from other jobs, and poor marks on your reputation. These are all signs of serious trouble.

When a company experiences rough times, everyone including the owner becomes concerned. Instead of shrinking away, you need to be hypervigilant about the status of your current productivity. You need to be a cheerleader as well as a motivator. If you have lost your optimism, so will everyone else. The effect will be evident to customers. This is the most important time to exercise leadership.

Loss of Market

When you are building a business, it is easy to dismiss the admonition that it is never good to have a single client that represents over 25% of your total sales volume. Being dependent on a few major clients makes you vulnerable. But, when new customers approach you, the matches are good, and they are solid citizens, it is almost impossible to say no. There is a way to protect yourself. Even if you are growing as a result of a few large clients, create as minimal an amount of permanent overhead and infrastructure as you can. Don't buy a bigger building to warehouse; rent a second one. Keep yourself nimble enough that if you lose business, you don't topple as a result. You want to be able to shed capacity and continue.

Be very aware of what is happening in the industry and the businesses of the customers who make up your market, large and small. Read reports about them, go online for data, and keep your lines of communication inside their operations open.

Watch for signs of trouble, such as orders that are newly stretched out and payments that are slow in coming. Know if your competition is mounting a campaign to replace you and at least try to do something about it. Be alert and don't be caught off guard.

Your awareness and willingness to act are the critical elements in stopping a change of markets from being a change of your business. New regions can be opened, additional products carried, new methods added—think of the possibilities. A business door closes and a new opportunity window opens.

Unpaid Taxes

This is a firm rule: NEVER borrow from any taxing body. They are not even the lender of last resort. In short, this means that taxes collected and withheld should be paid to the taxing authorities, and not sent to an insistent vendor or even a threatening banker. If you find yourself in a situation when taxes are due, and you don't have the money to pay them, you need to get to a professional quickly, who will contact authorities and work out a repayment plan. Ignore this debt, and the interest will continue to grow and the debt will become far more dangerous.

Some taxing bodies have additional penalties that can make the amount double very quickly, particularly when you do not file the returns as well. In the case of withheld federal income tax, the penalty is 5% to 25%, and non-filing is the same, at 5% per month. A $100,000 debt may become a $150,000 debt in less than 6 months! If you didn't have the money to pay the tax in the first place, you will really be under the gun for rapidly growing debt.

Be Careful of Personal Liability

The company, whether incorporated or not, may not be the only entity held liable for unpaid taxes. In many cases, although not all, the individual who was the responsible party for paying the tax will be pursued as well. The tax authorities don't have to wait until all of the actions have been exhausted against the business to begin their pursuits. You may find yourself subject to levies and liens and even seizures of personal property and bank accounts. This pressure will feel enormous and leave you with little resource and energy to continue operating a business at all. Letters from the IRS can raise your blood pressure easily, but it is important to answer them. Try to work out a payment plan or hire an attorney to represent you.

Criminal Sanctions May Be Applied

Even far more serious than the civil penalties and the strong-armed collection activities of the government, is the possibility that you might be the defendant in a criminal proceeding. It does happen, and I have personally seen several cases. In one such case, the withheld taxes were trust fund taxes and should not have been be misappropriated, but even more serious in most states is the state sales tax. Failure to remit sales taxes may cause you to be charged with theft. Even jail time might be imposed. If you are in need of funds and tempted not to pay taxes, do not give in. Consider the consequences.

Deteriorating Capital Base

Periods of flat growth and negative cash flow (perhaps due to debt service), as well as periods of losses, will eventually drain all of the working capital out of the business. The day may come when you do not have sufficient cash flow from current sales revenue and collected receivables to make all of your necessary payments to employees, vendors, and lenders.

It is important to know that you cannot grow from a situation like this, nor can you borrow your way out. The only way to cure a problem of capital shortage is to find a new source, such as an outside investment or additional owner equity. Both may be risky, the first because outside investors usually want too much control over their money, and the second because you may be tying up too much of your personal capital in your company. Look at these two solutions only after you have reviewed a newly created pro-forma statement and you feel assured that there is enough potential future profit to bring in a real return on these investments.

The other alternative is to liquidate some assets that will add some cash to ease the pressure. This alternative will affect the Balance Sheet. Strategies on this alternative will be covered in depth in Chapter 21.

Pricing Pressure from State-of-the-Art Technology

When a new company starts, their pricing strategy will usually be aggressive—they want to generate business quickly. Many customers (in some businesses, it is almost all) are price conscious and will immediately patronize the cheaper alternative. This situation can be exacerbated when the competition has newer, faster, and lower cost technology. The tough question for you is whether to jump off the price cutting bridge to see if you can save some of your customers. Resist the urge, because the major outflow of blood you will see in the water might be yours.

A business needs to be prepared to reposition itself, and with planning and belt tightening you can hold out long enough to do what you need to add a new twist to what you have been doing. Adding more services or access to new products or services (such as delivery, installation, or financing through your bank) will enhance value and justify your pricing structure. Not everyone wants the lowest priced item, at least not all of the time. Service is valued, as is quality.

Assuming that you have name recognition and market presence, you may want to do some aggressive investing in new technology. Perhaps the time has come to find an industry partner to join you in this enhancement of your abilities. The synergy may strengthen both of you, and give you the capital to get to the next level.

Lack of Strategic Planning

All businesses go through cycles from the start-up phase through growth and maturation, and that may result in stagnancy or a serious drop-off in volume. This may be seasonal, a result of economic cycles or new competition, or a lack of attention. Whatever the case, the facts are there. Business is not static—it is an ever-changing landscape.

The jobs of CEOs or top managers go beyond day-to-day custodial management of their companies. Their tasks involve reviewing current circumstances and research, as well as considering future possibilities on a continual basis. A company that does not do mid-range or long-range planning is a company that seldom gets where it wants to go. If you simply stand in place, things will change around you, and your business will be left at the back of the line. The business cycles, which were once a generation in duration, and in my tenure, ten or fifteen years, have now shortened to a span of three to five years. As soon as you have achieved current goals, you must set new ones.

As with most other decisions, using sound financial analysis on this one decision is critical. The easiest and best way is to create a fresh business plan for the new direction under consideration.

Develop new cost models of any new product or service you will be promoting. Treat your existing overhead as if it wasn't a permanent fact of life, and develop an administrative cost that only supports the business you expect to be. Find out where you will be able to go in the revenue and profit future. Then consider how you would have to modify the existing company. Can you do it with a minimal amount of dislocation? Do you have any choice? Can you find the capital?

You must continue to pay attention to both the current situation of your business and your future opportunities. Any lack of attention to what's ahead could cause you to stagger forward, unprepared to face and solve the business challenges of the future.

▶▶ TEST DRIVE

Most business owners get to know the rhythm of their own companies. When yours hits a sour note, pay attention and take action. Are you monitoring the ongoing activities?

1. Has your revenue been flat for more than two years?
2. Are the productivity levels you can monitor going down?
3. Are there any tax returns unfiled or unpaid?
4. Is the capital base at a level that makes meeting basic expenses a problem?
5. Do you have a plan for where you will be in five years?

A Business Plan Is a Roadmap—Keep One and Update It

One of the most interesting things about successful entrepreneurs is that they come in all genders, sizes, shapes, and colors. They can be found as young as teenagers, to folks well into their eighties. They may represent different businesses and different operating strategies, but the seven traits in this chapter are ones that I have identified in most of the successful entrepreneurs I have known. Consider your own attitudes, because they are clearly a part of a winning strategy. How many of these traits do you have?

The first common element of most successful entrepreneurs is having a good business plan. Many aspiring and new business owners dread even the thought of a business plan, much less actually writing one. They may think of themselves as business savvy, but putting it on paper seems both a waste of time and a writing task they would rather not undertake. I understand that as an entrepreneur as well as a writer.

When I have my business hat on, I would much rather be looking at new products, selling to a new client, or closing an interest deal. I happen to also have a writer's hat, but I know how arduous writing can be sometimes. So why make such a big deal out of a business plan? It doesn't have to be the great American novel. (But I still plan to write that!)

There is no doubt that putting a concept down on paper makes it real and gives you a chance to look at its flaws before it costs you money. You should have a section on strengths and challenges that discuss them in great detail. This will allow you the opportunity to plan how to overcome any expected situations. You are likely to discover some of these situations as you are writing the business plan.

You are going to need to identify potential vendors as well as expected customers, so you will know which other companies to watch. And you are going to describe in detail your sources of revenue, which will give you something to test against reality. This exercise will convert theory into practice.

Last, but surely not least, are the financials: current and pro-forma. This is an exercise in financial reporting that you need to do. Use numbers that have been thought about, and not just created on an EXCEL spreadsheet using a random formula. The real world always operates in unexpected ways. Customers don't show up, and vendors become unreliable. Walk through your numbers with that in mind.

Do all successful business owners write brilliant plans? No, but most have something on paper that they look at and review on a regular basis. They would tell you that it gives them direction. Others are impressed by the effort. These documents are the basis of a loan proposal, and will be ready when you need to make one.

Getting an Outsider to Write Your Plan

There are people who will help you write a business plan, and there are also services that will do one for you. I am strongly against having someone else do this work. This is *your* company, where *you* will be spending an enormous amount of *your* time, money, and energy. To me, having someone else write your plan is like getting someone else to date the person you will marry. You need to stay excited by the potential of your planned venture, while looking at the flaws and deciding if you can live with them. This is your future of ten- to twelve-hour days—take the time to write out the ways you will be spending your time and creating your future. Know what to expect and don't be surprised. You will end up far more comfortable. If you need help with some market research because you are doing the financials, call a Small Business Development Center at your local university.

Even if You Didn't Invent It, You Can Do It Better

Depending on the single act of securing patents or trademarks may be highly overrated at times. Being the first with a concept is only one part of a brilliant business success story. You need to produce and then market what you have patented. The very high cost of development, plus the extensive legal cost of a patent, may drain resources that are needed for marketing, and there is no guarantee of instant success. Save some of your cash for the long haul. The real win is in the marketplace.

So, don't think that you have to be the originator of a concept to cash in on the idea. It is often just as effective to look at business types that are opening around you and to develop a new take on it. Starbucks Coffee represents a motivated larger coffee shop with a higher level of food service. High-priced, specialty coffee was not a frequent purchase until this Seattle-based company created the demand. Add what you believe customers want and they will find you. The originator did all of the preliminary work. Don't steal someone else's idea—refine it.

The Franchise

When a new company has created a successful formula, and then uses the concept in different regional areas, it can be an instant opportunity for you. The types of available businesses are diverse, but the upside of the revenue and profit may have limits. There might be a very formulated program that allows for some of the risk to be removed. It's something to consider. Be careful as well, because not all franchises succeed. Try to talk to existing franchise owners, and read and review franchise material you are provided. Research public records and do on-site visits as often as you can. Your largest cost may be the up-front fee you pay. But don't forget the ongoing royalty fee that goes along with being a captive purchaser.

Make the Necessary Commitment

So many times I have heard, "It must be nice not to have anyone to answer to." People who work for others think the entrepreneurial experience is a dream come true. Having spent my entire working life as one, I must agree. But I certainly don't think that it is the easiest career. My days are longer, so my time commitment is greater than other careers. I seem to answer to just about everyone.

But, I also understand the business reality that the risk and responsibility of the business's success is that of the founder or owner. The smaller business with less ambition requires less of a capital risk, as well as less time and pressure. But many new start-ups often have much loftier goals. The caveat here is that creating a million-dollar plus company is a major commitment of time—working sixty hours a week is certainly not unusual. A major investment of effort will be demanded—this venture will monopolize your thoughts 24/7, and much of your money and financial future will be tied up in the business. If these thoughts send chills up your spine, take a deep breath before jumping into anything.

Being an entrepreneur is a profitable way to make a living, but it's not for everyone. It is really a lifestyle decision. A smaller, part-time business may meet your needs. If you aspire to be a mogul, be prepared to make that the priority of your life.

The Reluctant Restaurateur

Linda Callen loved the idea of being in food service. In college, she worked all levels of the business, from kitchen staff to the front of the house. However, her major was in marketing and she worked for eight years with a large consumer product company. Then, one of her best friends suggested they buy a neighborhood restaurant whose owner was not well and wanted to retire. The price was right, and the spot had always been busy. A great opportunity, right? Linda was thrilled to have the chance to own her own business, so she not only signed on the dotted line, but committed all of her savings to enlarging and updating the place. Their décor was terrific, and the grand opening was a success. The business was in the black from the first week. Linda felt pressure in spite of the success. The hours were grueling; staff called off and she filled in; and there was no end in sight. A year later, she was desperate to get back to her former, more orderly way of life. The business had become her monster based on success, not failure, and she wasn't prepared to make the sacrifice. Linda sold her half back to her partner for very little gain, other than a major lesson learned.

Always Hire the Best Customers

No business can adequately be of service to all types of customers. Some customers will be pleased with your products and loyal to your company, and others will be disappointed. This is true even though they are all responding to the same product, service, and price. People have different priorities and tastes. Some customers require large number of choices, little service, and the lowest possible prices; others demand just the opposite. Who are your customers? Who are you looking to attract?

You need to familiarize yourself with your most likely satisfied customer or client and spend the majority of your time and money marketing

Inside Track   **Know When to Walk Away**

One of my clients is a kitchen design center who does custom, high-end work. A male customer went into a business one afternoon looking for a redo on work originally done by one of the "big box" home stores. That should have been a red flag to this business. This customer was not originally planning on spending for high-end work, but he had unrealistic expectations of the original job. Now, he was doing it over and the cost would be even higher. There was no way to satisfy the customer here.

My client worked on it, even though she saw his agitation from the beginning, She completed a new design (for a fee) and then worked on his estimate. Their policy is that the design fee is nonrefundable but is applicable if the job is contracted. Not surprisingly, the client balked at the charge. There were some modifications, and then he demanded the design fee back. A little time later and he was thinking about going ahead with the job. My recommendation to them was to walk away from the customer. This was not a good connection and the job would never be satisfactory. That was what happened and the customer was angrier than ever. At least he wasn't angry over a large amount of money. You can't please all of the people, all of the time.

and serving them. When you draw in (perhaps by a major sale) a group of customers who aren't the perfect fit, you are likely to work harder for lower profits and get more complaints. This should not be a surprise.

Put your attention on those who value what you are doing. If someone comes along that can't be satisfied, give up and move on. It is the same theory that should be applied to employees. Try to find the best employees, but when you have made a mistake, cut the losses for both of you and move on. Keep your message to the point for the people you are looking to attract. That's where your return will be.

You Can't Win the Game if You Can't Keep Score

The primary reason I wrote the first edition of this book was based on the notion that you can't win a game if you can't keep score. A business owner who does not learn how to read and interpret the company's financial reports is limited in her job because she is missing an important tool. The real insight and information about what has been accomplished and what should be done next is found in these documents. You would expect a sports coach to understand the Xs and Os of the game—well, you are the business coach of your own team.

The job required is not to be able to do the day-to-day paperwork or data entry. What needs to be done, at a minimum, is to read a Profit and Loss Statement with insight, and to interpret a Balance Sheet. Here is where you find important financial information that allows you to make educated decisions about the strategic plans of the company. You need to know when you might be able to cut prices, and when doing so would be a fatal error.

You will make decisions on spending, on expansions or cutbacks, on new products, on bank lending, and ultimately, on when (and *if*) to find an equity partner or a buyer. All of these decisions are made on the basis of empirical financial information. You should have enough expertise to make these decisions and choices that ensure a successful outcome. The numbers are the score, and keeping them positive wins the game. This is not the job of your accountant; it is one of *your* obligations.

A Successful Business Is a Team Sport: Don't Go It Alone

The business team typically includes employees, customers, vendors, lenders, and a supporting cast of professionals. Each constituency occupies its own role, yet all with equal importance. The owner or manager who understands this has a far easier business life and is usually more successful.

When the pressure is on from all sides, it is easy to forget the team concept and to blame your workers or your vendors for the fact that your life has become complicated. But, at the end of the day, this isn't a good way to solve problems. People make mistakes, but if they work together, the situation can be turned into a positive one.

Don't run to your bank when you are in trouble, and then get angry that they won't bail you out. Work with it on an ongoing basis. That way, when you are in a squeeze, it can offer suggestions to make it easier. Most good bankers will do this, particularly if they have felt in the loop all along.

The entrepreneurial life can be one of isolation. Sharing the problems and the successes with other members of the team can provide support, as well as increased effort from them.

Keeping Secrets Never Works

I know many business owners who believe their employees should not have access to any of the business information. This includes sales figures as well as profitability. They believe that sales figures and salaries should be kept secret. That never happens in real life. Information is always available from inside, as well as outside, sources to reconstruct any numbers your associates need to have. Sometimes they develop the wrong ones, which makes it even worse. Why doesn't the information come from you? If it does, it will be accurate (as opposed to rumor), and you can invite real suggestions on how the company might work better. Your employees are players on your team; if you win, they win. The same goes for losing. Give your employees real tools to work with, and you may see some new energy and creativity in return.

Don't Get So Deep into the Forest That You Can't See the Trees

One of the best fringe benefits of being an entrepreneur is that the days are all different, and how you will spend yours is up to you, most of the time. Many of us are drawn to a particular business based on an individual skill or interest. We can spend much of our time working on these interests. For better or worse, it is possible to avoid the type of work we don't like doing, which often includes the administrative tasks. There is a danger when we spend too much time on one aspect of our business and ignore everything else. I had a client who was a great technical printer, so he expanded his business into a fair-sized printing company. He almost never spoke to his salespeople, didn't venture into the accounting department, and frequently only grunted at customers. He wanted to print and he was very good at it—but not very successful. The business had to be sold at a loss.

Another printer I know spends his day walking around the whole shop, calling on customers, and even making some deliveries. He has a big-picture view of the operation and far more possibilities of success. This is an essential behavior.

►► TEST DRIVE

Do you have enough good entrepreneurial instincts to create and maintain a growing and successful business? Ask yourself the following:

1. Are you comfortable with business planning?
2. Can you recognize a good idea and take it to the next level?
3. Are you able to decide to find good customers?
4. Are you willing to learn about the financials, even if it is not your area of expertise?
5. Can you see the big picture?

Inventory Must Stay Lean

There are a number of occasions when the need to sell assets to raise cash and increase liquidity not only makes sense but may be necessary. When capital is stretched and borrowing is not feasible, an asset sale may be your only choice. But you must be careful with what you sell and how you sell it. Don't liquidate what might be valuable in a few months, and don't send up signs of desperation. For some companies, the major source of tangible assets is inventory. If you have seasonal merchandise and it hasn't sold during the last cycle, there is a good chance that it will not sell at all (unless it is a classic). Even if it does sell, you will need deep discounts. Yet, it is an asset, so you are reluctant to just "dump the goods."

The same concept goes with clothing and shoes, and frankly, some jewelry that has a shelf life and doesn't come back into style until it is considered "vintage." You have this merchandise on your books at its cost, so as long as there is potential value, you are not facing serious writedowns. But when you are at the point of no return, you must take action. Some cash is better than no cash.

The Origin of "Lean Inventory" Is Cautious Buying

It is often conjectured that the best salespeople are the easiest to sell to, and from what I've seen, this has some merit. When a really enthusiastic salesman tries to sell you his entire line, the time has come to put on the brakes. Buy only what you need; you can always reorder. It is not easy to sell unnecessary goods without a careful plan. Once you have good sales history information from previous periods, use it as a guideline. Purchase popular products with a track record and order a smaller amount of new items to test trends.

Don't Take On the Look of a Fire Sale

Consider selling to a broker or a liquidator rather than having a massive event at your regular place of business. An aggressive "bottom dollar" sale may draw a different clientele from the one you normally see, because serious bargain hunters usually have radar. They will take time to service, even if they are only lookers. That time will take you away from your regular customers; these are the clients you need to retain. You may net more dollars from a sale on your own, but it will take longer, incur overhead costs, and may distract your ongoing business.

Many businesses have access to merchandise brokers—they may be general resale companies or specialized industry operations. Ask around; look in the phone directory under *liquidators* or try the Internet. Buying and selling goes on all of the time there. You may even be able to list excess inventory on eBay. Perhaps you could even engage an active eBay seller to do it for you. Your excess may be what someone else is looking for.

A final suggestion might be to appeal to a barter group with whom you can trade what you don't need for something that is of value to you. You get credit for your merchandise and can trade it in for other goods and services.

A "Final Sale" Sends a Bad Message

Companies come and companies go, and we all get used to seeing this happen. Whenever there is a massive "Inventory Liquidation Sale," it usually means the company has made a big mistake, and at worst, they are in a lot of trouble. Don't ever let your company look like that. As desperate as you may feel to raise cash, don't plaster signs all over the front of your place of business. It sends a bad message about the future of the company, and some clients may not come back.

Sell Off Outdated Equipment

Having cautioned business owners earlier to maintain a level of capacity by retaining extra backup machines, there are still times when you will have excess or out-of-date equipment that can be turned into cash.

As with your inventory, sell-offs will affect your Balance Sheet, which will be covered next in this chapter. You must know what they are before you make your decisions. Also, when it comes to tangible assets, take the time to check whether you have a free-and-clear title to the equipment, or whether it is being used as security for the bank. Most business loans will have a financing statement filed with your state that shows what business assets are being used to secure any lending. If what you are looking to sell is "off the books," you are likely to be free to do so, but if you have any questions, check with your lender.

If you want to sell something that is still on the books and secured to the bank, it may still be possible to do. Although technically all of the proceeds should be used to pay down your current secured debt, many bankers will be willing to make a deal allowing you to keep some of the cash you need. Your continual liquidity is in the bank's interest as well as yours, and a good banker knows that. Make a proposal that explains that and it is likely to be approved.

How to Sell Equipment

You will have two primary choices in selling your equipment: you can sell to a broker or to an individual (or company) end user. Needless to say, you will net more from the latter, but it will take more time and attention.

There are some industry specific brokers, as well as general equipment brokers. Some will make a purchase outright and pay you immediately. Others may sell on consignment, and that means you won't get paid unless or until their deal is consummated. Ask about this important difference. You need to check out the shipping costs as well as terms of the freight—who pays? Heavy equipment shipped to another coast could be more than a small charge off of the sale. The larger the equipment, the closer you need to sell it, if you have to deliver it.

If you decide to try a private sell, explore smaller and newer companies with fewer resources and more reason to save money. Don't bother with local newspaper ads, because they only work for the most common equipment. Try trade specific papers or Web sites. Make sure you specify that the sale is "as is" so the buyer understands you are providing no warranties. Get a substantial deposit, if not the entire price, before you ship. Disputes over used equipment can become costly and time consuming. Litigation usually benefits the lawyers handling the case rather than the injured party. The cases seldom go to trial; they are settled out of court, and the only one who makes money is the attorney.

Understand the Balance Sheet Implications of a Sale

When you purchase inventory, you list it on the Balance Sheet as an asset. Some companies with sophisticated accounting systems will record each item and then draw them down at sale. You may just put in a dollar amount.

Whether you do an actual drawdown or an end-of-month or -year inventory to make an adjustment, the value goes up with purchase and down with sales. A large withdrawal of inventory for a sale at below cost will impact both your Profit and Loss Statement and your Balance Sheet. Whatever money you have lost will lower all other profits.

One way to minimize the sudden impact is to take inventory periodically, so that the effect does not happen at once. You might do this at the end of a season.

Selling equipment may have a positive effect, assuming that the equipment has already been depreciated aggressively and you sell it for more than its book value. Your books will reflect a "gain from the sale of an asset." This won't help your profit, but it does improve your Balance Sheet.

Selling Real Estate with a Lease Back

You may wonder why you would want to sell real estate—isn't it a great investment? That may be true, but you can't book the appreciation. The only value you will record is the cash flow (the rent that you pay). You may be able to refinance the mortgage and get some cash, but remember that you will increase the monthly costs for payments.

▸▸ **A good plan may be to purchase the building in your own name for a fair, but not inflated, price, and then lease back the property to the company at a fair rate of return.** You now have ownership of a property that is likely to grow in value, and your business has exchanged cash for its asset and retains an interested landlord.

The hurdle here is that you may have a cross-collateral clause in your bank loan agreement that means your real estate is secondary security for the loan on your business. This is another area that requires negotiation. If you are able to pay down some of the proceeds from the building sale to the business loan, the transaction may be approved.

If you are not willing or able to own the property, look for a third party buyer and make your long-term lease one of the terms of the deal. A pure investor has no problem buying property that is already rented and will stay that way. Immediate cash flow is desirable from the standpoint of any investor.

Your decision to sell should be based on how much your current building is worth while it is being used, not how much renting or buying a different space will cost you. The critical need for the cash from the sale should also be a consideration in the decision. Make your plans long-term and not just a quick fix.

Intangible Assets Are a Source of Cash

The name of your company has value, as does the trade name of products you may market. You may not realize this, but I am assuming that you have already registered the trademark or will do so within days (right?). What other intangible assets might you have? How about some secret recipes? Rights to space at an annual fair? Another asset might be the rights to purchase tickets to popular sporting events. Even your phone number can be an asset.

If you were selling your company as a going concern, these are some of the intangibles that would add a premium price to your sale. Of course, a list of customers and as much information about their purchasing partners as possible is a real leg up to another company. But don't sell what you still need.

Be Careful with Customer Data

If you have launched a Web site to attract customers and offered them a chance to register to receive a newsletter or any such incentive, you need to review the context of that offer. Early on, most of the sites included a "right to privacy" for those who did offer information. Web site designers

Don't Wait Until the Roof Falls In

For fifteen years I rented space from a company that was a wholesale toy distributor. It was a huge building, and the costs of upkeep were high. I had the 2 lower floors (a total of 15,000 square feet) and the company occupied 35,000 feet above me. With fewer and fewer private toy stores, their business continued to shrink, as did their cash flow and need for space.

But they didn't want to move, so we all stayed, while the structure began to deteriorate around us. Only weeks after my landlord turned down a nice offer for the building, a major rainstorm exposed a serious leak in the roof. Water damaged their inventory and even trickled down the walls of our floors.

A year later, the property was sold at a distress sale and returned less than half of the last offer. In the back of the building, there were yellow warning barriers to protect from falling bricks.

They moved from 35,000 square feet to 10,000, and I consolidated to 10,000 as well. They should have left earlier, and I actually found a better layout where I resettled.

If you think you need to get out of your real estate, take action now.

did this as a matter of course, so yours may be in that group. Do not give out (or sell) information that you promised to keep private—particularly if you plan to stay in business. Offending customers is never a good idea.

Bidding on Steelers Tickets

Before there was such a thing as a sports stadium seat license, people could purchase transferable season tickets. With the opening of the old Three Rivers Stadium, my company had twelve season passes. In the late 1970s, I sold half of them for $10,000 each, and I knew someone else who put his up for bid and got almost $100,000 for six. There was nothing to exchange but a signed piece of paper, and a nice bit of cash was received. However, when I sold my company, I did not include the tickets, because my buyer was from out of town. This was in the 1990s, when the team was not so hot, and I received less per ticket. Still, it was a hidden asset I seldom thought about, one that wasn't on the Balance Sheet.

▶▶ TEST DRIVE

The title of this chapter is "When to Sell Nonessential Assets." This is an important point to remember; don't get so caught up in the drive to raise cash that you sell off something you will just have to replace in the future. Consider these issues when considering such a strategy:

1. Is your inventory bloated with items that are not likely to sell?
2. Are you planning to handle any liquidation as quickly as possible?
3. Is all of your equipment still necessary? (Include cars and trucks.)
4. Are you fully utilizing the value of your real estate?
5. Have you considered the value of your intangible assets?

Stabilize the Operation

The popular word a few years back was re-engineering, and while you can use it here, the word has the connotation of involving staff, reports, and reviews, and perhaps even a cadre of outside consultants. When a smaller business is in trouble, the action must be less costly and more direct than re-engineering.; I prefer to call this process a turn-around.

When a business gets so far into trouble that it needs a serious turn-around, the signs of disarray are usually throughout the organization. Poor operating results in pressure that is both internal and external. Employees haven't had raises, and they are offended. Vendors and bankers are not being paid timely, and they are creating pressure on these same disgruntled employees. Inventory is low or out-of-date, and everything needs to be updated. Can it really be changed? Yes, but you must know where to start—by bringing back some basic stability. Here are the steps you need to take:

1. Harvest cash—it is critical.
2. Pull back all major projects for review.
3. Cut expenses across the board.
4. Develop open lines of communication.

Harvest Critical Cash

The worst thing any business owner can be is out of cash. Payrolls can't be met, and even smaller partial payments cannot be made. This is the end of the line, so you must take action before this day comes.

The first step is to increase receivable collections. Every last dollar is important, and those customers who have been dragging their feet must now be prodded to pay. I know this is an issue with some companies, because I see it in my consulting practice every day.

Now is also the time to offer discounts for early payment to a few select customers. Knowing that money is on its way soon after a job is shipped is very comforting.

The second step is to slow down on your own payments. The fact is that most creditors (you know this because you are one) cannot force a customer to pay who, on intent, is not doing so. I don't recommend becoming a deadbeat, because the day will come when that reputation will haunt you. However, you can take some extra time and hold on to your cash. This way, if you need it for some critical expense, you will have it.

Perhaps your bank will allow you to pay interest-only on your loan for a few months to save cash. If you still have anything left on your line of credit, draw it out. Every event is important to survival, and if you are successful, you will find a way to pay it back. A failure without this cash might mean that little or none of the loan will be repaid.

Barter Is a Way to Conserve Cash

Barter is just an institutionalized way of exchanging favors. It makes the deal completely fair, because the trade is done on a value basis. You can contribute your goods and service to one company while collecting what you really need from another. Restaurants can usually earn large amounts of barter because everyone eats and many like to do so without using cash. I have often seen restaurants trade their food for advertising time and space they need to promote their business.

Take Advances Carefully

I have warned previously in this book about dealing correctly with deposits on contracted jobs done; this is something that happens most often in the subcontracting industry. All sorts of independent professionals, from lawyers to consultants to graphic designers, request advances when they begin their work. This is free cash to fuel the operation over the short term and is always of value, unless, that is, the work is not completed and the client requests a refund. If you are confident about the project, by all means request the cash advance.

The Second Step to Stabilizing Is a Review of Projects

In the months before a company comes to the realization that there is real trouble, it often tries a number of different solutions. Sometimes outside advisors give suggestions. Projects may be in different stages of implementation at one time, and this isn't good. With limited resources, you can't be going in several directions at one time. A turnaround requires suspension of all but necessary business activities until a full assessment of future directions can be made.

Cut Your Expenses Across the Board

In earlier chapters, the recommendations were to make selective cuts in expenses to trim overhead and increase profitability. A turnaround situation is more dire and requires strong remedies. Take a reasonable percentage (2–4%) and make a universal cut; this includes everyone and everything, and that includes salaries, even yours.

This may only be short-term until sales increase or capital is raised, but it must be fair if you are to get the cooperation of others. During tough times, you must have the group's consensus.

Develop Open Lines of Communication

When a plane runs into trouble, sometimes the pilot gets on the intercom and explains the situation to the passengers and keeps them updated. Well, your employees are your passengers; if you crash, they crash. Understand their concerns and keep them in the loop. Share the good news and the bad news and be open to suggestions and questions. You are all on the plane together, and you all want to keep it flying.

Develop a Team Approach

Believe it or not, you did not build the company all by yourself, and the tough times are not just happening to you. You need a team approach here to give you both advice and support. Don't ignore the support. It is very easy to be critical of yourself and lose the confidence that was your strength. Professionals will be necessary, but so will trusted friends.

The Role of Accountants and Lawyers

Far too many smaller businesses have inconsistent relationships with their accountants. In many cases, you see your accountant once or twice a year, and tax returns are always on extension because you haven't gotten all of the information she needed. And you may not have paid all of your bill.

Even if all of this is true, you need to make contact with your accountant now and bring her up to speed about your situation. Invite her to your place of business for a real heart-to-heart. Your accountant has many resources to bring—things like a deeper understanding of what your operating numbers mean and information about what resources may be available. The situation is often the same with the company attorney; he is called only when you are angry enough to sue someone, or the company has received some threatening communication. You might not think of your lawyer as a good business resource, but that is exactly what he might be. As a fellow member of the business community, he may often know individuals who can liquidate inventory or equipment without making it public knowledge. He will also know where some quiet investors might be. Your attorney could help you find a good deal and then structure it as well.

Using Your Attorney as a Buffer

If money has been a problem and your vendors are threatening action or have already taken some, a lawyer is necessary, if only to act as a buffer. The moment you engage counsel, you can refuse to handle disconcerting calls and utilize your time being proactive.

Getting Your Lawyer and Accountant on the Same Team

During the normal course of business, few of us think about introducing our professional advisors. As a consultant with a company, it can take months before I meet the accountant, and at times, I never meet the company lawyer (unless, of course, there is serious trouble). It's better to bring all of the professionals together for a meeting and to have the benefit of their shared expertise. No one discipline has all of the perspective, and they may suggest things you have yet to consider. This meeting will be expensive, but it is likely to be of great value.

How Your Banker Can Help

Some bankers are genuinely interested in the well-being of their clients and will go out of their way to be of assistance. But it is also naïve to forget that, at the end of the day, they represent the interest of the bank.

More Than Just a Loan Officer

I know some bankers who have gone far and beyond their job description. One, Tom Nunnally, whose advice was given earlier in this book, has spent a lifetime helping customers. When one of my clients needed a loan for a piece of equipment, this small entrepreneurial bank did more than any customer could imagine. Tom, another loan officer, and I approached several organizations that would be in a position to offer a guarantee. These were primarily state-funded programs, and I am not sure why we hit such a stone wall. The only other place to look was the SBA, and that would require the bank to really carry the load. Time was quickly running out, and this company would have gone under without the bank being willing to take the lead position as the lender.

   We put together the package, and the bank completed the documentation and tried to secure a quick answer from the SBA local office. There were many questions to answer, and we decided the best way to handle it was face-to-face. So, the bank president, the bank's legal counsel, and the loan officers and I met with all of the relevant SBA officials to answer all of the questions at one time and in one place. Within seventy-two hours, we had the guarantee and the loan was approved. This is the work of a dedicated banker.

If your bank borrowing is minimal or cash hasn't become truly strangled, here's someone with financial knowledge who could really help. Ask a banker to lunch—surely it will be worth the price of the meal.

Look to Your Employees

I worked with a CEO of a small distribution company for six weeks, and he described his company as "on the brink" as a result of a big customer leaving them with inventory and no way to pay for it. We always met outside of the CEO's building. The supplier was holding needed material while waiting for payment on the unsold inventory.

Finally, at my insistence, we called a meeting with the office manager, sales manager, and warehouse employees. First, these employees knew a lot more about what was going on than my client thought. The salesman knew he had other customers to move the goods. The warehouse manager had ideas for a second supplier that would ship the goods, and the office manager reminded the CEO about some credits coming from the vendors. This didn't solve all of the company's problems, but it surely eased the immediate crisis.

Your Friends Can Be Advisors

Some of us have friends and associates who are also in their own ventures. You may spend some time together sharing war stories—at least they understand much of your experience. But it isn't often easy to share the real problems, particularly when they feel so serious.

But, if you have a few friends that you trust, you can find some real support and perhaps good ideas of how to handle some of your problems. Let me caution you about using this group as lenders. Money complicates relationships—if it doesn't end them. You will feel you have to take advice even if you disagree, and be pressured by repayment. Don't do it.

Analyze Your Current Operation

In preparing a financial analysis, you must utilize the following information:

1. Compare year-to-year results.
2. See if your expenses are in line with sales.
3. Calculate your break even.
4. Identify expense areas to be cut and revenue areas that can be increased.

If your accounting system is on a computerized database, this work should not be much of a problem. Almost all software spreadsheet programs have analysis features built in. A manual system will require some additional work, and because categories may change a bit from year to year, you (or your bookkeeper) will have to verify items as you enter them.

Use a Three-Year Comparison

Year-to-year reports give you some good information, but a three-year look will show up some serious trends. The best is a side-by-side format as follows:

	2002	2003	2004
Sales	1,800,000	1,600,000	1,456,000
Cost of goods	1,260,000	1,136,000	1,044,000
Gross profits	540,000	464,000	406,000
Expenses (Admin)			
Wages	305,000	288,000	262,000
Benefits	18,000	20,300	22,500
Rent	23,000	23,000	23,000
Utilities	6,800	6,600	7,000
Sales expense	45,000	54,000	38,000
Insurance	6,000	6,200	5,800
Interest	20,000	18,000	12,000
Depreciation	7,800	6,500	5,900
Office	31,000	40,000	35,000
Warehouse	15,000	21,000	18,500
Total expense	476,000	494,100	429,700
Net Profit (loss)	64,000	(29,900)	(22,300)

To better understand your progress, put these numbers into percentages and then make your reviews.

	2002	2003	2004
Sales	100%	100%	100%
Cost of goods	70	71	72
Gross profits	30	29	28
Expenses (Admin)			
Wages	56.48	61.42	64.53
Benefits	3.33	4.42	5.54
Rent	4.26	4.42	5.67

Utilities	1.20	1.47	1.75
Sales expense	8.23	11.64	9.36
Insurance	1.11	1.34	1.43
Depreciation	1.39	1.47	1.43
Interest	3.70	2.45	2.96
Office	5.56	8.62	8.62
Warehouse	2.78	4.53	4.56
Total expense	88.04	103.42	105.87
Net Profit (loss)	12.96%	-3.42%	-5.87%

The very first thing to notice from this chart is that the cost of goods is drifting upward over the period. While it may only have changed by 2%, with falling volume, this is a critical percentage. Perhaps the most important item to note and go to work on immediately, is the issue of wages, which have gone from 56.5% of sales to 64.5% of sales, an increase of 8%, which exceeds the loss. Lower that number and you are back in the black (profit) range.

It's interesting that the selling expense is going down and so are sales. Are the efforts needed still being made? A number of other items have made marginal increases, some of which should be investigated by checking details of the category. It's time to get competitive quotes; think about outsourcing or merely tightening your belt.

Establish Your Break-Even Revenue

Determine your absolute necessary overhead and the best gross profit margin that you can be making, and you can find your break-even point. If you need $500,000 to open the doors and your gross profit is 33%, you must have $1.5 million to break even. Your analysis must give you absolute goals so you can do some planning to move forward.

Have Marketing Efforts Been Neglected?

You've been around for a while—customers have found you and a number of them keep coming back. This means you've done your marketing already and now you just have to run a steady business, doesn't it? Not at all.

Over the years, your products and services will change, and so will your customers and what they are looking for. Perhaps you drew a base from a wide geographical area and gas prices have spiked recently. People are staying closer to home, and some of those people used to be your customers.

You need to get more active in a closer demographic to replace what is being lost. A mailing to a local zip code may be the spark you need.

Maybe one of your top products has fallen out of favor—trends do change. Time to market and sell the rest of your line. Stores that opened to meet the low carbohydrate craze became general health food stores.

What do you need to do?

Begin change in demographics or methods or tangible products; your business is always moving in a slightly different direction. Use the media, mail, Internet, and print to keep your new message in front of potential customers.

Joint Ventures and Strategic Alliances

I often recommend this method of leveraging what you do and how you do it on a regular basis, but never is the time for it so critical as when you are trying to recover from a tough period. When capital resources are in short supply so are enthusiasm and energy; the best cure is the synergy that can be found in a short duration partnership.

Look around at other companies that are similar to yours and see where the two of you might be able to generate more business and profits by combining efforts. Share space, equipment, or advertising. Approach it with enthusiasm, and the result may amaze you both. It's a good way to kick-start a lethargic company.

▶▶ TEST DRIVE

Any company going through a difficult transition is a painful experience for everyone. Know how to do it efficiently and life will be a bit easier. Here are some of your steps:

1. Are you keeping cash on hand for emergencies?
2. Have you stopped looking for the quick fix?
3. Do you know how to analyze your performance?
4. Are you aggressive and constant about your marketing efforts?

Understanding Business Cycles

Growth is what propels a company into the future; it secures increasing profits for this year and allows for continuation of profit expansion. There are a number of reasons that a company stops growing and a variety of strategies to get back into the mode. One is growth by acquisition, and it's not just for corporate giants.

There are a number of cyclical manifestations to be seen in the life of a business. The first is what typically happens to the company during its own life span. There are basically four stages that a business will go through:

1. **Start-up**—The time just before and immediately after the opening of the company. This is when capital usage is high and revenue is low or nonexistent.

2. **Early stage**—The business is finding its niche in the market and revenue is coming in consistently. Inflow and outflow begin to equalize. Profits are on the rise.

3. **Rapid growth**—The business has found its customers and the revenue is growing at a faster pace. This stage can last a number of years as the company continues to expand to meet demand. There are high cash needs at this time, and revenue should be able to keep up with available bank lending as a timing tool.

4. **Maturation**—Revenue and profits are normally flat, and the business requires change to begin their next round of growth. Without change, the company will face a crisis.

At the same time that an individual company is going through the life phase, industries are also going through their own life cycles—as are the general economic conditions. You need to give thought to where your particular industry is in its cycle that tends to mirror the same pattern as a company cycle. Here are some stages that companies typically go through:

1. Conceptual—New ideas are coming in and businesses are being formed to take advantage of opportunities. Capital is needed to fuel invention.

2. Developmental—Individual companies are pursuing their own ways to capitalize on new concepts and technology and bring them to market. This is the time for equity capital investment. The potential for return is great.

3. Rapid growth—Customers are beginning to accept the new methods, products, or concepts. Revenue is quickly coming on stream. Profits are the highest at this point.

4. Maturation—The idea or technology has been available for a length of time, and growth potential has slowed substantially and perhaps is being replaced for newer concepts or technology. Individual companies within an industry are growing stagnant, while some are looking for and embracing change. The change may be found in a consolidation.

Cycles Are Not Just for Hi-Tech

Some industries have cycles based on costs—for example, much of our domestic manufacturing from steel to clothing are organized this way. Some of the cycles clearly apply to technology and involve innovative businesses such as computers, software, and medical discoveries that are driven by development. Yet, there are business types such as the high-end coffee shop, which was initially driven by Starbucks and experienced rapid growth with a number of other local and regional start-ups joining as well. While few think of coffee as an innovation, with the variations newly offered to Americans as specialty drinks in the 1990s, there soon will be a saturation or maturation phase for something as basic as coffee. What will be next in food innovation? How will all specialty products change? Is there something that you could do to revolutionize your own business, but lack the market strength to do so?

Finding Opportunistic Moments

The best time to consolidate is before both the company looking to acquire a business, and the industry it is in, has reached its full potential. For the individual company, when rapid growth has slowed but not completely stopped, the possibilities should be considered. This is the time when capital for acquisition may be available, as well as reasonably priced, either from investment sources or from bank loans.

An industry in the decline may be consolidated to provide some improvement in performance, but this is a riskier move. A number of steel companies tried this and failed, and the airline industry is traveling the same path as I write this. The joining together of two sick companies does not make one healthy one. But, the shared strength of reasonably performing businesses is measurable if one isn't a drag on both. Good matching and strategic planning will definitely make the difference.

Mature Industries Require Consolidation

When an industry has matured to the point where the growth stops, there are a number of economic pressures to force consolidation. Too much capacity brings on price pressure and lowers profits for everyone. With overhead growing and margins shrinking, some companies will close, voluntarily or otherwise. This allows survivors to become stronger. The question you must ask yourself is can you wait out the natural forces, or would it be in your best interest to buy one of your competitors to get a jump on the opportunities to serve a stronger, less predatory market?

New technology has also forced consolidation on entire industries. When a rapid, centralized system allows a regional company in any business, like book selling for example (such as West Coast–based Amazon .com) to serve the entire country, then small, independent operators struggle to survive. Fewer customers are browsing the independent bookstore shelves (many being served by the mega-stores), so the single store operator is at risk. Change must take place, or existing companies will become dinosaurs. This phenomenon has been seen in every large industry. Can you put it to work in your smaller business world?

Assets Are Purchased Below Market Price

Assume you owned a small manufacturing operation and wanted to expand your business. Buying the equipment from the original source or even a machine broker is one way to go about it, but it may be more costly than you prefer. If you purchase or merge with another company, some valuable underutilized equipment, and perhaps even space, is likely to come along with the deal. Your purchase price includes the intangible assets such as a customer base, and the tangible assets will end up being acquired at a discount. For tax reasons, you should put the acquired assets on your books at a higher price to defer future taxes. Even so, you are getting added value as a result of the fact that there are new sales immediately.

This is particularly true when you are taking over a business in another geographical area. The value of having an instant presence in another region is very high, because you have access to a larger market without going through the costs in time, as well as the money required for marketing to establish yourself. A well-timed and well-managed purchase within an industry brings almost instant results.

Consider the human assets as well. Find a well-trained, experienced management team and it will be able to work up to speed from day one. This cuts out the cost you can normally expect to train new people. Determine whether your methods are compatible, because there may be some time and cost to find a common operational style. Described as corporate culture, each business has an identifiable personality.

The Dynamics of a Good Deal

One New York contractor had grown substantially doing primarily large control work on a fixed bid basis. The estimates were opened and the lowest bidder was awarded the job. Some were very profitable and some were not. Then other smaller contractors in the area tried to grow by bidding on these larger jobs. They weren't as sophisticated at costing and were often the lowest bidder—the bids were barely more than cost. Fewer jobs meant lower profits, and a new strategy had to be put into place to propel this company forward. They went into the acquisition mode and bought a smaller boutique contractor who did custom work mainly awarded on a T&M basis (time and material plus percentage of profit). The combined entity turned out to be extremely profitable. The buying company could put a trained workforce on high profit jobs, and its purchasing discounts lowered costs. This was an instant success. The company became a bigger and stronger player, and when some of the predatory competition gave up, it was still around to take over the company's original type of work.

How to Finance the Deal

One of the most interesting aspects of business acquisition of one company by another is the flexible way that the deal can be financed. ▶▶ **All terms can be negotiated, from the price to how it is paid.** While some deals are pure cash deals, that is likely to represent only a very few. Most deals will include a number of creative features ranging from owner financing to a price based on future earnings. This pays only a portion of the price at closing and the balance over a period of years, and is based on the profit results of the combined companies. There is an incentive for everyone to contribute to the future.

In these types of deals, the previous owner stays on in some specific role, which may be prominent as an indication to customers of continuation, or it could be a secondary position, such as a consultant. This is decided on the contacts and reassurance that is required. Salary continuation may also be considered part of the purchase price.

The company being acquired may also retain an equity interest in the new entity, so that at some later time, a sale of the combined business will provide additional return to the original seller. The process is as much of a merger as a sale.

This Can Be a Very Creative Deal

There are no limits to the ways two or even more companies can consolidate to form a stronger more profitable business. Recently, a public shell acquired a vast number of local companies in the same industry (this is called a *roll-up*) and then sold stock, and all owners redeemed the equity they were given by the corporate acquirer. Some have worked well while a number proved to be less efficient. In a few cases, the companies were sold back to their owners.

Whether you are looking to be bought or to be the buyer, or perhaps negotiate a merger, read all you can about deals being made by larger corporations under the direction of sophisticated advisors, and see if you can simplify these models to work for your situation.

Do a Practice Run

Perhaps you are aware of a company that you think would be a perfect match with yours. They have strengths where you have weaknesses, and vice versa. Why not approach the company with the idea of a joint venture on a project? Each one of you can contribute your best skills and assign each task to any one entity in the venture. While it is likely in the first go around that there will be some awkward moments, when no one is sure who is covering an area, you will also be able to find out if this is a good match. This gives you the basis to move to an offer to purchase the company or merge with it. The worst that can happen is that you will learn from this experience.

Before you take even this step, you want to have some form of confidentiality or nondisclosure agreement between you and the other company. Any sharing of resources is likely to open some inside information, and many small companies guard this closely. Also, if you are serving any customer who had previously dealt with one or the other company, you need an agreement that the second business will not solicit this customer for a specific period of time once the venture has ended.

Economies of Scale: Serving More Clients with Less Overhead

The key reason for an industry consolidation is the ability to increase customer base and volume without increasing overhead. The gross profit on this increase in volume drops directly to the bottom line.

For example, imagine you own a printing company that operates eight shifts per week, five full days and three evening shifts. You pay rent and insurance on your building and have an administrative staff that does the purchasing and billing and other customer service work. They work nine to five on a regular weekday schedule. In addition, you have loan payments for the press and a few other pieces of equipment.

Your current production employees may be busy when they are on the job, but a full week can provide twenty-one shifts, although every business needs down time. Perhaps you may consider the company at full production with eighteen operating shifts. What you need to run these additional times are workers and material, all direct costs. What would happen if you acquired a company just about the same size as yours? You could fill your 18 shifts and double your revenue. The gross profit of the operation should double.

Many Costs Will Remain the Same

If you consolidate as mentioned before, your rent or building insurance won't increase. Your payments for equipment will remain the same, and it is possible for the same staff to handle the volume of purchasing and billing as well as customer service. You may need to hire a clerk to float and help out anywhere she is needed, but that is about all. Assume some of the following:

In 8 shifts per week, current volume is	1.6 million
Gross profits of 30% =	480,000
Fixed overhead is	300,000
Available for semivariables and profit	180,000

With 18 shifts on the job, the volume is	3.4 million
Gross profits of 30% =	1,200,000
Fixed overhead remains	300,000
Available for semivariables and profit	900,000

Your volume goes up, your gross profit goes up, and the fixed overhead expense does not. How much could you afford to pay for a company that provided such a dramatic improvement to your bottom line?

While this works best for companies with high fixed overhead, even professional firms can benefit from consolidation. Administration can become more efficient and advertising dollars spent more wisely. This is known as *economy of scale*—consolidation of costs to generate much higher contribution to overhead and profits.

Pricing Pressure May Be Relieved

When supply goes down, competition decreases and adequate pricing may very well hold. This, too, will add to the bottom line, while gross profit margins might even go up. A local purchase of a company can generate this effect. Where the two of you may have quoted against each other, now there is only one quote for a job. The industries where newer, cheaper competition may get into the game undermines this goal, but in most small businesses, the entry cost for new players will keep this from happening. When both companies have a similar market position and loyal customers, an increase in the number of competitors is not a likely scenario.

Local Strategies Become Regional, National, or Global

Similar companies in different regions of a state or in different states can be combined to enlarge the selling market fairly quickly. The bigger customer base provides greater selling opportunities, and the operations can be consolidated to different locations—manufacturing where the capacity is available, warehousing where space is available, and administrative functions where the workforce is available.

This is really the best use of technology and the Internet. Contact and service can be almost seamless using the tools that are readily and economically available now.

Take an example from call centers and outsourcing. Most people have little idea where the person is who answers their phone call, and as long as the products they want are produced and delivered, where production was done or shipped from is of less importance. A city company with high costs can combine with one in a more rural area where costs are low.

Items such as food and clothing, once thought to be only supplied by a local store, are now a national business with online purchasers and fulfillment warehouses dotted across the country. Look at your possibilities and reinvest yourself.

How Long Will the Party Last?

The timing of how and when things change is more art than science. A well-timed business consolidation with a good integration of functions may give your business another five to ten years of growth and health profits. But if you are in a business category that is involved in a rapidly changing environment, the next cycle may only be a few years before the next action will take place. If you are one of the larger players in the game, you will have the resources available to take advantage of new opportunities. A few years of very healthy profits can do wonders for the options of any company.

▶▶ TEST DRIVE

Has your bank been sold more than one time, yet you still go to the same branch and even see the same people? Only the name on the front of the door is different. This is a good example of an industry consolidation. Are you able to use the same strategy? Ask yourself:

1. Do you understand where your business, and your industry, is in its life cycle?
2. Are there assets you need that can be bought as part of the purchase of another company?
3. Do you understand the variety of acquisition financing available?
4. Are you profitably using all of your capacity, or could you support additional volume with existing overhead?

Keep Lines of Communication Open with Creditors

There are a number of reasons for a company to be in debt over a level that is no longer comfortable to the owners. The early stages of rapid growth will be fueled by debt, both long term and short term. There are situations when the borrowing outpaces the growth. Mature companies who are becoming stagnant may feel the burden of debt service, which drains available cash and makes running the operation a burden. The time has come to find a way to restructure the debt.

When a creditor calls asking for money which isn't readily available, the natural tendency is not to take the call. "Tell him I'll call right back," is often the response of the person who is the company principal. Most people in this position are reticent to admit they don't have the funds, so they also often find themselves in the position of making payment promises they know they can't keep. Both solutions are wrong—silence raises anxiety and unfulfilled promises raise anger. No one wants a creditor feeling this way. The feeling becomes a lawsuit looking for a place to happen.

Answer the Call or Return It

When a creditor finally gets to the point of calling the company principal, he wants and needs an answer. Perhaps his own business is short on funds and he is trying to pay bills, too. He may have outside owners, investors, or bankers to answer to. Explaining the reality, whatever it is, is the best strategy.

Before you answer or return the call, determine what the past due situation is. How much money do you owe and how long has it been outstanding? A fairly recent bill allows you to respond with the commitment to get a payment out as quickly as you can. An older invoice needs some more specific information. Be prepared to give it.

If you are waiting for a payment to come in, explain the situation. If you are on track for a new loan or any new investment that you might have, explain that as well. And, if you have no possibility of paying any amount for a while, be honest. Offer to call back with an update in a week. Remember to do so, even if it's only to give the same information. You may be able to buy a few weeks until the cash crisis passes.

Forcing Payment Is a Slow Process

One company may threaten to sue your company for payment as a way to force you to write a check. That is mostly an idle threat, although your creditor may not even realize it. There is little that can be done legally, or very quickly at least, to get to someone else's money. A threatening letter has little clout, and filing a lawsuit only means that the wheels of justice have been put into motion. It may take a year or more to win a case that can then be appealed. Any debtor determined to hold off the process can usually do so for a fairly long time. Even if you lose the first round of legal battles, you can always file for another round of hearings, particularly if there is some discrepancy. If that is the case, make the claim early and keep documentation available.

Make a Payment Plan

When you owe a debt and intend to pay but have run into your own cash problems, the best bet is to offer a payout over a period of time that you can handle. Really astute vendors understand that having you do so voluntarily is the best way for them to get their money. Most will accept a reasonable plan. If you can sweeten the deal with some immediate cash, you are giving a good incentive to make a deal now rather than later.

Do Not Borrow Money Set Aside for Taxes

Payroll day is here and you have that major expense to cover, as well as a loan payment and some other important vendors to satisfy. There are times when you think the answer is to pay the net payroll amount to your employees and then use the balance to meet the other obligations, with the full expectation that when other monies come in, the taxes you will pay. This is a serious mistake, and takes you to the edge of a slippery slope.

Pay the taxes when they are due, and plan to call any of the other creditors whose money will be late, and then use the next money to catch up with them. In an earlier chapter, I explained how costly it can become not to pay taxes; the penalty and interest can add up quickly, making it almost impossible to recover. However, if you have already done this, prepare to make a call to the tax office and work out a payment plan. They have collection enforcement greater than any individual creditor.

Any taxpayer who initiates the contact in order to work out a repayment plan will have an easier time than one who waits for the letters and calls.

Call your local state or federal tax office, and ask to meet with someone. Bring your records and a list of what has been paid and what is still owed. The official will be able to access her own accounts of payments easily. Come in with a payment plan in mind—you can usually get two years to pay off the debt. Bring a check for the first payment, because this says you are serious about solving this problem. More often than not, you will walk away with an agreement. The federal government has a Tax Resolution Office for when you can't come to an agreed amount due. Keep in mind that the IRS is vigilant about any payment plan you make.

Most Taxing Bodies Are Reasonable the First Time

Accountants, lawyers, and business advisors are fairly strong in their caution about having their clients fall behind in tax payments. Yet, when it does happen, the negotiations to resolve the tax debt usually go smoothly—at least the first time. Most agreements have a clause requiring the taxpayer to keep current in the future. Not to do so is a serious mistake because the second time you find yourself in this situation, the negotiations are much tougher and the revenue agent far less accommodating. Agents are very cynical about repeat offenders—don't become one. Always remember, they can reach directly into your bank account if they want. This action sets up a red flag in front of your banker, who may also be your lender. It may also freeze your account for a while and perhaps cause checks to bounce.

Working with Your Landlord

It isn't very difficult to evict a nonpaying tenant. Unlike a pure money dispute with a vendor, the owners of the property can usually get relief in sixty days. But, like most creditors, they would rather get their money than pay legal fees. Even a foreclosure on a mortgage costs money.

Some of the issues to consider before approaching your landlord are how easily she will be able to find a new tenant, and how much it will cost to prepare your existing space to make it ready to move in. A landlord with office space and a waiting list of interested tenants is unlikely to be very flexible. However, if you have painted your walls black and added a lot of specialized hookups or modifications, you may find a very motivated building owner. You don't need to point it out, your landlord knows her own situation.

The Beauty Salon

On the second floor of a building in an affluent neighborhood in Pittsburgh, was a well-known beauty salon. The stairs leading up to the place were steep and few people ever dropped in to check out the place. But, the owner had a big following, as did many of his operators. In addition, the site was full of sinks and special areas for drying and nail care. After a falling out, one of the stylists left to open his own shop. Business volume fell off. Even paying the rent became a challenge during slower months. But this was not a space easily changed and rented to another tenant even though it had a fairly good location. Rent concessions went on for eighteen months before they were finally resolved at a lower level. I negotiated many of those changes, and in the end, the landlord was holding all of the cards, but he chose to try to keep the tenant.

Have a Plan in Mind Before Meeting

Know what it will cost the landlord for a change in tenancy and know what you can afford to pay short term as well as long term, assuming business improves. You can ask for anything from a total renegotiation of the lease to a forbearance of a few months' rent, which will be added on to the end of the lease. Try to balance what you need with what the next tenant is likely to offer.

Perhaps you have been in a retail area for several years and new malls have drained much of the business traffic. Any new tenant coming along will expect a lower rent to accommodate the reality of less business. If your lease was written before this new space arrived, you may be able to get a new lease at a lower cost. Landlords know that finding new tenants is a costly job and there are often months of vacancy with no income coming in at all. If the space is still desirable but you are experiencing short-term business problems, ask for a temporary reduction. Astute landlords know the value of reliable tenants; be one, and they will be more accommodating when you need them to be.

Never Over-Promise

When you are attempting an informal restructure of debt, you need to work hard on creating a realistic cash flow pro-forma. Be conservative on projecting the expected revenue, and then determine how much cash over the ongoing day-to-day expense you will have available to pay back past due amounts to your creditors. Prioritize your debts in order of importance and make your deals with the most critical creditors first. When you run out of available cash flow, you must stop, because making deals you can't keep will only buy a month or two, and then everything will unravel. Going back to explain or remodify the first deal is not likely to be possible.

Reorganizing Under Chapter 11

When you can't come to an agreement with creditors or you need to lower overall debt in order to pay something to everyone, the time might be right to consider a legal reorganization. This is a filing under the bankruptcy laws, but it does not signify the end of the business. The fact is that this may be the first step to a new beginning. The process is unknown and scary to most, so let's cover the basics so you can decide if this is the right step for you.

The entire event may take less than six months and, for most, after the first few weeks, much of the business goes on as usual. You retain control of your day-to-day decisions and need court permission only to do things "outside of the normal course of business," such as selling assets or hiring professionals. This process seems much scarier than it is. You will hardly see any effect on how and what you do to operate the company. But you must be working on the problems that got it there.

Step One Is to Find the Best Legal Advice

There are attorneys who specialize in bankruptcy, but many of them do only a specific type. You need to find one who has extensive experience in small business reorganizations and has had successful Chapter 11 cases. Ask specifically about this, and, as the filings are public information, you should be able to check out the references. You will depend on this professional to get you through uncharted waters, so you need to trust him.

If this is not an emergency and you have the luxury of time, I seriously suggest that you visit the courts and attend some of the bankruptcy hearings. You can see the players in action and find out how they perform in actual court. Respect of the judges and their fellow attorneys is important. So is good communication and genuine interest. Don't go to a high-volume bankruptcy firm because you have seen its ads on billboards. Interview more than one before you make a choice. If you know people who have successfully been through the process, call and ask for their referrals.

Filing Stops All Pending Action

If someone has sued your company for payment and won a judgment, all collections will stop with a Chapter 11 filing. If you haven't paid taxes and the state or federal government has tried to levy your assets, this will stop with a Chapter 11 filing. Even if there are lawsuits pending for damages due to your alleged negligence, these will stop with a filing. Any action that threatens the assets of your company will stop the moment you file.

The court will issue what is referred to as an *automatic stay,* which stops all other proceedings, including foreclosures, in place. From the moment of that filing, all creditors will now have to propose a motion with the bankruptcy court before they can proceed in any action. The federal court will decide what is in the best interest of all creditors before they allow pending actions to proceed. While there are some actions that may be allowed to continue, they will dramatically slow down, giving you time to resolve or pay them. What this does is give you breathing room to improve your business and its cash flow.

What It Means to Be a "Debtor in Possession"

The existing business operator is allowed to continue to run day-to-day operations. The fact is that very little changes in the company after bankruptcy. A new bank account is established by the debtor and all money is deposited as it always has been. Payments are made to current vendors as they would expect. You run your own business.

Most businesses considering a Chapter 11 are concerned that they will lose vendors and not be able to purchase what they need. In reality, that seldom is the case. Most creditors these days know that they are going to take a loss, so any future business, along with the profit it brings, is desirable. Be careful about pricing, as some creditors think they can add part of the past due amount to new invoices. By law, they can't. Creditors can't do anything to force "preferential treatment" above other creditors.

How the Process Works

You begin by filing a petition to the Federal Bankruptcy court for relief under Chapter 11. This is the act that stops all actions against you. At the same time or within fifteen days, you will have to file a complete set of schedules, listing all of the aspects of your business's operation. You will include a list of all assets and current values for them. You will include operational information and history of the company. What is difficult for most entrepreneurs, is the fact that all of this becomes part of the public record. The fact is that few people are curious enough to go to the clerk's office and pay to get copies of what you have filed. Your filing may be noted in the business section of the paper, but it isn't the shock to others that you may think.

The most important aspect of filing is the list of creditors and how much you owe. You should learn a great deal from this, as you will learn the legal status of each of these creditors. They fall primarily into four categories:

1. **Administrative debt**—This is what you will owe to lawyers and professionals during the course of the case. It will also include any new debt incurred after the case is filed. This debt has a high priority and is watched by the courts. New tax debt is classified here and will quickly cause unwanted attention by the court.

2. **Secured debt**—Any creditor who filed a lien at time of purchase, (such as real estate) or a subsequent lien due to a contractual obligation or as the result of legal action. This assumes there was collateral for the lien to attach to. All liens that were filed within ninety days of bankruptcy may be lifted, as they are presumed preferential. Secured creditors have the right, after a court proceeding, to repossess their asset, if you are in default of your payment arrangements.

3. **Priority unsecured**—Those are parties holding claims that could have resulted in liens, such as tax debt and some municipal claims, even when the liens have not yet been filed. They are not actually secured on assets, but they must be paid back as a priority to payment of unsecured loans.

4. **Unsecured debt**—Basically, this is all of the trade credit you have amassed leading up to the filing. Unless an individual creditor has taken legal action and been allowed to file a judgment (ninety days before your filing), they all have equal standing in this category. When you propose a payment plan, each will get the same percentage of their claim.

The Next Steps

Once the filing has been made and all of the schedules are complete, the Trustee's office will schedule a meeting of creditors called a *341 meeting*. The debtor appears with counsel and is first questioned by the Trustee as to the accuracy of all the information; the cause of this business failure and what initial plans are being considered to correct the situation and pay back the creditors. This questioning is more informational than adversarial.

Next is an open questioning directed to the debtor from any creditor who wishes to be present. Most of the time, this will include only attorneys for the secured lenders, but every once in a while an angry creditor will come as well. They are unlikely to get any real satisfaction, because the proceedings are orderly and the debtor does have counsel to handle any issues. For many debtors, this is the last time they see the courthouse.

Moving Beyond Bankruptcy

I have worked as a consultant on more than twenty Chapter 11 filings, and all but one has been successful. The toughest are when there are debts in all categories and balancing the total payoff is very tricky. The easiest cases are when most of the debt is in one category, no matter how large.

One of the most dramatic changes I have seen was with an asphalt contractor who had taken on too many big jobs while using too many subcontractors. He estimated poorly and lost a good bit of money. He owed the subcontractors and his material supplier almost $200,000, and his cash flow was a mere dribble because he could barely get materials for small jobs anymore. This was unfortunate, because his original business had been very profitable.

All of this debt was listed as unsecured, and there was a minimal amount in the other three categories. Within a month, we had filed a plan calling for payment of 20% of this debt over 6 years. That was less than $300 a month. Vendors were not happy, but they had few choices. One or two material suppliers even started selling to him again on a firm credit limit and payment terms. The business was able to go forward successfully.

Unless you have an ongoing relationship with your creditor, they are not allowed to make contact with you again.

After the Hearing

The law allows for 120 days for a debtor to have exclusive rights to file a Plan of Reorganization, but that time may be expanded with permission of the court. Each month, the business will have to file a Statement of Business Affairs providing information on the Profit and Loss Statement, plus all debts incurred or any changes made during the past thirty days. A full bank reconciliation will be included with this filing and no pre-petition debts may be paid. Several large companies have been in bankruptcy for years—this might happen if there are complicated legal issues—but it is unlikely to be the case for a small business. Six or eight months is the limit.

The Plan of Reorganization

There are actually two documents that will be filed at this time. The first is a Disclosure Statement which reviews the initial filing and what has taken place during the course of the case. This includes any contracts that have been cancelled or obligations that have been avoided or property that has been sold. The debtor will schedule all remaining debts including the ones such as the legal and accounting fees generated by the needs of the case. A plan to pay back debt will be a major focus. Typically, the obligations fall into the following categories:

1. Administrative Debt

This is paid in full upon the confirmation of the plan or with prior agreement with the creditor. Legal fees must be paid once the attorney has filed his fee application with the court and had it approved. The debtor should have this money on hand by the time the confirmation is approved.

2. Secured Debt

This debt must be paid in full to the value of the security, either under the original terms, or others that have been agreed to. If there is no longer value in some of the security, that portion of the debt is not secured. This may happen to a bank loan originally secured by receivables that are much lower now, and inventory that has also been reduced. While this is usually subject to negotiation, you may be able to pay a part of a loan as an unsecured. Secured debt, including tax debt, is paid by the terms, or in the case of taxes, you have a six-year term to pay it off.

3. Priority Unsecured

This debt tends to be primarily tax debt or certain other obligations such as union dues. This debt also must be paid in full, although you may be able to discharge or negotiate away a portion—in the case of taxes, it would be the penalty. Since it's not secured, the interest will stop accruing at the time of filing. The term of payback is most frequently seventy-two months. Many of these payments are made according to agreements, not any court orders.

4. Unsecured

Here is where there is the most latitude. Once you have looked over all of the other debt services, then you make an offer to this class of creditors to pay back a portion of their claims over seventy-two months. I have seen plans succeed with as little as a 5% offer, but typically for a small company, the payback is 20–30%. Let's assume that your vendor debt is $500,000 and you offer 20%. Over 6 years you will be paying back about $1,800 per month. Quite a difference, and that debt forgiveness makes the business cash flow sufficient to bring it back to health.

Here is where a cash flow projection is the most critical. Once you have had a chance to plug in the debt service requirements of your other "must pay" obligations, you can determine what is left to pay back this class of creditor. Your offer to them is based on your ability to pay, not what you originally owed. The reality of a reorganization is that you must pay back more than they will get if your property is liquidated, but promising a generous return may cripple your ability to move forward.

Avoiding Unfavorable Contracts While in Bankruptcy

One of the benefits of a Chapter 11 filing is the ability to go to court and reject virtually any executory contract you have made if it will impair the company's ability to successfully reorganize. For many large companies recently, it has been union contracts that have renegotiated under threat of cancellation, and the ending of seriously under-funded pension plans. Think about some of the payments you have been making that you might be able to end as a result of this right. Do you lease space you no longer need? Do you have autos, trucks or machinery under lease contracts that you could return? Do you have labor agreements that need to be modified? Discuss all of these contracts with your legal advisor; you may be able to negotiate modifications and changes in terms to make the potential of a successful reorganization more likely.

What Happens to the Plan

The Plan and Disclosure Statement is scheduled for a hearing in front of the judge, giving all of the creditors opportunities to object to how you have treated their claims. This is not about how much you are planning to pay back, but the mechanics of how the claims are listed. This is the time when it will be argued whether a loan or debt is fully secured or not. Once the judge has ruled on the adequacy of your filing, it will be sent on to your creditors for a vote.

The Liquidation Analysis

The key element in a reorganization is whether the creditors will receive more by the debtor's plan, or by taking control of the assets and liquidating them to satisfy debts. In most cases, this is usually not a close call. Assets that are sold under duress will bring only a fraction of their value, and most debtors will agree, under the terms of the plan, to pay far more than that over time. This written portion of the Plan is an important section; make sure you have completed it carefully. Your attorney will likely draft most of these documents, but you should be there to carefully review all of the information.

The Voting and Confirmation

A Plan is sent out (along with a copy of the Disclosure Statement) to all creditors, and the court order allows them to have thirty days to vote on it. Some creditors will be impaired, meaning they are not recovering the full amount of their claim. Others are unimpaired, meaning that they will be paid in full and their vote will be considered in favor of the Plan.

Most of those in the category of unsecured creditors are really the critical votes to receive. There is a formula for the successful vote. The majority of the creditors must vote for the Plan for it to pass. The reason is that no one wants a small angry creditor to be to undermine the Plan. Larger creditors have more at stake and their vote means more. At the end of the day, most of the Plans do succeed, because creditors realize that it is better to get something back on their debt. They aren't any worse off than they already were, and they may be able to get a recovery and keep a customer.

The Final Step Towards Freedom

Once the votes have been sent out, the debtor can encourage their creditors to vote, but they may not use any incentives as an inducement, meaning that you can not offer a slightly higher payout to any one creditor in exchange for a yes vote. Ballots are sent back to the attorney and they are then reported to the court. A clear vote in favor will absolutely receive a court confirmation, and even some negative votes may be rejected by the court, and the plan might be confirmed over the objections of creditors. In the end, the court decides what is in the interest of all creditors, not just a few.

Negotiating Deals with Debtors

Often, major creditors (particularly those who are fully or partially secured) will begin independent negotiations with debtors through their attorneys. The negotiations are often driven by the value of the collateral. In most cases, banks or other lenders do not want assets or receivables turned over to them. They are not equipped to conduct liquidations and usually see a very low rate of return. Even when they make noise that they will repossess or foreclose on their collateral, that tends to be a positioning technique. What the bank wants is to be paid back as much and as quickly as possible.

Once a loan has become delinquent, and certainly after the company has filed for reorganization, the loan or debt is written off by the creditor as uncollectible. In the case of the bank, the loan balance goes into special reserves and is deducted from the capital base of the bank. This is a part of banking regulations meant to keep the system safe and sound. Any recovery goes directly to profit.

Other credits, such as large general vendors, some taxing bodies, and many utilities, have the same procedure—a bankrupt debt goes to special departments. The good news is that they understand the drill and will typically strike a reasonable deal with the creditor and incorporate that agreement into the plan as a stipulation.

The Plan Creates a New Business

You started with a company in trouble, and once you failed, you became a debtor in possession. Once the Reorganization Plan is confirmed, you then become a third entity, called the Reorganized Debtor. This actually does have some significance because it means that the debts you brought into the case and did not agree to pay in the Plan are discharged as though they never existed. Creditors cannot come back to you and ask you to make any payments on those old debts. This is a chance for new life.

Going through the process can be confusing, though it is seldom as painful as it is feared, and there should be lessons learned. The new entity that emerges may no longer be burdened by debt, but it is likely to have payments that hamper it for a while. This will require you to operate the company profitably and carefully. Good new habits for you to learn anyway.

▶▶ TEST DRIVE

It is never comfortable to get deep in debt and begin wondering whether the business will survive. Have you considered all of the alternatives you have, even close to the end?

1. Are you trying to communicate with creditors?
2. Are you keeping tax funds separate from operating?
3. Have you talked to your landlords about a new lease?
4. Have you explored your options under Chapter 11 Reorganization?

Financial Challenges

Starting and growing a business over the years is a far different life experience than securing and managing a job. Your own company is like your child; you don't actually start it as much as give birth to it, and the responsibility is continual as well as constant. Here are some tips for some of the issues you might face.

Being in business is a different financial life choice than the one you make having a job. You are creating a venture and in many cases, you are responsible for generating a good bit of the revenue. Even when you are at a point where you have other sales staff or marketing associates on board, it is most likely that the direction and strategies will still be yours. That is a big burden to shoulder, although some of the times it will be easier than others. But the value of your work will not always be compensated in dollars. In fact, when the company is going through tough times, you are likely to be working harder for less money. You are providing for the welfare of others, and most business owners take that very seriously.

This is a fact of entrepreneurial life, and one you need to come to terms with early in your career. Your fortunes may rise dramatically very suddenly, and there are times they will may diminish as well. ▶▶**You need to be personally balanced and resilient.** You're the leader and you need to continue to have the confidence to motivate yourself as well as others. There are times when you will cut hours and expenses and employees won't be sympathetic; you are the one who must have the vision and determine the next course of action. You need to be objective enough to be driven by the goals of the organization, not just your own. You also need to be analytical and fair.

Family Succession May Not Be in the Cards

Depending on the type of company, many entrepreneurs involve their family from the very beginning. I probably went to work the first time with my father when I was ten or eleven years old. His factory became a second home to me as I was growing up, and when he suddenly died, I took over the operation, even though I did not know half of what I needed to know to be in charge. But I was comfortable in the environment.

Many wives keep the books at home or help out a few days a week. Boys may be asked to work in construction projects, and girls might be asked to work in sales or in the office. For parents, the gender roles may be specific, and there is no legal protection for the children, although this is changing as roles and expectations change. The founders are proud of what they built and want to share the experience. And after all, why not hire your child and pay a salary instead of an allowance? This way you get a double deduction—a business expense and a personal one. Careful that you set the salary from day one based on worth—the value of the job, not on what your child requires to maintain her social life.

The challenging time comes when your children are about to make career decisions and the family business is standing in front of them like a 1,000-pound elephant—very hard to ignore. Many business owners just assume that younger generations will come in and take over so they can retire. This is not good planning. If you have potential candidates for the job, allow them to make the decision in their own way and in their own time. This company is your dream, but it may not be theirs. Some will leave to pursue other goals, and some of them may eventually come back. This is their decision.

Even when you have a son or daughter who aspires to work with you and contribute to the future of the company, bring them on board with care. Find a defined role for them to play, not just the junior CEO, and then pay them according to the value of that job. Be sensitive to the concerns of other managers about having "the boss's kid" in tow, and try to set established goals for them to reach. You need to measure the progress of an insider the same way you would that of an outsider. They will have your ear more than others, but you must listen objectively and treat everyone fairly. Some business children can become real tyrants.

Not Many Second Generations Succeed

Only slightly more than one in four companies pass to a second generation successfully. Those are very high odds to keep in mind. With the business cycle becoming shorter and shorter, there is little reason to think that will change for the better. If all of your assets are invested in the business, don't risk your financial, and the family's emotional, future by forcing a lukewarm succession in plan. If you do have a son or daughter with the talent and intent to take over the company, arrange to sell it to him. Let a lender decide whether this is a deal with a future. You will get the capital out of the business that you need, and he will get full ownership and responsibility. Also, never make loans back to the company once you are gone. That is a poor practice, both personally and professionally.

Invest Outside of the Business

One of the best strategies for any business owner financially is to have investment interests outside of the company. No doubt that the business will be the major focus of most of your resources (human and capital) in the early years, but once the company is on its own feet and you are taking a fairly regular paycheck, put some of it aside in a Keough Plan or another independent retirement plan. Find and use the services of a good financial planner and also consult with your attorney. You may be able to create a plan within the company that allows for deductible matches. Don't focus on investment tied to the company stock, either.

The types of investments you want to make are those that are safe from any actions of creditors, in case you fall on tough times. An established plan usually meets this criteria. Also holding a joint investment with a spouse may shelter some of your assets. You are looking to create a second stream of retirement income and a way to make you feel more personally secure as you get older.

Another strategy to employ is to invest in other businesses. You are more astute about what it takes to succeed in a new venture. You know how to measure the idea and the entrepreneur based on your own real world experience. On paper, these investments may not be worth much but, down the road, you may be able to cash in. You can see where the potential is.

Responsibility in the Community

The business community has always taken a certain amount of responsibility in being a good community citizen. It may range from putting signs in your window about a neighborhood activity to making major contributions to the organizations that provide services in the neighborhood. Being involved in a variety of ways is a win-win solution. The area where you spend your time working or seeing customers and selling your goods will be a better place, and you will make friends who will give you social as well as professional help and advice within the business sector. There are organizations like the Rotary that spend almost all of their time improving the world around them; as with other similar organizations, the Rotary has an unwritten code that motivates members to transact business with one another whenever possible. Belonging to Rotary says something about a person and her values. This is a unique organization in that you are welcomed at Rotary meetings all over the world, and have a chance to really enhance your network of contacts while serving your fellow citizens. Everyone is welcome.

For women and minority entrepreneurs, there are networking groups that meet on a regular basis to support and encourage the empowerment of the community. You can find support with your unique situation and can have an opportunity to find new business contacts at each meeting. Do not join these groups exclusively, but make them a part of your enlarged business network.

Sharing the Wealth

The most difficult choice for most entrepreneurs is establishing a wage scale for staff and employees. The most logical way is not always the one employed. In the start-up days when business and cash are scarce, it isn't unusual to find loyal believers who come on board on faith and far less salary than they could get somewhere else. This is the birth of the loyalty that most entrepreneurs value highly, sometimes even overvalue.

What most entrepreneurs are sensitive about is the claim that they pay less for work than "the big guys." This is likely to be true, but then I know of a few business owners who can continue to draw huge salaries when their companies are losing money. We don't get retention benefits

Inside Track   **A Network of Support**

I took over my family business when I was in my twenties, at a time when few women were CEOs of any companies, much less manufacturing companies. I often felt alone and isolated. I knew that I needed to get out more, and I chose to join a Jaycee chapter. During those eight years of membership, I learned a lot of organizational skills that help me to this day (I can host a major event almost single-handedly), and I met other young professional men and women. More than half of my current network are those friends. We grew to like, as well as trust, each other as we worked in the community together. We have great memories of botched projects, as well as some that made a difference.

I also felt a need to network with other women to find and give support to those who were pursuing dreams as entrepreneurs. I am still a member of a number of women's networks today. At the time I started, fewer than 10% of businesses were controlled by women; the number today is almost 50%. We have done a good deal to promote each other! Much of my writing, teaching, and speaking has come from that earlier work as a business woman.

to stay when times get really tough—tenacity is one of the marks of an entrepreneur. You must understand this is a different system and run your business according to its needs, not what others are doing.

The time comes when salaries have to be set at a fair market level so that costs can be established. The second and third in the depth chart often work almost as long as the founder, so they must be compensated. Keep in mind that the business model must make sense; overpaying an employee because you are grateful for his early faith in you does not make sense. Consider other ways to show your gratitude. When salaries are out of synch with the market, the whole venture is at risk.

What About Benefits?

The two problem areas in most smaller companies are in the cost of vacation and healthcare benefits. A small company usually creates a vacation policy that is at least in the neighborhood of the larger ones. After ten years, the paid time off is likely to be three weeks, but where do you go from there?

The fact is that there isn't anywhere to go, because few companies have the reserve in workforce to cover the work of a vacationing employee for a month, much less the earned profit to pay for it. Confront this reality with your employees as a fact of life, and stick to your guns. These days when corporate loyalty is often in short supply, many workers value this, and that is one of the benefits you can offer. Set your own rules about when people need to schedule vacations so they don't leave you with an empty department. You must keep control of your own ship, no matter how close you get with the shipmates.

When you first started providing a healthcare plan, perhaps the cost was reasonable, but now it has gotten out of control. Larger entities have been forced to change the terms of this coverage and then they simply put out a memo. You have to face your people, and that isn't easy. Ignoring ways to lower the healthcare costs to the business is a mistake, because you will not be competitive and the business will not prosper. Find a fair way to share this expense and then work with your staff to help everyone understand why this must be company policy. This is a cost burden that can destroy a small business.

When Times Are Good

If you are in a profitable and growth mode, it is likely because of the people around you. They should share in the success. A profit sharing plan which results in either pension contributions or bonuses should be put into place. They are triggered by a certain level of profits, and pay out a fixed percentage of these earnings to a group of your associates. A small business is an intimate work environment, and the good times should be shared, because the tough times will be as well. What you don't want to do is set in motion a permanent increase in compensation not linked to actual profit outcome.

The following are ways to structure compensation plans to reward efforts that result in healthy profits:

1. **Stock option plan**—This is primarily for companies that have potential for an IPO (Initial Public Offering) that takes them public. In the hi-tech environment, many talented people

signed on to new ventures for this benefit alone, and some became very wealthy as a result

2. **Stock appreciation bonus**—When a company has had a good evaluation by an expert, it is possible to set a value per existing shares. Stock is not actually issued (nor is any control given) by the existing owner, but valued employees will receive the equivalent of any increase in value of their theoretical stock after a given period, and another formal evaluation. They share in what they have built.

3. **Profit sharing**—A percent of the actual profit is set aside and placed in a fund to be divided, according to some established formula, among the employees.

4. **Bonus plan**—A bonus can be anything of value to an employee, ranging from extra time off to cash. To be effective, however, a bonus plan has to be uniformly applied and must, as much as possible, reward the employees equally when their efforts benefit the company.

5. **Cafeteria plan**—These plans, sponsored by the employer, set a fixed amount of money for each employee to access. The list of benefits that can be covered by these funds may include life insurance, expanded health insurance coverage, and disability. Employees not needing any or all of these benefits could increase their cash compensation.

6. **401K plans**—These are retirement plans set up by an employer with strict guidelines under federal law. The key benefit is that it allows both the employer and the employee to contribute money to the plan without immediate income tax consequence. As profits increase, the employer can increase their portion of contribution.

Understanding Personal Guarantees

The last few pages of your bank loan application is a place for you (and usually your spouse) to sign as personal guarantors. You may not be happy with this requirement, but over the course of a business life, you will have

Don't Accept the Status Quo

When I took over my family's manufacturing company, the second highest paid employee was our mechanic; his hourly pay rate was within reason, but he was in the factory building for sixty hours per week, meaning that twenty hours were time-and-a-half. He opened the factory and closed it. Being recently divorced, he would punch in at 4 A.M. and out at 5 P.M. although our work shift was 7:00 A.M. to 3:30 P.M. Those extra hours added up. This had been the situation for several years.

My father had said little to Albert over the years, because he had originally been hired by my grandfather and seemed like a permanent installation in the building. The first time I came in at 6:00 A.M. and found him sound asleep in the back of the basement, all of that changed. I decided he could spend as much time as he needed in the building if he had nowhere else to be, but not on the company clock. I limited him to 6:00 A.M.–4 P.M. each day and he was angry. It started an ongoing argument that ended with him leaving, which was not easy for me. I still think it was the right thing to do. Now when I take on a new client, I often check to see if she has her own Albert. More than half of companies do. Their wages have little to do with the value of their work and more to do with the inertia of the owner. The cost is an important factor in these decisions, but so is the loss of productivity of an employee who has become totally complacent.

come to terms with the bank requirement and their lack of flexibility in this matter. If your loan is carrying an SBA guarantee, this is absolute. For most lenders, the issue is not whether they want the right to foreclose on your house (few will ever take that action) or take your assets; it's that they want you to have an absolute commitment to what you are doing and be willing to make a personal sacrifice (read, lower your own salary) in order to make debt service payments when they are due. Paying a loan should be a high priority to any business owner, and banks think that personal guarantees will make it so. They may be right.

Be Careful of Accidental Guarantees

Some contracts, such as leases, are specific in requiring a personal signature from the lessee so that you can't just move out and leave the balance of the rent unpaid. You will see the specifics in the agreement.

There will be a specific line for guarantor. This may be negotiable if you have a track record with the landlord.

But, what are often missed are the credit applications that are signed for potential vendors. They can be signed by corporate officers and obligate only the business. Some of them have a simple place for the owner to sign that carries the language of a personal guarantee. If the business defaults on its payments, the one who signed may be held legally responsible. You may be able to leave this blank and still be granted credit, but if you do have to sign, understand what it means. Big box stores are starting to slip these guarantees in casually; read carefully.

It Takes Two Signatures

Most married business owners will have personal assets in the joint account of both spouses, and these are safe from creditors having a claim against only one. The bank, understanding this loophole, will require two signatures, but others, including landlords and vendors, may not. Try to avoid having both of you sign if you can, because it may be a protection you need for future payment negotiations. If the company is in the name of some outsider (even your spouse) and you aren't asked for that signature, don't volunteer the information.

Do Not Become Your Own Banker

Payroll is due and the bank account is short. You hold your own check and cover some of the others with your own funds. There's not enough time to try the bank for a loan. You'll take the money out next week. But next week has its own demands, and in the following months you also supplement the business account three or four more times. The cash crunch eases, but it does so with your money remaining in the business account. It's easier than taking the time out to put together an application for the bank and go through their hoops. Perhaps this will work for the short run, but there are likely to be difficulties down the road. You may not be able to get it back.

First of all, you need to have a liability account titled "loan payable stockholder," and each and every time you add money, you will need to document it with a note stating payback, and perhaps interest rate. Down the road, you may need this for tax purposes, and when you do go to the bank eventually, they will want documentation as well. The fact is that you are likely to be required to subordinate any personal loan to the company to the bank's loan, meaning you do not get any of your money until they get all of theirs. Your temporary infusion of capital may well become permanent equity in the company.

Drawing paychecks that will be held is wrong for another reason; you will accrue tax liability on wages not paid. Take yourself temporarily off the payroll.

Credit Cards Must Be in the Company's Name

A new business without much of a track record may not be able to get the open credit card lines it requires. New business owners often finance the early needs of their company with their personal cards. And too often, they mix business and personal expense on the same card and then pay the monthly bill from the business account without recording anything about the charge.

The first thing wrong with this is that a tax audit will red flag these payments, and without documentation, they may disallow them all as a business expense. The second problem is that if you are running up cards to their limit and not recording the total debt on the books, you are presenting an inaccurate picture of how the company is doing. Remember, that you need this information to make decisions and plans, so you need to carry all of your informal cash arrangements with the company in a prescribed way.

The best solution is to use one card exclusively for business expense and post the entire monthly charge where it belongs. This means that one Visa card may have part of its bill posted to material purchases and part to travel. This allows for a more accurate control of cost. The card company becomes a vendor as any other would, and the bill is carried under accounts payable and then reduced by any payments.

Virtually all new business owners finance their own companies as they go along; this isn't a criticism. But keep it properly on the books and try to keep it at a minimum. Remember, running up personal debts lowers your credit score and makes future business loans more difficult.

Building Value for the Future

What doesn't show on your books, and isn't usually a part of the day-to-day thinking of a business owner, is that you are creating value in the company. Some day that value may be great enough for you to sell the company and do something else, or retire.

One of the good reasons to get a professional evaluation is to find out what the company is worth, what the areas are that give it strong value, and what the weaknesses are. You can then work on correcting any of these problem areas and enhancing the areas that provide growing value. This is your chance to grow equity for your future, and you want to understand now how to do that. You can't see this money and you can't spend it, but it should be there when you need it.

▶▶ TEST DRIVE

The finance of a business is not just about the company—the owner has involvement in a number of levels. Have you considered what this will mean to you? Ask yourself these questions:

1. Are you prepared to balance your own budget based on the fortunes of your business?
2. Have you considered whether employing family members is a good idea now and for the future?
3. Are you looking at investment opportunities outside of your business?
4. Are you keeping your own money and the company's money separate?

When Is It Time to Begin?

The day will come when you are no longer enthusiastic about running your company, or your age and physical circumstances will make you ready to retire. For most people, the idea of simply closing the doors has no appeal—you have worked too hard to see that happen. But, if you are to have any chance of success with an exit strategy, this must be planned in advance.

The answer to the question of when it is time to begin your exit strategy depends on a number of factors. Some involve your personal situation, some involve the circumstance of the business, and some involve the general health of your industry as well. Let's begin with you.

Are you getting close to the age when you want to slow down or retire? The closer you are, the sooner you should start to analyze your company and determine what options are available to you. If you think there is a possibility of a clean sale, have your current financials reviewed by your accountant to see how much the business may be worth. And find out, in this process, if there are ways to improve the Balance Sheet as well as your profit margins short-term; these are improvements that will create greater value for the buyer. This will be covered in depth later in this chapter.

Are your liabilities growing, and is the company clearly losing value? A quick sale that stems these losses is distinctly possible. Be honest about what is going on and what you must do to stop the damage.

Is the industry still in its growth cycle, or has it reached full maturity? The challenge here is for the company to maintain sufficient access to cash in order to take advantage of the potential. If you are tapped out, perhaps a new owner, or even a partner, can provide the needed cash resources.

When a Business Is Created as an Investment

There are two types of business owners. One type works in the field for the love of the work (or because it is the only skill he has) and he plans to stay for most of his life. The other is one who is making an objective business investment for the primary financial purpose of gains. The latter will plan to have an exit strategy before the company begins, making sure that the legal entity is one that can easily be sold or, in the case where there is a potential for a public offering, that the correct corporate structure is in place. ▸▸ **When an IPO is even being considered, it is critical that the books and records are set up professionally and audited by a CPA firm on a regular basis.** Only a very clean financial record will pass the scrutiny of the SEC (the Securities and Exchange Commission, which oversees stock trading). This is a strategy for the sophisticated business person.

For the accidental business owner (someone who has spent her life working at a trade) the situation will be quite different. Her first step is to realize that she wants to exit at some point.

Three to Five Years Before Any Sale

If you have not done so before, now is the time to have a business evaluation done. Talk to your CPA about which version you require. There is a formal evaluation that is fairly expensive (it's used primarily for tax purposes and litigation), and a different opinion of value which is far more economical. This will include an analysis of the line items on your Balance Sheet, as a business sale may be based on the net worth of the company. There will be time, after you see the analysis, to clean up that Balance Sheet.

If you have machinery and equipment that has value, yet these items have been depreciated off the books, consider selling them and adding to the value of the company. Even if you trade them in, the full value of the new equipment will be reflected on the books and the trade-in credit will be added to the net value of the business. This increases the tangible assets, therefore, the net worth.

If you are carrying old personal loans to the company, you may want to write them off or begin to write them down, because this will also strengthen your Balance Sheet. This whole process is similar to cleaning and polishing your house before putting it on the market. You want the business to look as shining as possible.

Pay Attention to Your Income Statement

Often a company will be paying far too many expenses of the owners and principals, the theory being that this is tax-free money. These are not really deductions (they are not likely to pass a tax audit), except under the most extraordinary stretch, but they begin to matter more as the business is being groomed for sale. How many cars and insurance policies are being paid by the company? How many gas cards are in family members' names, and how many cell phones are being used by those who don't really need them for business purposes? This is not the voice of your conscience, or the tax auditor's, it is the voice of your financial advisor.

When a business is being prepared for sale, these excesses do become issues. Often the buyers are looking on the basis of cash flow, and in order to substantiate it, they will ask for three years worth of records (usually your tax returns). Since you may be able to substantially boost the price of the business, it is in your best interest to trim these lifestyle payments for a while once you have really committed to preparing for a sale.

What Are Some of the Alternative Strategies?

The dream scenario is that just about the time you feel ready to sell your business, an interested buyer (perhaps a customer who has always loved what you do) comes by and you make a deal that pleases you both. Okay, now is the time to wake up. This does happen, but it is few and far between. It is more likely that the person who loves your business doesn't have any money to buy it, and you spend time, energy, and legal cost to try to find a way around this deal-busting problem. ▶▶ **Do not let a potential buyer talk you into a payout program, where you will be paid out of revenue.** It simply never works. You may never see your money, and you will have lost control of your company.

The other "wouldn't it be fabulous" idea, when your original idea is innovative enough, is that you have the capital to take it to the next level, and you go public with the whole company and cash out for millions. This scene was more likely to happen a decade ago with the dot com mania and other innovative technology and biomedical ideas. The business must plan for this from day one, by forming a C Corporation, and have a CPA on hand to set up and audit the books on a regular basis. Then there is the fairly large amount of legal fees necessary for preparing all of the SEC (Securities and Exchange Commission) documents and securing the underwriting for a public offering.

Another Version of This Strategy

Some new companies that are formed are meant to be in business independently for only a short time. They are created to try out a new technology or a new product, and then put themselves up for sale to one of the bigger players in the field. The start-up doesn't cost nearly as much because the corporate structure is less important. Accounting must be kept, but not necessarily the regularly audited statement. The goal of this business is to prove it has a profitable concept, and then have someone else take it to the next level. In this case, the founder must patent or trademark her innovation.

Succession Planning

This is not truly an exit strategy, unless there is a specific family member who has been identified, and who has both the talent and the interest to pursue the work in the company until the time has come to succeed the existing owner. The rate of only one in four family successors being successful is very discouraging. Many children are working in the family business because it pays better and it is easier than getting a real job. These are not good candidates for the new CEO—in your heart, you know how much work it takes.

When there is a motivated son, daughter, nephew, etc., the turnover won't just happen in weeks, months, or even a few years. Time and effort must be made to provide training and education to prepare this person to take over all of the aspects of the business. Perhaps the candidate needs to move from department to department learning all of the jobs, including some of the ones you may never have mastered. This will serve two purposes. One, it will allow any candidate to grow confident enough that on the day of succession he feels totally prepared. Two, this will give all other employees a chance to get to know who the "next boss" will be, and hopefully gain some respect for him. This process may take a good deal of time, and he may be in the company for years, but the "owner in waiting" needs to have a comprehensive role to fill. You want to retain his interest and utilize his skills as well.

Inside Track — Are Your Children Really Ready?

I went to work for my father first when I was a teenager, initially during summers and holidays. I just wanted to earn some money. Then in my early twenties, I came back to the company, by then unsure of what else I could and wanted to do. My job was to run errands and help out, not much of a challenge for an aggressive young woman. I did take courses on time and cost studies, and did some internal studies in our own factory. But I was given little authority, even when I had good ideas. Overnight, that changed dramatically. My father had a stroke, and I ended up being the one in charge. I had the responsibility but not the training.

Anytime a family member is employed in the company, she may be called to fill in or take over at a moment's notice. Could you take over someone else's company without any training? If the answer is no, don't put your own offspring in that position. I was there, and it's a scary place to be. It's not the best way to protect the family's assets, either.

What About a Merger?

If you cannot identify a single buyer who would be a good candidate to purchase the company, can you think of other candidates who could use your resources to combine with their own and create a new larger and more successful company? The strategy may be to combine ensuring each of you still holds an ownership interest, and then to sell the larger entity. This is one way around the problem of "too small to sell." If there is another company that fits nicely into this scenario (your shared business becomes a market force), why not approach them to instigate some dialogue? You will each need professionals to complete the deal, but why make the expense without a meeting of the minds?

Is There an Inside Candidate?

Your key person inside may not be a family member, but someone you may have grown the company with and who is committed to its future. Perhaps this person is younger and has intentions of working well beyond the time you intend to be shouldering most of the burden. Or you may be able to find an industry insider (perhaps the most active salesperson at another company or one of the innovators in the field) who would jump at the chance to direct his own operation.

There are a number of ways to go about these transactions. The cleanest would be an out-and-out sale based on a fair purchase price with money to be exchanged at closing. This is always the best deal. But with someone you have known a long time and someone you expect to be successful, you might be able to be a little more flexible in your terms. Consider the possibility of selling an interest for a period of time while you both work together. Then the balance of the company may be sold when the financing is in place. The minority interest will not impede your ability to retain control, and your deal could include a price that incorporates the shared value while you have worked together.

The Parts Are Worth More Than the Sum

There are times when the pieces of a company—its buildings, equipment, inventory, and product lines—have a greater value when they are sold separately than when they are packaged together as a going concern. This happens most frequently when there is owned real estate which has a value that is greater than its current usage by the business. Rather than go through all of the changes to relocate the company and then sell it, the answer may be to sell it off in pieces.

Don't forget to value the intangible assets in the mix. Your trademark, your customer list, your special recipes, etc., all have value to be sold to an interested party. Some tangible assets that are no longer of value to your company may be sold to an industry or an area where they have great value. I once sold off "out of spec" fire retardant garments (which were still completely serviceable) to an exporter at a premium. He was moving as many goods as he could to an area where they were fighting an oil fire.

Doing a sale in pieces is by its very nature an asset sale. The other primary way that a business changes hands is in a stock sale. They are not as frequent, but you must groom a business for a sale such as this.

How to Create Value

What we are considering here is the going concern value of a company being sold as a stock sale. This means that the buyer purchases the stock of the company, which includes all of its assets as well as all of its liabilities. Few buyers are usually interested in this type of a transaction.

The downside is that there are liabilities that may grow even after the sale is closed. Few smaller businesses are able to make any real provisions for this.

There may be lawsuits based on something that happened in the past few years that has just not surfaced yet. The primary areas of concern are product liability and workers compensation. In both cases, the business is likely to have insurance that will cover the actual loss, but the increase in rates as a result could undermine the entire operation in the future.

A small business stock purchase happens for one of two reasons. The first would be the assumption of leases, agreements, and contracts that are controlled by the selling company. Some of these are grandfathered and have beneficial terms only for the original business.

The second reason may be a tax benefit. A C Corporation may have a series of tax losses that can be passed on as a carry-forward to the new owner to defer taxes as new profits come on stream. Remember that a corporation is an entity that has ownership and rights, and only the stock in the corporation changes hands.

Confidentiality and Letters of Intent

You find an interested buyer and he expresses interest by looking more closely at your company. What should you be doing to protect your information from falling into the wrong hands? One way is to have your attorney draw up a Confidentiality Agreement, meaning that all material shown to the buyer for the purpose of the sale must be kept private and not shared with a third party. Can you really rely on this as full protection? Not likely.

In fact, some of the inappropriate disclosure may be accidental. People learn facts in a variety of ways, and at times don't even think about where they first heard the information.

There are other ways to add to your own protection:

- Control access to your facility.
- Provide records in a bound book, making it harder to remove or copy any documents.
- Provide customer sale information using denotations and not names for actual customers.
- Provide a limited amount of time for this "tire kicking" phase.

You Are Entitled to Financial Information

Another way to protect yourself when selling a business is to prequalify any buyer. It wouldn't be a good use of your time and effort to work with someone who doesn't have the financial capability of completing the purchase of the business. Ask for personal financial statements as a form of verification. This will weed out the casual lookers and make the entire transaction seem to be one of more importance.

The Letter of Intent

This is an agreement stating that both parties have expressed desire to bring the negotiations to a final agreement and sale, which will be put together in the written contract of sale. There are some advantages to moving to having a letter of intent (remembering that it is not a necessary step). They are:

- It signifies the seriousness of the parties.
- It begins the consideration of all of the details.
- It will draw in the professionals for their opinions.
- It will identify primary representatives for both parties.
- It allocates responsibilities.
- It adds more gravitas to the future talks.

There are disadvantages to making this letter of intent and not gong directly to the contract of sale. They are:

- It is not a binding agreement.
- The negotiation dynamics may change with outsiders involved.
- The seller may be locked in while the buyer is still making final considerations.

Doing the Deal

Once you have an interested buyer at hand, you must begin to negotiate the terms of the sale. There are a vast number of issues to consider, and at this point you need to have professionals (likely both a lawyer and an accountant) giving you advice, and perhaps even doing the negotiation. You may have a business broker or a consultant dealing with the buyer and their representatives. They will make sure that you are receiving what you expect, and there are no trap doors waiting to be sprung. What does that mean?

When you buy a car, you can see what the deal includes; the same goes for a house, although there can be problems that you don't see, like a leaky roof or a malfunctioning furnace. A business is a complicated sale, so you need to know a number of the issues.

1. Which assets are being transferred?

Unless this is a stock sale, which includes very few small businesses, you are selling some, but not all, of your company's assets. These must be specifically listed to be included. Any equipment, inventory, trademarks, contract rights, receivables, intellectual property, and goodwill may be specified.

2. Which assets are excluded from sale?

There may be real property such as buildings, automobiles and trucks, equipment, or intangible property that you are keeping or expect to sell on your own. You may have wanted to keep them, or the buyer didn't want to purchase them, but they must be listed.

3. What is the purchase price for each asset?

There is a serious tax question in the issue of how the price is allocated for each item. Unfortunately, what is best for the buyer is not always what is best for the seller. This must be very specific in the agreement.

4. Will there be any assumption of liabilities?

Most asset sales do not include the assumption of other liabilities. However, there is the possibility of a buyer taking over the business space and assuming the balance of the lease, or purchasing the equity in equipment and assuming the balance of a loan. This must be in your agreement, but must also be included in a new or modified contract with the landlord or lender.

5. Will there be any earn outs?

There are times when the purchase price may be increased by the new owner reaching a benchmark, normally with the assistance of the previous owner. You will begin with a base price and increase it as the value of the company grows. This payback may be included in a sale in lieu of a consulting agreement.

6. Will there be price adjustments, and on what basis?

There may be proceedings or pending insurance claims and a virtual laundry list of items to be checked. During this process, you may see lawyers, accountants, and maybe even mechanics. Real estate will require an appraiser. The sales contract will identify items that need to be checked and any adjustments that need to be made.

For example, you have sold a business that you have operated with sales of one million dollars annually for the past few years. You may find someone auditing invoices to assure that the number is valid and those sales are likely to continue. There will also be a physical inventory done within days of the closing.

Within a day or two before the date when the company actually changes hands, a final price will be set, which may be higher or lower than what you thought you negotiated. You will get an explanation of the changes and the reasons for them. Have this verified by your representative, because the closing is the end of the process, and you are not likely to ever see any of money you expected but did not receive by this time.

Be Prepared to Walk Away

There are some advisors who have a negotiating technique that may be very disadvantageous to sellers. They take the negotiations straight through to the minute of closing and then ask for some sort of major concession. The theory here is that most people won't walk away when it is that close. For a business owner who is ready to sell, and close to having it happen, this is a difficult step. But you must be ready to do so, because you could end up with very little to show for your years of hard work. I had a client who was selling his propane gas company to a joint venture. Both he and the buyer were from rural Pennsylvania and they tended to do a lot of business on trust. The other party hired a negotiator from D.C., and two days before closing, he demanded a $200,000 concession based on an error he claimed was on the pro-forma. My client ceased negotiation and walked away. It wasn't easy after a process of six months, but I thought he was right and respected him for his decision. There is always a better deal down the road.

Closing the Sale

It may easily take a period of six months from the time a business sale is in the serious negotiation stage, until the day the deal closes. There are so many items to cover and research, that even the initial identification of all of the considerations may take weeks and weeks. Every issue in the life of the business, from the existing assets and liabilities to any future expectation of earnings or claims, must be covered. Will obligations be settled or assumed by the new owner? Will there be a noncompete agreement and will it also include a consulting agreement? Will the cash be paid on closing or are there some notes being issued by the seller? The list goes on and on.

One thing that you must understand is that during this process you must continue to run the company with the same effort and enthusiasm as you always have. Letting it slide may be dangerous, as you could lose money in the sale for not meeting established targets, and the business may not be sold in the end, and you will be back in your operational role again, only now with a very troubled company.

Getting Paid

Selling a company and getting the deal closed is only part of the challenge. You need to be paid in full to complete the deal. There are many times when the seller is asked to take paper (meaning a loan) in lieu of cash. The buyers are essentially financing the company with the seller's money. This is a very risky way to transact the deal, because the only money you are assured of getting will be the cash you receive at the closing. Once the company is in the ownership and the control of the buyer, your payments will be based on their success. If times get tough, your payments may be delayed, or not forthcoming.

Buyers may offer you a higher purchase price as an incentive to secure owner financing; however, it is often more prudent to take less money payable at the closing than over time. If you do agree to any deferment, ask for a personal guarantee so you have additional security beyond the assets of the company. These details will form the basis of a note between you and the buyers. The other elements of such a promissory document will be the interest rate and the time for repayment. You should understand that you are not likely to be able to force payment by the threat of foreclosure (as others will have senior liens to yours), but you can at least be paid eventually if any of the assets that are used as collateral are sold.

The Tax Consequences of a Sale

You may think that your only concern is how much money you will receive for your business and how quickly it will get paid, but there are other considerations when you make the deal. Depending on whether you are a corporation or not, you may be liable to double taxation if assets are being purchased. The business will pay capital gains tax as a result, and then you will have to pay personal tax as well. In some instances, this can take a very large bite of the purchase price.

Buyers often prefer the asset purchase because they can depreciate the cost of the purchase over years and shelter future earnings. The asset will often be overvalued to account for the value of goodwill, and that cannot be expensed. The analysis of this part of any sale must be turned over to your accountant.

One way to handle this problem to your benefit is to take payments in the form of a noncompete or a long-term consulting contract. This will be taxable to you only at the personal income rate. Buyers may resist this level of allocation if the expense will not be beneficial to the new company.

Starting a new business may be time consuming and complex, but this is the time you will be energized by the concept. You need to understand that a successful exit strategy is equally time consuming and complex, and you must give it adequate attention, including experienced professional in the process.

▶▶ TEST DRIVE

When the time arrives to pass the torch of the business and move on to a new venture or to retire, you must develop a game plan. Have you considered your own strategy? Ask yourself:

1. Is the exit planned within the next three to five years?
2. Do you have alternatives to a sale, such as a succession plan or a merger with another company?
3. Have you explored ways to create value in your company for any new buyer?
4. Do you understand the basic terms of a business sale?
5. Is your accountant providing information on tax planning for a future sale?

Epilogue

Yesterday I met with one of my clients (a two-million dollar manufacturer) and his banker. It wasn't scheduled to be a cordial visit, more of a heart-to-heart talk about where the company was headed and how to make the changes that would keep the business from being constantly on the brink. Their revenue was fairly consistent, but the business owner paid little attention to the other operating numbers in his business.

Both the banker and I had reviewed the financials given to us a few days earlier, and we knew exactly where the problem areas were. We even had good ideas about how to solve them. Now we were waiting for the owner to give us his thoughts. I was disappointed, but not surprised, by the conversation. He concentrated on the sales prospects and the quality of his products.

▶▶ **What motivates most entrepreneurs into business is a spirit of adventure, a desire for freedom, and a healthy dose of creativity.** The belief in yourself and the products or services you provide gives you the confidence to turn it into a business venture.

For most of us, it is on the sales and marketing side of the business that we feel most comfortable, and we learn the operation angle because this is the only way to deliver the goods. For others, with more technical backgrounds, their drive is on the basis of a product (new development) of their own creation. These are the operational people. Few, however, come from the world of finance and accounting.

Then, instead of tackling the challenge to learn what we need to know in that area, we tend to assign the task to someone else or hire outsiders and carry on treating numbers as if they were some sort of foreign language. This is a serious mistake.

You're in the game to win, and you're not likely to do so unless you learn to keep the score. Where are the point opportunities, and what numbers really matter? You must track the performance of your company through the Profit and Loss Statement and measure your stability through the Balance Sheet. These numbers indicate what has happened recently and what is likely to happen in the near future.

You don't have to have a math aptitude to understand accounting, and you don't have to do the transaction work yourself. But you do need to know where the numbers come from to understand the meaning of the reports.

There are financial pressures and financial decisions to be made from the first day you begin the business. The profit that you deserve and that you need to go forward may become elusive if you can't make choices based on all of the knowledge you require. You will make purchases, pay employees, and quote prices—all of these will have an impact on your bottom line. To make these decisions, you must be able to understand the implications of all of your decisions.

Your employees want to earn as much as they can because they feel they earned it. Your customers want as good a value as they can get; they feel they're entitled to it. Your suppliers want fair and full prices as well as prompt payment because they've worked hard at their business. Yet, it is virtually impossible to meet all of the needs while adequately protecting your own business's bottom line. This is the work of finance.

Part of your contribution to the ultimate success of your business is to translate these various needs and requests into numbers so you can determine the impact any sort of change in costs or prices will have on your business operation. If your employees get an 8% raise, what will that do to your overall costs? If a customer needs a 5% discount to seal the deal, how much will that hurt your profit? What if the offer is for a particularly big order; will the volume make up for the price cut?

Consider how well you really understand how to reach these answers in a professional way. Isn't it worth the effort to learn more so you can make better decisions?

Do you begin to worry, as soon as one payroll is met, whether you will be able to meet the next one? Are you unsure of what to tell vendors when they call for payment information? Do you know how long it takes you normally to pay your bills? Do you know how quickly your sales turn into cash? If you take the time to master your company's financials, you will learn about the turnaround ratios that will give you this information in typical days.

Do you have the sense that the business is improving, but you can't explain why it's happening, much less continue to maximize the trend? Or, do you feel the situation is deteriorating and you aren't quite sure why this is happening?

All of this information is found in the books, records, and reports generated internally in the company or compiled by your accountant. This is powerful knowledge if you learn how to use it.

This book was written to give you the information in the language most business owners will understand. If something isn't quite clear, go back and reread the relevant section, or go over the concept with your financial professionals. Work with your numbers until you raise your confidence level.

You may very likely find that it is easier to get a loan when you know how to communicate better with your bankers. You can anticipate their concerns and be prepared to give them assurance. You will know how much of a loan is required and how soon it will be paid back.

All businesses go through cycles, beginning with the early start-up phase. You must know the effect of smoothing out the bumps caused by outgrowing, slowing down, or draining your cash reserve. One requires borrowing, and the other needs attention. You need to know when to raise prices and when not to.

▸▸ **Your business will never remain static—it will be on the rise or on the decline.** The early steps in either direction are not giant ones, just small trends and nuances that must be caught early and corrected. A period-to-period review of ratios will show you those trends. I experienced another business phenomenon in the company I ran after I sold my manufacturing company. This is having the resources in reserve to respond to a sudden, often tragic, but needed opportunity. In my case, it was the oil fires after the 1991 Kuwait-Iraq war. I was involved with safety clothing and a call went out to locate as many coveralls and respirators as possible. Availability was more important than price, and we made some serious profits.

There have been a series of crises since then, foreign hostility as well as natural disasters. Perhaps your company can participate in these contracts? You will need to know what resources you can access and how quickly. This is a more "big picture" issue than the ones that keep you consumed day to day.

I did not know much about what I have been writing in this book when I first took over my first company. I learned some of it the hard way, by making costly mistakes, but I was determined to master the concept of small business finance. I admit that some of it is boring to me, but some of it has become very interesting. I understand the dynamics of almost any business and can show the owners how to improve their results.

I dedicate this book to your learning. You may not understand it all the first time, but I urge you to use it as a reference guide. It was written to make your entrepreneurial experience much more fun and far more profitable.

—Suzanne Caplan

APPENDIXES

Appendix One
Glossary

Appendix Two
Troubleshooting by the Numbers

Appendix Three
A Successful Loan Proposal

Appendix Four
A Case Study of a Turnaround

Appendix Five
Business Resources

Appendix One
Glossary

Accounts Payable

This listing of outstanding debts to vendors is kept as a sub-ledger of the General Ledger, and it appears on the Balance Sheet as a current liability. Normally listed alphabetically as well as by date of invoice, a well-tracked system provides information about repayment terms. Accounts payable terms are significant sources of working capital used to finance inventory and receivables. Some invoices may carry an interest charge if not paid by due date. These rates are normally in excess of traditionally borrowed funds.

Accounts Payable Turnover Ratio

This ratio is calculated by dividing the total dollars of annual purchases by the total dollars of outstanding accounts payable. To quantify in days, you may divide 365 (number of days per year) by the ratio. This number is used as a comparison with similar companies as well as with previous periods within the business. When the days increase, accounts are being paid on a less timely basis. This may be an indication that working capital is being financed by trade credit that is meant as a short-term strategy, not permanent financing.

Accounts Receivable

Maintained as a sub-ledger, this is the list of customers who have purchased goods or products from the company on a credit basis. The amount of outstanding credit is shown on the Balance Sheet as an asset. A receivable represents incoming cash flow, and the timing may be established by a receivable aging.

Accounts Receivable Turnover Ratio

This ratio is calculated by dividing the total dollars in annual purchases by the current outstanding dollars of accounts receivable. It may be quantified in days by dividing by 365. This management tool is used to compare with peer companies and to highlight trends. If the number of days increase, it could mean that collection activities have not been sufficient, and cash flow will be slower, possibly causing a cash crunch.

Accrual Basis Accounting

This method recognizes income at the time it is earned and expense at the time it is incurred, whether or not actual cash has been transferred from buyer to seller. This matches the revenue and expense to a fixed accounting period and allows for comparisons to be made period to period.

Accrued Expenses

These are expenses that are anticipated but not yet due, such as taxes incurred during one month, but payable at a later time. Other payroll expense such as vacation pay may also be stated as accrued. Accruing expenses will produce a more accurate statement of current business conditions.

Amortization

This is the process of allocating a portion of the total amount over a fixed period. In a long-term loan, the principal will be allocated over the life of the loan. This will show the amount of the payment applied to interest expense as well as principal reduction over the life of the loan. On the expense side, the total cost of acquisition or development of a major long-term project will be allocated over the useful life of the project.

Asset Purchase

When purchasing a business, this means that the acquirer is buying only certain identified and specific assets, not the corporate common stock. No liabilities are assumed by the new owner, whether current or anticipated.

Assets

This is the total value of any tangible property and property rights, less any reserves set aside for depreciation. Hard assets will not reflect any appreciation in value that are not strictly quantifiable under current accounting principles.

Bad Debts

Unpaid obligations that are deemed uncollectible for a variety of reasons. These may have been pursued through collection activities or not, but they are written off accounts receivable to give an accurate reflection of financial status. This causes a loss of revenue during the period in which transactions are booked.

Balance Sheet

This includes the summary of assets, liabilities, and net worth of a business at the end of a monthly or yearly accounting period. A Balance Sheet includes current assets such as cash, accounts receivable, and inventory, as well as long-term assets such as property and equipment. Liabilities that are listed as current include accounts payable and current loan amounts, as well as long-term portions of loans, mortgages, and notes.

Book Value

This is the value of an asset shown on the Balance Sheet, listed at cost and then reduced by total accumulated depreciation. Accelerated depreciation schedules may reduce value to less than current market value. Tangible assets may be fully depreciated while still having usable life.

Bulk Transfer

This concept is covered by the Uniform Commercial Code (UCC), and it regulates the sale and transfer of more than 50% of a company's assets. Under this article, in certain states, notification of all creditors is required in advance of completion of such a sale and transfer. This is meant to prevent any fraud from taking place in a business sale.

Business Plan

The written document used to describe what the business does, its market strategy, sources of revenue, and projected outcomes. This document is typically written before a business begins, and it should be updated annually.

Capital

The worth of a company as determined by the total amount of all assets less all outstanding liabilities.

Cash Basis Accounting

This method recognizes revenue when the money is received and expense at the time that payment for them is made. There is no match of revenue against expense in a fixed period, so comparison on a period-to-period basis is not possible. This system provides less financial control because unpaid expenses are not recognized.

Cash Flow

The difference between the cash at the beginning of a period with the cash at the end of a period is cash flow. Cash flow may be increased by the sale of assets or the acquisition of new debt. It may be decreased by large purchases, but not for current use or principal debt payment.

Cash Flow Statement

There are several different types, the basic one being simply the measure of cash flowing in and out of the business. Most important as a management tool is the operating cash flow statement that measures inflow of revenue versus the outflow of expense, and does not reflect cash reserves or borrowings.

Chart of Accounts

The numerical list of all assets, liabilities, sources of revenue, and expenses in the company's operating business that is used to organize and track all financial transactions. In the company's accounting system, most common transactions (sales or purchases) will automatically default to an account in the chart. And the expenditure of any cash will default to an expense account.

Collateral

The tangible assets of a company, a third party, or both, that are pledged and encumbered for the payment of a loan. Although some collateral such as stocks, CDs, or money market accounts will be maintained under the control of the lender, most collateral such as equipment, inventory, and accounts receivable remain in the possession of the borrower. Rights to sell or liquidate these assets remain in the control of the secured lender.

Compensating Balances

These balances on deposit by the borrower are normally the operating accounts that are maintained by the lender. The lender will desire a certain average daily balance to partially compensate for a special rate of interest charged on a loan. Some loan fees may be waived by lenders to borrowers who maintain a high level of compensating balances.

Confession of Judgment

This describes a clause in many loans that permits the lender to record a lien on record against all of the assets of the borrower without having to bring suit against the borrower in court. This is normally exercised only when there has been a default. In the states that permit this clause, banks often use it because it saves them time and money. If the "confession of judgment" clause contains the phrase "as of any terms," the bank can record the note without any default, much the same as it would record any mortgage.

Co-signer

Any signator in a note, beyond the primary signer, is a co-signer who is fully obligated to all clauses of the note until it is fully paid.

Covenant Not to Compete

This is an agreement between the buyer and seller that prevents previous owners from competing in a similar business for a period or in a specific geographic area. Also may be included in an employment agreement.

Credit Memo

A source document required to back up any adjustment made to a customer invoice that lowers its value is a credit memo. May be issued for a return or adjustment to settle a dispute.

Credits

Credits always appear on the right-hand side of the General Ledger. A credit will increase items on the revenue side as well as on the liability side.

Current Assets

These are the assets that are in cash or expected to be turned into cash within one accounting period (one year), such as inventory and accounts receivable. They will normally not include items such as notes receivable from officers, since these may not be required to be paid to zero during a specific period.

Current Liabilities

These are the corresponding liabilities, that is, those due within one accounting period (one year). These would include all accounts payable; the current portions of any long-term loans; and any accrued but unpaid items such as taxes, insurance, or benefits. Operating lease payments will not be listed on the Balance Sheet, but will be recorded as a liability.

Debit

Listed on the left side of the general ledger, a debit increases the asset account and the expense account.

Debt

The amount of money owed to others, either formally (by written agreement) or not. Some debt is secured by the pledging of assets and the filing of liens under the Uniform Commercial Code. Others, such as vendor credit, are considered unsecured, since no asset is backing the obligation.

Debt-to-Equity Ratio

Banks rely heavily on this number, which is calculated by dividing debt by equity. Increasing ratios, more debt in relation to equity, means that the company is being financed by creditors rather than by its own positive cash flow. In most conditions, a ratio of three to one is the upper end of the limit.

Depreciation

The conversion of the cost of an asset into an expense, expressing the useable life of the item covered. Set up over a fixed period in a depreciation schedule according to current tax regulations. Once an item has been fully depreciated, it no longer is carried on the books of the company as having any asset value.

The depreciation can be made in equal amounts over the useful life, known as straight line depreciation, or taken more in the early years, known as accelerated depreciation.

The Balance Sheet will show the asset at its original cost, and then the reserve for depreciation, resulting in the net asset value. This number reflects book value, not necessarily actual value.

Direct Costs

Normally the costs of material and labor that are directly attributable to the level of sales or production are considered direct. These include the costs of direct subcontractors. These are also referred to as variable costs because they rise as volume increases and drop as it decreases. Total revenue less direct costs results in the gross profit from operations.

Double-Entry

Double-entry system is one that allows only for an item to be posted to both sides of the sub-ledger. Revenue posts as income as well as a corresponding asset (cash or accounts receivable).

Due Diligence

The period during which a buyer under contract to purchase the business conducts an investigation into the company's financial condition and operations. Financial statements and their backup documents are scrutinized and verified, and tax and public records are checked for accuracy. Physical inventory is taken and all of the equipment is checked. Leases and loans are verified for balances as well. The outcome of any due diligence is reflected in the final purchase price of the company.

Equity

Also referred to as net worth, this is the difference between the total assets of an entity and the total liabilities. Shown on the liability side of the ledger, it may be thought of as the amount owed to owners, since theoretically, this would be disbursed to them if assets were sold and liabilities paid.

Equity Financing

Raising capital through any instrument that carries equity risk and reward such as stock is called equity financing. Some debt instruments will carry convertible features that allow them to be redeemed for stocks. Since there is an additional risk to this type of financing, the cost is higher than more traditional ways of raising capital.

General Ledger

The central listing of all activities posted on the sub-ledgers is the General Ledger. This covers all financial transitions and may be used to audit activities that may have been incorrectly posted. A trial balance will show whether the ledgers are in balance or not.

Gross Profit

This number is derived from the gross (total) sales revenue less any direct costs such as labor, material, and subcontracting that is directly attributable to that sale.

Also referred to as operating profits, the gross profit represents the money available to pay overhead expense and taxes, and to generate a net profit for the company to retain as working capital.

Guaranty (Guarantee)

The document that represents the agreement by a third party to pay all or part of the borrower's obligation to a specifically named creditor is the guaranty. The pledge is for payment of any or all of the installments not made in a timely manner, or the total debt if accelerated, including principal, interest, and perhaps, collection costs. A number of different types of guarantees may hold the guarantor not only responsible for a single note, but for all borrowings of the company (a continuing guarantee).

Income Statement

The document generated monthly or annually that defines the earnings of a company is the Income Statement. It shows all relevant income and all expenses that have been generated by that revenue. Also referred to as the Profit and Loss Statement.

Indirect Costs

Expenses that are not directly related to sales, including items such as rent; utilities; and administrative overhead such as office salaries, professional fees, and selling expense. Called overhead or fixed expense because this cost continues regardless of the sales level of the company.

Inventory

These are the assets held for resale, which may be finished goods, works in progress, or raw materials. When valuing work in progress, there is the added value or direct labor involved. This may increase the real worth of inventory, yet not be realized until the work is complete and goods are released.

Inventory Turnover

This ratio is calculated by dividing the total costs of annual material used in costs of goods sold by the current inventory. Decreasing ratios (fewer turns per year) may indicate that there are slow selling items in current inventory, which puts a pressure on cash, since it will not turn to cash in the current cycle.

Invoice

The source document required as backup to any sale that is posted as income of accounts receivable is the invoice. Hard copies or copies of a complete database should be retained for at least three years.

Journal Entry

These include transactions entered on a sub-ledger and into the General Ledger. Entries include the date of transaction, account number, and which accounts were debited and credited as a result of the transaction.

Labor Costs

There are two types of labor, direct and indirect. The first is related to production and performance of products or services, and the latter is related to the work involved in the distribution, sale, and administrative duties involved in operating the business. Labor costs include any taxes and benefits that are incurred as the result of the payment of wages.

Letter of Credit

Issued by a bank, this document uses very specific language, and is issued to suppliers or vendors. It serves as a guarantee for payment with the bank standing as guarantor rather than the customer. Often used for international transactions, a letter of credit promises payment once goods are received by the customer and may be drawn by the beneficiary. This instrument allows a company to import goods without tying up capital while they are in transit.

Line of Credit

A line of credit is issued by a bank or other lender for short-term (one year) capital needs. Most lines are revolving; that is, they can be drawn down, repaid, and drawn on again. A nonrevolving line may be drawn only once.

A line of credit should be paid to zero at least once during the year, since its purpose is short-term financing of inventory and receivables. Although it is granted for one year, it may be renewed on a regular basis.

Liquidity

This is the ability to pay current obligations as they become due from cash, or the normal turnover of inventory or receivables into cash. Long-term assets (property and equipment) are not measured, since they provide no cash from which to retire current debts, until they are sold outright and become cash items.

Loan Agreement

This document covers some short-term, but all longer-term loans, and it is the basis of the agreement between the borrower and the lender. The rules that govern the borrowing are known as loan covenants, and they are used to determine if the borrower is in compliance with the credit requirements of the loan.

Even when a loan is completely current, failure to meet all of the loan covenants will place the loan in default. Some of the typical covenants are the timely submission of financial information, payment of all obligations (particularly taxes), and maintaining adequate insurance. Minimum equity levels may also be required.

Most loan agreements will allow the borrower to cure certain elements of a potential default before the loan is called and payments are escalated.

Note

This is the actual document of the debt of a loan, including the amount, interest rate, maturity date, and parties obligated to pay. Notes are quite simple, but there may be additional loan documents such as a security agreement and the loan agreement itself. A note may be sold or assigned to a third party, and the borrower becomes obligated to the new holder.

Overhead

The indirect or fixed costs of operating the business, ranging from rent to administrative to marketing costs. The majority of these costs stay fixed regardless of sales volume, although a few that are sales related may be considered semivariable.

Post

The act of entering a financial transaction on a sub-ledger as well as on the General Ledger. In a dual-entry system, each transaction will be credited to one account and debited from another.

Prime Rate

The prime rate is not an official benchmark that governs the lending rate of different institutions. Each institution is free to set its own, although that is seldom done because most banks follow the lead of the larger institutions. This rate is based on the current federal rate for funds, and goes up and down according to the Federal Reserve Board decisions.

Profit and Loss Statement

Prepared annually and often monthly and quarterly as well, this is the report of the income and expense, and the results as expressed in profit or loss. This report identifies all income from product sales or other activities and reports all direct and indirect costs by category. Operating (gross) profits are listed, as are the net (before tax) profits.

Pro-forma

This may be created in the form of both a Profit and Loss Statement and a Cash Flow Statement. This is a prediction of financial results in future periods based in part on historical happenings and anticipated new income or expense.

Rates of Interest (Fixed and Variable)

The interest rate that is in effect at the start of a loan may not always be the interest charged during the life of the loan. Only a fixed rate loan has one rate during the entire term, but this normally is limited to five years or less. The only long-term loans that are fixed are mortgages, and these loans are sold through Fannie Mae or Freddie Mac, which relieves the bank of the interest rate risk.

A variable rate loan has a floating rate pegged to an index such as the prime rate and goes up and down according to that rate. Some loans may have semifixed rates for one year and then they float. These loans may also have a minimum floor as well as a maximum ceiling.

Retained Earnings

Profits that are not distributed through dividends, but are left in the business and carried on the books as retained earnings, are retained earnings. These numbers are reduced over time by any losses.

Secured Loan

A loan that has assets pledged as collateral that may be liquidated if the loan is not paid according to agreement is secured. Assets will remain in the borrower's possession, but under the control of the lender.

Semivariable Costs

While these costs are listed under the fixed expense, they tend to follow the trend of sales; going up with an increase in revenue.

Sub-ledger

A sub-ledger is used to record transactions of revenue and expense items to accounts payable and accounts receivable journals. Sub-ledgers are posted to the General Ledger as well, to track all financial transactions.

Subordination Agreement

This agreement between creditors covers the priority of each one on all or certain assets of the borrower. This may be necessitated when one lender has filed financing statements (VCC-1) on all assets of a borrower and a second lender is asked to make a loan. The primary lender may release some assets as security for the additional capital. This also comes up when an officer has a note payable to a closely held company and the bank requires that the note be subordinated to its claim, regardless of the timing.

Trade Discount

A 1-2% credit on an invoice offered by some vendors for prompt payment usually covering ten days is called a trade discount. This incentive always exceeds current costs of borrowed funds.

Uniform Commercial Code (UCC)

When a lender wishes to perfect his secured interest in certain assets, he may do so in a number of ways. One is to take possession of stocks and bonds that are held as security. Another is to file an encumbrance on a title such as a vehicle. Where there are a variety of assets in possession and control of the borrower, the lender will file a Uniform Commercial Code financing statement with the secretary of state where the borrower is located. These financing statements are normally signed by the borrower at the time the loan closes.

Unsecured Loan

An unsecured loan has no underlying collateral pledged to the borrower to offset any losses in case of default. It normally carries a higher interest rate than those loans secured by collateral. Personal guarantees are usually required with any unsecured loans.

Venture Capital

Venture capitals is funding flowing into a company in the form of an investment rather than a loan. Controlled by an individual or small group known as venture capitalists, these investments require a high rate of return, and they are secured by a substantial ownership position in the business. Equity interest transfers to original owners when all loan payments or premiums are paid. Most venture deals have a fixed exit strategy.

Working Capital

This is the difference between current assets and current liabilities, and is an indication of liquidity and the ability of the company to meet current obligations. The assumption is that current assets will turn into cash concurrently with obligations such as payables and loans.

The variable here is the collectibility of current receivables and the salability of inventory. This may mean that a company is less liquid in reality than it appears to be on paper.

Working Capital Ratio

This number is calculated by dividing current assets by current liabilities. A decreasing ratio indicates that working capital is being reduced by losses, the purchase of long-term assets, or distribution to owners. This tool may be used to compare peer companies and to monitor trends.

Appendix Two
Troubleshooting by the Numbers

There are a number of key ratios covered in the earlier chapters of this book that are important to know as you analyze the results of your business. You need to be able to see your business in comparison with others in the field by using RMA (Robert Morris Associated) Ratios. You can find these industry ratios in the library or on the Internet. You may also be able to purchase a survey from a trade association. Your accountant can help you interpret this information. Your banker can share with you the ratios they require in their lending criteria. Most important, when you know where the trouble is, you can develop a strategy to correct it.

Some of the computations are found only on your Balance Sheet and some only on the Profit and Loss Statement. Others require the use of both financial reports. I have provided examples and explanations of both so you can find the numbers and how to compute them. Try them with your own financial reports.

Profitability Analysis—Gross Profit Margin

Profit and Loss Statement—ABC Manufacturing

Sales Income	**$1,500,000**	(1)
Direct costs		
Labor	595,000	
Material	300,000	
Cost of goods sold	895,000	
Gross operating profit	**605,000**	(2)
General and administrative expense		
Rent	25,000	
Office salaries	60,000	
Office expense	25,000	
Sales expense	50,000	
Advertising	35,000	
Travel and entertainment	40,000	
Utilities	20,000	
Depreciation	80,000	
Telephone	15,000	
Officers salaries	104,000	
Interest expense	78,000	
Miscellaneous	15,000	
Total costs	547,000	
Net before taxes	58,000	
Gross operating profit	605,000	(2)
divided by sales	$1,500,000	(1)
= Gross Profit Margin	**= .40 or 40%**	

What is normal is dependent on your type of business and can range from less than 5% (high volume grocery store) to mid-thirties in manufacturing and construction to a far higher level in a retail operation. Compare yours from year to year as well as with industry norms. There is more similarity between companies in direct costs (costs of goods sold), and yours should follow an industry norm. Lower profits may mean that your pricing structure is too low.

Profitability Analysis—Net Profit Margin

Profit and Loss Statement—ABC Manufacturing

Sales Income	$1,500,000	(1)
Direct costs		
Labor	595,000	
Material	300,000	
Cost of goods sold	895,000	
Gross operating profit	605,000	
General and administrative expense		
Rent	25,000	
Office salaries	60,000	
Office expense	25,000	
Sales expense	50,000	
Advertising	35,000	
Travel and entertainment	40,000	
Utilities	20,000	
Depreciation	80,000	
Telephone	15,000	
Officers salaries	104,000	
Interest expense	78,000	
Miscellaneous	15,000	
Total costs	547,000	
Net before taxes	58,000	(2)
Net before taxes	58,000	(2)
divided by sales	$1,500,000	(1)
= Net Profit Margin	**= .038 or 3.8%**	

The important concerns here are the trends from year to year, and for any individual company, this is sufficient to meet debt service. It is also useful to compare with industry norms. However, there are more overhead differences between companies than direct costs. If your gross profit is within a target range but your net is low, you may have an excess of overhead costs to control.

Liquidity Analysis—Current Ratios

Balance Sheet—ABC Manufacturing

Cash in bank		$12,000	
Accounts receivable		400,000	
Inventory		500,000	
Prepaid expense		38,000	
Total current assets		**950,000**	(1)
Fixed assets			
Building		750,000	
Less Dep.	–525,000	=225,000	
Machinery & equipment		800,000	
Less Dep.	–200,000	=600,000	
		825,000	
Total fixed assets		**1,775,000**	
Liabilities			
Accounts payable		450,000	
Current portion-note payable		250,000	
Total current liabilities		**700,000**	(2)
Long-term balance on note		500,000	
Total liabilities		1,200,000	
Net worth		465,000	
Current assets		950,000	(1)
Current liabilities		**700,000**	(2)
Total current assets		950,000	(1)
divided by total current liabilities		$700,000	(2)
= Liquidity Ratio		**= 1.36**	

This is an indication of how a company can retire current debts from current operating cash flow. A ratio of 2:0 is desirable because it allows for the possibility of substantial asset loss while still being solvent. The most likely way to improve this ratio is to liquidate inventory. You may also be able to turn short-term debt (accounts payable) into long-term borrowing.

Debt Ratio

Balance Sheet—ABC Manufacturing

Cash in bank		$12,000	
Accounts receivable		400,000	
Inventory		500,000	
Prepaid expense		38,000	
Total current assets		**950,000**	
Fixed assets			
Building		750,000	
Less Dep.	–525,000	=225,000	
Machinery & equipment		800,000	
Less Dep.	–200,000	=600,000	
		825,000	
Total fixed assets		**1,775,000**	(1)
Liabilities			
Accounts payable		450,000	
Current portion-note payable		250,000	
Total current liabilities		**700,000**	
Long-term balance on note		500,000	
Total liabilities		**1,200,000**	(2)
Net worth		575,000	
Total liabilities		**1,200,000**	(2)
Total assets		1,775,000	(1)
Total liabilities		1,200,000	(2)
divided by total fixed assets		$1,765,000	(1)
= Debt Ratio		**= 68%**	

This means that 68% of the company is financed by debt. A number this high makes it very difficult to acquire any new assets for growth or improvement. The focus should be on cutting costs and paying off existing debt. The acceptable range in this ration depends on the nature of assets. Real estate is likely more highly leveraged than equipment because the values on land and buildings rise over time.

Return on Investment

Requires Profit and Loss and Balance Sheet

Profit and Loss Statement—ABC Manufacturing

Sales Income	$1,500,000
Direct costs	
Labor	595,000
Material	300,000
Cost of goods sold	895,000
Gross operating profit	605,000
General and administrative expense	
Rent	25,000
Office salaries	60,000
Office expense	25,000
Sales expense	50,000
Advertising	35,000
Travel and entertainment	40,000
Utilities	20,000
Depreciation	80,000
Telephone	15,000
Officers salaries	104,000
Interest expense	78,000
Miscellaneous	15,000
Total costs	547,000
Net before taxes	**$58,000** (1)

Balance Sheet—ABC Manufacturing

Cash in bank		$12,000	
Accounts receivable		400,000	
Inventory		500,000	
Prepaid expense		38,000	
Total current assets		950,000	
Fixed assets			
Building		750,000	
Less Dep.	−525,000	=225,000	
Machinery & equipment		800,000	
Less Dep.	−200,000	=600,000	
		825,000	
Total fixed assets		**1,775,000**	(2)
Liabilities			
Accounts payable		450,000	
Current portion-note payable		250,000	
Total current liabilities		700,000	
Long-term balance on note		500,000	
Total liabilities		1,200,000	
Net worth		575,000	
Net profit		58,000	(1)
Total assets		1,775,000	(2)
Net profit		58,000	(1)
divided by total assets		$1,775,000	(2)
= Return on Investments		**= .033 or 3.3%**	

This means that the money invested in these business assets are returning 3.3%, which is a very low return for the risk. Small business investment is considered a high risk compared to other ways to invest.

The rate of return may be higher on government-guaranteed bank instruments or money market funds. Is this a good use of the owner's capital?

Inventory Turnover Ratio—Balance Sheet & Profit and Loss

Balance Sheet—ABC Manufacturing

Cash in bank		$12,000
Accounts receivable		400,000
Inventory		**500,000** (1)
Prepaid expense		38,000
Total current assets		950,000
Fixed assets		
Building		750,000
Less Dep.	−525,000	=225,000
Machinery & equipment		800,000
Less Dep.	−200,000	=600,000
		825,000
Total fixed assets		1,775,000
Liabilities		
Accounts payable		450,000
Current portion-note payable		250,000
Total current liabilities		700,000
Long-term balance on note		500,000
Total liabilities		1,200,000
Net worth		575,000

Profit and Loss Statement—ABC Manufacturing

Sales Income	$1,500,000	
Direct costs		
Labor	595,000	
Material	**300,000**	(2)
Cost of goods sold	895,000	
Gross operating profit	605,000	
General and administrative expense		
Rent	25,000	
Office salaries	60,000	
Office expense	25,000	
Sales expense	50,000	
Advertising	35,000	
Travel and entertainment	40,000	
Utilities	20,000	
Depreciation	80,000	
Telephone	15,000	
Officers salaries	104,000	
Interest expense	78,000	
Miscellaneous	15,000	
Total costs	547,000	
Net before taxes	58,000	
Annual material cost	300,000	(2)
Current level of inventory	500,000	(1)
Material	300,000	(2)
divided by inventory	$500,000	(1)
= Inventory Turnover Ratio	**= .60 or 60%**	

This means the inventory has not completely turned over annually. This happens when old and obsolete inventory remains on the books year after year and is never sold. This could represent a warehouse full of unusable goods that may be liquidated to raise capital and lower debt.

Accounts Receivable Turnover Ratio

Balance Sheet & Profit and Loss

Balance Sheet—ABC Manufacturing

Cash in bank		$12,000	
Accounts receivable		**400,000**	(1)
Inventory		500,000	
Prepaid expense		38,000	
Total current assets		940,000	
Fixed assets			
Building		750,000	
Less Dep.	–525,000	=125,000	
Machinery & equipment		800,000	
Less Dep.	–200,000	=600,000	
		725,000	
Total fixed assets		1,665,000	
Liabilities			
Accounts payable		450,000	
Current portion-note payable		250,000	
Total current liabilities		700,000	
Long-term balance on note		500,000	
Total liabilities		1,200,000	
Net worth		$465,000	

Profit and Loss Statement—ABC Manufacturing

Sales Income	**$1,500,000**	(2)
Direct costs		
Labor	595,000	
Material	300,000	
Cost of goods sold	895,000	
Gross operating profit	605,000	
General and administrative expense		
Rent	25,000	
Office salaries	60,000	
Office expense	25,000	
Sales expense	50,000	
Advertising	35,000	
Travel and entertainment	40,000	
Utilities	20,000	
Depreciation	80,000	
Telephone	15,000	
Officers salaries	104,000	
Interest expense	78,000	
Miscellaneous	15,000	
Total costs	547,000	
Net before taxes	58,000	
Total Sales	1,500,000	(2)
Accounts receivable	400,000	(1)
Total Sales	1,500,000	(2)
divided by accounts receivable	$400,000	(1)
= Accounts Receivable Turnover Ratio	**= 3.9 (or almost 4 times per year)**	

This means that your receivables are turning every ninety days or so, so that an invoice sent on January 5 is not likely to be paid until April 5. This can create cash flow problems and should be improved by aggressive collection policies. Monitor this number to see positive progress. The longer an invoice remains unpaid, the less likely you are to be able to collect it in full.

Accounts Payable Turnover Ratio

Balance Sheet & Profit and Loss

Balance Sheet—ABC Manufacturing

Cash in bank		$12,000
Accounts receivable		400,000
Inventory		500,000
Prepaid expense		38,000
Total current assets		950,000
Fixed assets		
Building		750,000
Less Dep.	–525,000	=225,000
Machinery & equipment		800,000
Less Dep.	–200,000	=600,000
		825,000
Total fixed assets		1,775,000
Liabilities		
Accounts payable		**450,000** (1)
Current portion-note payable		250,000
Total current liabilities		700,000
Long-term balance on note		500,000
Total liabilities		1,200,000
Net worth		$575,000

Profit and Loss Statement—ABC Manufacturing

Sales Income	$1,500,000	
Direct costs		
Labor	595,000	
Material	300,000	(2–partial)
Cost of goods sold	895,000	
Gross operating profit	605,000	
General and administrative expense		
Rent	25,000	
Office salaries	60,000	
Office expense	25,000	(2–partial)
Sales expense	50,000	
Advertising	35,000	(2–partial)
Travel and entertainment	40,000	
Utilities	20,000	
Depreciation	80,000	
Telephone	15,000	(2–partial)
Officers salaries	104,000	
Interest expense	78,000	
Miscellaneous	15,000	(2–partial)
Total costs	547,000	
Net before taxes	58,000	
Total purchase	**390,000**	(2–partial)
Accounts payable	450,000	(1–total)
Total purchase	390,000	(2)
divided by accounts receivable	$450,000	(1)
= Accounts Payable Turnover Ratio	**= .87 or 87%**	

This means that there are outstanding debts on this company's books that are more than a year old, and are turning less than one time a year. The possibility of legal action against a company in this circumstance is great, and the future is very insecure.

There is no doubt that the company described here in this appendix is in a dire circumstance. However, all of the tools for correcting the problems can be found in the ratios. The ongoing operation is solid as seen by a profitability ratio. Debt is serious but not critical, and return on equity is low but could improve.

Receivables are being collected too slowly, cash flow is inadequate, and payables are dangerously high. With the money received from the sale of old inventory and quicker payments for current work, deals could be struck with vendors to prevent any legal action and repair business relationships. This company is also under collection pressure, which takes time and effort away from building a successful future.

Analyze your company this way and see what you discover.

Appendix Three
A Successful Loan Proposal

The following is a copy of a loan proposal that was successfully submitted to a bank in 2005.

The company was originally financed by the owner and the original partner. A large national bank granted the company a small loan of $50,000, but it was not enough to grow to the level of revenue and profitability they wanted. The company was just breaking even, but the most impressive evidence of their future success was that they had made projected goals for two years. This is the document that convinced the bank that the risk was balanced by the potential of the company and the hard work of the owner. A smaller bank granted a loan of $150,000 as well as a line of credit.

Table of Contents

I. Description of Business

In August of 2001, the assets of the XYZ Engineering Group were purchased by Dave Martin, and the Acme Valve Company was formed. For the past four years the Acme Valve Company has been manufacturing, marketing, and selling their growing line of high efficiency check valves. Their "Next Generation" design of check valves and foot valves offer significant advantages over the competition in both functionality and life expectancy.

An exclusive marketing agreement with a large O.E.M. account (Gardner Denver Blower Division) in early 2002 has propelled the Acme Valve Company into expanding a smaller pipeline size range through 24" pipeline size. This expansion opened up additional markets, and has allowed the company to piggyback this sales success with almost all major O.E.M. blower manufacturers and packagers. The potential sales volume has doubled between 2004 and 2005.

Another marketing success, which took almost two years to complete, was the development of the Application Engineering Company business. Our expansion check product with its significant flow advantages combined with the benefits of the Acme Valve internals system have opened up new market potential in the O.E.M. pumping market.

Other ongoing marketing efforts include growing our all-stainless valve business. High margins associated with these products make this a high priority. Key to this project is the addition of a stainless steel cast wafer style valve body. Target accounts are ADM, Sterling Fluids, Osmonics, and Ecolochem. Their combined market potential is over $300,000.00 annually.

Other projects in the works are optimization and linking of our Web site to make it more easily linked and more user friendly. A connection to the Thomas Register site will allow us to access customers throughout the world. Another is the development of the fire and crash truck marketplace with higher pressure rated valves, as well as deep well 450 PSI female threaded ends valves for the oil and gas exploration markets.

The known domestic market for our seatless, fully ported, double door style check valves is over four million dollars annually. Our three-year sales projection calls for a minimum 25% market penetration. This equates to about a 30% growth rate. A number we have surpassed each and every year, and are on track to surpass again this year. We believe our plan to be a very conservative plan. With only two competitors world-wide, a proven superior product, and a competitive price advantage we have all the pieces in place for success and continued profitable growth. The only missing piece is adequate capital to take advantage of these opportunities.

II. Location

Acme Valve Company has a long-term lease for approximately 4,500 square feet of office and manufacturing space at 1234 Main Street in Erie, PA. The building is a block structure with a shingled roof, a high bay with an industrial tile floor, and a small, attached office. It is zoned for manufacturing and is surrounded by three additional acres of undeveloped property. The landlord has agreed to build additional office and manufacturing space as needed. Process air, and all necessary utilities are available on site at no additional expense. Our location is an additional advantage as our costs remain far below those of our competitors.

III. Current Markets

Check valves are used in both fluid and air piping systems to prevent damage, caused by back flow and back pressure, on expensive piping components such as pumps and blowers. The valve market place domestically is a mature market with both new and replacement sales potential. The major markets for our seatless, double door check valves are oil and gas, petroleum refining, water and wastewater resources, power generation and cogeneration, chemical and petrochemical, pulp and paper manufacturing, pump manufacturers, and original equipment manufacturers (OEM). Some key OEM markets would include gas turbine manufacturers, air and gas dryer manufacturers and packagers, heating ventilating and air conditioning (HVAC), air filtration, compressor lube oil systems, aeration systems, blending and vapor recovery systems, and fire and crash truck manufacturers.

There is an export potential for check valves as well. Key target markets would include Canada, Mexico, the Middle East, Australia, and Pacific Rim. Britain and the Common Market countries of Europe have potential as well, but piping components there are often purchased to British standards, which differ from American piping standards our valves are currently produced to.

Major market growth is expected to exist for many years in the water/wastewater segments of our business. Domestic demands for cleaner water, and wastewater processing and handling, along with stricter government standards and enforcement are fueling our domestic growth. Industrialization of underdeveloped nations around the world is also adding to the demand with China, Indonesia, the Middle East, and India leading the way.

IV. Competition

The Acme valve has two competitors worldwide. ABC Corporation, the creator of the seatless design check valve some 50 years ago; and Apex Company, who cloned the ABC valve in 2000. ABC has undergone some significant recent turmoil. Beginning with their moving out of Erie, PA in the fall of 2001 to Boston, MA, and not offering any of their personnel positions at the new location. Most recently ABC's parent company, as part of a corporate restructuring, sold their family of valve manufacturers to a large manufacturer of Houston, TX. It is still too early to know what impact this will have on the ABC operation, but the fit does not appear good. Cooper's core businesses are oil and gas exploration, processing, and distribution. These are typically high-pressure applications, with distributor-based sales. ABC only produces a low-pressure valve, and is heavy in customer direct sales. We will be watching them closely ready to capitalize on any market opportunities. Apex, on the other hand, after some very early success appears to be scaling back their check valve operation. Most recently they have disbanded their sales and marketing efforts terminating all former ABC employees. We are unsure but expect Apex's production arrangements with a Romanian supplier may be at the root of this cutback. With steel demand high worldwide costs are up and deliveries have been extended, we suspect Apex's margins may have slipped to unacceptable levels prompting their actions. Again we are watching them closely, ready to pick up new accounts as the opportunities present themselves.

V. Pricing Strategies

The pricing strategies vary with the product, the competitor, and the customer. The all cast seated valve line because of the larger number of competitors whose primary focus is on large OEM accounts and distribution, forces us to concentrate on the smaller end user and small OEM accounts. Price and service are usually the motivating factors pushing order placement. Our success rate here has been high when we find and target the right accounts.

Strategies for the "Acme Valve" differ, as there are only three manufacturers worldwide. ABC Corporation has created a market with extremely high margin potential. The Acme Valve Company's strategy will be to focus on the Acme Valve advantages of superior performance, quality, and service to protect the existing market structure. When competing with ABC Corporation, the Acme Valve Company's list pricing will be structured to be incrementally lower than ABC's published price. Discounts for OEM accounts and distributors will be the same as ABC. Market analysis indicates Apex Company pricing to be 10% below ABC's published schedule. It is our belief that ABC has already adjusted their selling prices to reflect the increased competition. Therefore, for those products that all three of us produce, the Acme Valve Company will discount to slightly more than 10%. For those products, which we only produce such as foot valves there will be no discounting.

The Acme Valve Company will attempt to always remain competitive, but will recognize they are the likely loser in a price war. For that reason we will evaluate each order and customer before cutting price.

VI. Sales Projections

Sales projections are based on development of an OEM, direct customer, and distribution sales plan. Our sales goal for 2005 is $640,000.00, a 40% increase over last year's final results. Our goal for 2006 is $850,000.00, and 2007 is $1,200,000.00, or about a 25% market share. ABC has assisted this process by listing customers and markets serviced in their product catalog. Utilizing SIC code searches and computer based market searches, we are able to identify additional customers and markets to expand our business even further. The primary focus of the Acme Valve Company will attempt to develop distribution outlets across the country. Distribution has the potential to quickly increase sales dollars, and to expand market awareness of our products, but they demand significant discounting before they will consider inventorying a product. Additionally, they traditionally have little loyalty as margin potential dictates their decisions. The upside of doing business with them is they traditionally purchase larger quantities, which can help reduce your overall costs. Ideally a blend of direct and distribution sales will be the goal. The proper ratio will change from year to year. Our first few years' goals will be weighted heavily towards direct sales with very little distribution efforts. In succeeding years we pick up distribution when and where there is a good fit.

VII. Description of Management

The management of the Acme Valve Company consists of two key personnel, Mr. Dave Martin, President and majority owner, and Mr. Frank Conner, Vice President and minority owner.

Mr. Dave Martin is a graduate of Gannon University (1983) with a B.S. in Industrial Management. He has over 20 years of sales and management experience, most recently as a Regional Sales Manager with a large specialty steel manufacturer. He was responsible for maintaining and developing sales and marketing strategies in a seven state region generating over five million in annual sales. Prior to that he successfully ran a small manufacturer's representative company for six years, selling castings and forgings. His background in metals and materials manufacturing will be a great asset in new product development, and proper materials selection. For the past 20 years Mr. Martin has been a resident of Erie, PA with his wife Debbie, an office administrator. They have two grown daughters and are both committed to this business.

Mr. Martin is in excellent health. He is a hard worker, and is used to long working hours and travel times necessary to develop and service customers. He is proficient with software and hardware necessary to operate this business. With the use of a portable computer and an Internet connection he will be able to effectively operate the business even while he travels. His salary will be $5,500.00/month.

Mr. Frank Conner has an Associate's degree in Manufacturing Engineering from Dean Tech (1982). His background includes 13 years in management with Atlanta-based Steel Tee Company. His most recent positions were as plant manager, where he supervised over 20 employees, and six years with McGee Corporation of North Carolina where he oversaw project management for an eight-state region. Mr. Martin has been married for 24 years to his wife Sue, an office manager. They have two grown children, 22 and 20. Mr. Martin has been with Acme Valve for three years. He is a hard worker willing to work long hours when necessary. He is proficient with the software used to manage the company, and his management skills will be a great asset as we continue to grow. His current responsibilities include purchasing, inventory and manufacturing management. His salary is $4,600.00/month.

VIII.   Application and Expected Effect of Loan

The funds from the proposed bank loan will be used to expand our product offerings, improve profitability, purchase new software, upgrade our Web site, and to open a remote office. The new product offering will be a stainless steel wafer style check valve. Addition of this product is expected to generate about $200,000.00 in new sales in the first year with an extremely high profit ratio. The cost of patterns and inventory to support sales will be $52,000.00. Also as an effort to improve profitability, we would like to add our 14" and 20" cast iron wafer to our China source. Cost for patterns and inventory will be $15,000.00 with a one-year R.O.I. Additional funds will be used to update and upgrade our Web site. We have already begun this process with the assistance of eBizlTPA, a state resource for small business. They estimate our cost to be about $8,000.00 and have funds available to help us defray any additional expenses we might incur. We are looking to replace our QuickBooks bookkeeping software with customized software. This cost is expected to be near $20,000.00. This investment will allow us to more accurately track our manufacturing and overhead costing, and assist in inventory cost control issues. Finally, we will use $5,000.00 to purchase equipment including a computer, printer, fax, and copying machine, for a remote office in Eastern Pennsylvania. All combined these expenses will allow us to increase sales and profit dollars, and to accurately track and report our financial picture.

Appendix Four
A Case Study of a Turnaround

A company does not deteriorate into a difficult situation quickly; it is normally a slow process of erosion and lack of attention. Even when the problems (often more than one) have been well diagnosed and a good plan devised, it takes time to implement and time to see any meaningful results.

The following is a case study of a real company, where I was called in before the owners even identified all of their problems; they just knew they were in serious trouble, because, as always, it shows up in the cash flow. Pressure was mounting by the time I got there.

Able Plumbing was a fair-sized contractor with a presence in a good area of Manhattan (the Upper West Side), and had a longstanding reputation for high-end jobs in expensive buildings. Their work had been profitable for years. But there were lean years as well, when business had been slower and overhead costs (particularly the owners draw and benefits) remained at the same level, causing cash to be tight. A long-term bookkeeper devised a way around this by stashing away an undisclosed $100,000 that could be drawn on when bills had to be paid. The owner discovered this and the money was soon drained. The next cash crunch arrived; there was no reserve, and pressure grew.

Suppliers were cutting off credit, and the union was becoming more threatening about past due payments. The environment was chaotic. The owner and his son, who was working out of obligation and not desire, called me, and I flew to New York to see what I could find out. It didn't take long before most of the serious issues reared their heads. These problems were not hidden.

My review of three years of financials found the following recipe for disaster. Sales were drifting downward a bit, not in a major way. Direct costs (material and labor) had increased almost 4%, and overhead costs were up by even more.

Before any serious investigation, I realized that that company was no longer being managed—everyone in any key position was barely doing an adequate job. In fact, the owner was spending three days a week in Florida in the winter, even if problems were all around. The son was left in charge. He was honest and hard working, but mostly without a clue about how to schedule jobs to make things work smoothly and profitably. The father came in later on Monday afternoon, stayed through Thursday morning, and did little else but price invoices from a big price book he had on his desk.

One of the two most serious problems they had was they were no longer buying materials at the price in that book. The major supplier had cut them off over past due payments and their expeditor, now disgusted, picked up material anywhere he could, regardless of the cost. This was a major source of profit loss. And worse yet, this key employee's days were spent more obsessed by ordering breakfast and lunch than plumbing supplies. He didn't care.

The men in the field did not have what they needed, so they often had to run to the other side of town to find a place where there was available credit. They even went to hardware stores and paid retail prices! So the cost of labor increased along with the cost of material. This inefficiency could not be passed on to customers.

The other areas of concern were ones you would expect—softer sales and no control on overhead expense. I suppose that to an insider, getting this company back on its feet seemed monumental. To an outsider and professional, it was merely logical. The major challenge was in creating a plan and making changes gradually. Then the owner could present it and sell it to the guys on the ground. It was about setting priorities.

I. Major Issues to Address

    a. Poor purchasing that squeezed gross profits
    b. High unnecessary overhead that was draining cash
    c. Overall poor morale that made mechanics on the job ineffective, and inside people resentful

d. Questionable leadership attitude

e. Marketing and sales efforts to generate increased business

II. The Plan

I began by recommending a drastic, yet short-term, cut on executive salaries and perks. We needed cash, and they were taking too much. Given the stress of the past few months, father, son, and one manager were willing. Another manager was not so willing, but his pay was cut as well.

I immediately set about reopening the credit with their most necessary supplier. I called (there hadn't been much communication as of late) and made an appointment to see their credit manager. I took our record of the account to compare with theirs, and a check for a partial payment. She was impressed by both gestures and willing to talk.

We worked out a payment arrangement on the past due amounts and reopened the account with a fixed credit limit. The account was to be paid weekly. It would not be easy, but it was worth it because we improved profits immediately.

The personnel noticed the activity and began to open up, so it was time to work on their productivity. True, the supply issue was time consuming, but they weren't setting any land speed records in getting work done. They decided, with the encouragement of the younger owner, to go along with the program and see if work could be completed more efficiently. Ka-ching—profits were on the rise.

A few good weeks and my client wanted all of his perks back, and that presented a challenge for me. I wasn't in charge, but I had established some credibility. He knew that while we had made some inroads with suppliers, we had made none with the union, which could prove to be far more dangerous. They could pull the workers off the jobs if benefits were not up to date. They could, and would, cancel health benefits, too.

So the company remained in the cost control mode for several months, during which time we sat down and worked out a payment agreement with the union, and that was not at all easy. Terms were tough because it was part of a legal agreement, so not everyone felt relaxed.

After the operation became stable, the natural next step was to focus on growth. Higher revenues would provide better cash flow and many internal pressures would be eased. The business was well known, so the major focus was putting their name out in front of customers. A densely populated location such as Manhattan usually has more work to be done than people to do it, particularly with an aging infrastructure. We decided on a direct mail campaign, and a full-color postcard was designed. I saved a good deal of money by taking the project out of New York City, where everything costs more. Printing in Pennsylvania was half the cost, and at no sacrifice in quality.

We did a random mailing to specific zip codes and scheduled them to be mailed weekly, not all at once. We weren't equipped to be swamped, and wanted to be prepared to earn good, new customers. It worked better than expected. The phones were ringing constantly. Sales actually did climb by almost 5%, and combined with a lower direct cost, gross profits were healthy, as they should be in this type of business. Even net profits were there, while overhead was being held down. For more than six months, things were far easier for everyone. But, as often happens, they got too comfortable.

III. Phasing In a Strategic Plan

Step one of this process was to try to recapture some cash, which was accomplished by cutting overhead being paid to principals. While some of that had to be allocated to supplier payback, it was replenished by the decrease in cost of raw materials and increase in productivity. Cash flow was definitely improved.

We did not institute an expensive and overly ambitious marketing plan because of budget constraints, but we might have gone further if our initial efforts had not shown success. Sales growth was a central part of this strategy, one to be put into place only after costs had been controlled. No one benefits from a false sense of success.

What is important to learn from this is that the majority of turn-arounds are not single-solution issues. There are typically many areas that have developed problems and must be corrected. You can't take them on all at one time, and the fact is you wouldn't want to. The tasks would be far too time consuming. As always, there continues to be day-to-day jobs to do as well.

The important thing to do is step back and determine where the problems are and what policies and people are key to putting change into place. Set your priorities and put the wheels into motion. If you feel you are stuck in place, bring in an outsider who can serve as an independent advisor. Make sure that you empower the advisor with authority and autonomy—she is there to find solutions, not just reassure you that everything will be okay. Being in business is a risk, and being in a troubled business is a serious situation. You need to hear the hard facts and take the tough steps to turn it around. This is most often precipitated by a high level of pain.

Able Plumbing was a classic. The owner was at the core of the problem, and on one level, he was in denial and on another, I am sure that he knew it. He agreed with his son to call me to diagnose the situation. An outsider is a good first step.

My analysis was harsh and required immediate personal sacrifice. This was an issue of lifestyle as well as ego, and that was a hard reality. Selling phase one was the toughest step. We all were in agreement about the cost of material and labor. I could recommend it as the outside advisor, but I was supported by the symbolic gesture of the owner's personal sacrifice. Insiders knew of it and they gave the support for everyone else to get on board.

How long did this process take? My first analysis was delivered within thirty days and we were on our way in another sixty days. Within the first three-month period, the pressure of most outside threats had abated and everyone was breathing a sigh of relief and moving toward a new attitude. The next step, to arrange some payment plans, caused another increase in stress. The total amount of debt was fairly high, and that was of concern, although the monthly payments were reasonable. It was clear that the belt around this company was going to have to be kept far more tightly than it had been in recent years.

The last phase was the direct mail price, which increased sales and thus further lowered the strain of bill paying. I was pleased because within six months, I saw a business that was doing well and could sustain itself through the next business cycle. Did it?

The answer in this case is no. Before year one had come to an end, things had drifted back into the situation in which I found it, perhaps worse because even more trust was gone and I was actually called back. It only took a few hours to see what they had done—gotten behind in payments to their major supplier and reverted back to buying more expensive supplies. The owner and his son were not happy about their own reductions; instead of returning to full salaries slowly, they reverted to the cash grab I first encountered. Now, it wasn't a matter of what to do; it was a matter of whether they were willing to be disciplined. Memories of the bad times were not that faint and some direct conversation did the trick—as did new impending threats of lawsuits and union walkouts. I gave them an ultimatum: I would come back only if everyone was on board. They were.

The Reality of Turnarounds

Everyone involved in the company will end up working harder for less money, and that includes those with the high salaries and those who are making average wages. Stress will become very high, and the need for extra communication is paramount, and working in cooperation is a critical element of productivity. Few will have the extra energy to spare, but motivation needs to carry the day. The challenge is, when the work is complete, not reverting to earlier bad habits. Doing this work once is difficult, and few can accomplish it twice. The decision that must be made is whether the business is fun anymore or if an exit strategy is the next step. Some companies can be pieced together so that they can be sold, but never brought back to the vibrancy that made them fun in the first place.

Appendix Five
Business Resources

Online Information for Managing Your Business

Accounting Software
QuickBooks
www.intuit.com

Peachtree
www.sagesoftware.com
(*www.sagecrmsolutions.com*)

Credit Reporting Services
www.dnb.com (Dun & Bradstreet)
www.equifax.com
www.experian.com
www.transunion.com
www.telecheck.com

Business Incubators
National Business Incubation
Association
www.nbia.org

For Women
www.sba.gov/financing/special/
women.html

Loan Programs—Federal Guarantees
www.sba.gov
(general business loans and
disaster recovery loans)

www.rurdev.usda.gov
(business loans for rural
communities)

Minority Business
National Minority Business
Council, Inc.
www.nmbc.org

Minority Business Development
(Department of Commerce)
www.mbda.gov

Women's Business Enterprise
American Business Women's
Association
www.abwa.org
National Association of Women
Business Owners
www.nawbo.org

Technical Assistance
American Management Association
www.amanet.org
(training and seminars)

Technical Assistance and Counseling

Small Business Development Centers
State & Regional Offices

Alabama

Alabama SBDC
2800 Milan Court, Ste. 124
Birmingham, AL 35211
Phone: 205-943-6750
Fax: 205-943-6752
www.asbdc.org

Alaska

Alaska SBDC
430 W. 7th Avenue, Ste. 110
Anchorage, AK 99501-3550
Phone: 907-274-7232 or
1-800-478-7232
Fax: 907-274-9524
www.aksbdc.org

American Samoa

American Samoa Community
College
P.O. Box 2609
Pago Pago, American Samoa 96799
Phone: 011-684-699-9155
Fax: 011-684-699-8636
E-mail: *hthweatt@ascc.as*
www.ascc.as/academicssuportsbdc
.html

Arizona

Maricopa Community Colleges
Arizona SBDC
2411 West 14th Street
Tempe, AZ 85281-6941
Phone: 480-731-8720
Fax: 480-731-8729
www.dist.maricopa.edu/sbdc

Arkansas

Arkansas SBDC
University of Arkansas at Little Rock
2801 S. University
Little Rock, AR 72204
Phone: 501-324-9043
Fax: 501-683-7720
www.asbdc.ualr.edu

California

Santa Ana District SBDC
California State University at
Fullerton
800 North State College Blvd.
Langsdorf Hall, Room 640
Fullerton, CA 92834
Phone: 714-278-2719
Fax: 714-278-7858
www.leadSBDC.org

San Diego/Imperial Counties SBDC

Southwestern College
900 Otay Lakes Road, Bldg. 1600
Chula Vista, CA 91910
Phone: 619-482-6391
Fax: 619-482-6402
www.sbditc.org

San Francisco Regional SBDC

At City College of San Francisco
455 Market Street, 6th Floor
San Francisco, CA 94105
Phone: 415-908-7501
Fax: 415-974-6035
www.sfsbdc.org

North Coast SBDC-Huboldt Prosperity Center

520 E Street
Eureka, CA 95503
Phone: 707-445-9720
or 1-800-697-7232
Fax: 707-445-9652
www.northcoastsbdc.org

Fresno Regional SBDC

University of California at Merced
550 East Shaw Avenue, Suite 100
Fresno, CA 93710-7702
Phone: 559-241-7406
Fax: 559-241-7422
http://sbdc.ucmerced.edu

Golden State SBDC Program

CSU, Chico
35 Main Street
Chico, CA 95929-0765
Phone: 530-898-5443
Fax: 530-898-4734
http://gsbdc.csuchico.edu

Los Angeles Regional SBDC

California State University Northridge
18111 Nordhoff Street, Mail Code 8414
Northridge, CA 91330-8414
Phone: 818-677-6397
Fax: 818-677-6521
E-mail: *ssloan@lbcc.edu*
www.csun.edu/~csunsbdc

Colorado

Colorado SBDC

1625 Broadway, Ste. 1700
Denver, CO 80202
Phone: 303-892-3840
Fax: 303-892-3848
www.state.co.us./oed/small-business

Connecticut

Connecticut SBDC

University of Connecticut
1376 Storrs Road
Storrs, CT 06269-4094
Phone: 860-870-6370
Fax: 860-870-6374
www.sbdc.uconn.edu

Delaware

Delaware SBDC
Delaware Technology Park
One Innovation Way, Ste. 301
Newark, DE 19711
Phone: 302-831-1555
Fax: 302-831-1423
www.delawaresbdc.org

District of Columbia

District of Columbia SBDC
2600 6th Street N.W., Room 128
Washington, D.C. 20059
Phone: 202-806 -1550
Fax: 202-806-1777
www.dcsbdc.com

Florida

Florida SBDC
State Director's Office
401 E. Chase Street, Ste. 100
Pensacola, FL 32502
Phone: 850-473-7800
Fax: 850-473-7813
www.floridasbdc.com

Georgia

Georgia SBDC
University of Georgia
1180 E. Broad Street
Chicopee Complex
Athens, GA 30602-5412
Phone: 706-542-7436
Fax: 706-542-6803
www.sbdc.uga.edu

Hawaii

Hawaii SBDC
308 Kamehameha Avenue, Ste. 201
Hilo, HI 96720
Phone: 808-974-7515
Fax: 808-974-7683
www.hawaii-sbdc.org

Idaho

Idaho SBDC
Boise State University
1910 University Drive
Boise, ID 83725-1655
Phone: 208-426-1640
or 1-800-225-3815
Fax: 208-426-3877
www.idahosbdc.org

Illinois

Illinois SBDC
Department of Commerce &
Economic Opportunity
James R. Thompson Center
100 W. Randolph
Chicago, IL 60601
Phone: 312-814-7179
www.ilsbdc.biz

Indiana

Indiana SBDC
Network Lead Center
One North Capitol, Ste. 900
Indianapolis, IN 46204
Phone: 317-234-2082
or 1-888-472-3244
Fax: 317-232-8872
www.isbdc.org

Iowa

Iowa SBDC
Iowa State University
2501 North Loop Drive, Bldg. 1,
Ste. 1615
Ames, IA 50010-8283
Phone: 515-296-7828
Fax: 515-296-6714
www.iabusnet.org

Kansas

Kansas SBDC
Fort Hays State University
214 SW 6th Avenue, Ste. 301
Topeka, KS 66603-3179
Phone: 785-296-6514
Fax: 785-291-3261
www.fhsu.edu/ksbdc

Kentucky

Kentucky SBDC
University of Kentucky
225 Gatton College of Business and
Economics
Lexington, KY 40506-0034
Phone: 888-475-7232
Fax: 859-323-1907
www.ksbdc.org

Louisiana

Louisiana SBDC
University of Louisiana at Monroe
College of Business Administration
Admin. 2-57
Monroe, LA 71209-6435
Phone: 318-342-5506
Fax: 318-342-5510
www.lsbdc.org

Maine

Maine SBDC
University of Southern Maine
96 Falmouth Street, P.O. Box 9300
Portland, ME 04104-9300
Phone: 207-780-4420
Fax: 207-780-4810
www.mainesbdc.org

Maryland

Maryland SBDC
7100 Baltimore Avenue, Ste. 402
College Park, MD 20740
Phone: 301-403-0501
Fax: 301-403-8303
www.mdsbdc.umd.edu

Massachusetts

Massachusetts SBDC
227 Isenberg School of Management
University of Massachusetts
121 Presidents Drive
Amherst, MA 01003-9310
Phone: 413-545-6301
Fax: 413-545-1273
www.msbdc.org

Michigan

Michigan SBTDC-State
Headquarters
Grand Valley State University
Seidman College of Business
510 W. Fulton Street
Grand Rapids, MI 49504
Phone: 616-331-7480
Fax: 616-331-7485
www.misbtdc.org

Minnesota

Minnesota SBDC
First National Bank Building
332 Minnesota Street, Suite E200
St. Paul, MN 55101-1351
Phone: 651-297-1291
or 1-800-657-3858
Fax: 651-296-5287
www.mnsbdc.com

Mississippi

Mississippi SBDC
P.O. Box 1848
B-19 Jeanette Phillips Drive
University, MS 38677-1848
Phone: 662-915-5001
or 1-800-725-7232
Fax: 662-915-5650
www.olemiss.edu/depts/mssbdc

Missouri

Missouri SBDC
University of Missouri-Columbia
W. 1051 Lafferre Hall
Columbia, MO 65211
Phone: 573-882-4321
www.mo-sbdc.org/index.shtml

Montana

Montana SBDC
301 S. Park Avenue, Room 114
Helena, MT 59601
Phone: 406-841-2747
Fax: 406-841-2728
*http://commerce.state.mt.us/brd/
index.asp*

Nebraska

Nebraska SBDC
University of Nebraska at Omaha
6001 Dodge Street
Roskens Hall, Rooms 308 and 415
Omaha, NE 68182-0248
Phone: 402-554-2521
Fax: 402-554-3473
http://nbdc.unomaha.edu

Nevada

Nevada SBDC
University of Nevada, Reno
College of Business Administration
Ansari Business Bldg. Rm.411
Reno, NV 89557-0100
Phone: 775-784-1717
Fax: 775-784-4337
www.nsbdc.org

New Hampshire

New Hampshire SBDC
University of New Hampshire
108 McConnell Hall
15 College Road
Durham, NH 03824
Phone: 603-862-2200
Fax: 603-862-4876
www.nhsbdc.org

New Jersey

New Jersey SBDC
Rutgers Business School
49 Bleeker Street
Newark, NJ 07102
Phone: 973-353-1927
Fax: 973-353-1110
www.njsbdc.com

New Mexico

New Mexico SBDC Lead Center
Santa Fe Community College
6401 Richards Avenue
Santa Fe, NM 87508-4877
Phone: 505-428-1362
or 1-800-281-7232
Fax: 505-428-1469
www.nmsbdc.org

New York

New York SBDC
Administration Office
State University Plaza
41 State Street, Ste. 700
Albany, NY 12246
Phone: 518-443-5398
Fax: 518-443-5275
www.nyssbdc.org

North Carolina
North Carolina SBDTC
5 West Hargett Street, Ste. 600
Raleigh, NC 27601-1348
Phone: 919-715-7272
or 1-800-258-0862
Fax: 919-715-7777
www.sbtdc.org

North Dakota
North Dakota SBDC
1600 E. Century Ave., Ste. 2
Bismarck, ND 58503
Phone: 701-328-5375
Fax: 701-328-5381
E-mail: *christine.martin@und*
.nodak.edu
www.ndsbdc.org

Ohio
Ohio SBDC
77 S. High Street
Columbus, OH 43215
Phone: 614-466-3379
or 1-800-848-1300
Fax: 614-466-0829
www.odod.state.oh.us

Oklahoma
Oklahoma SBDC
Southeastern State University
1405 N. 4th Avenue, PMB 2584
Durant, OK 74701
Phone: 580-745-7577
or 1-800-522-6154
Fax: 580-745-7471
www.osbdc.org

Oregon
Oregon SBDC
99 W. 10th Avenue, Ste. 390
Eugene, OR 97401
Phone: 541-463-5250
Fax: 541-345-6006
www.bizcenter.org

Guam
PISBDCN
University of Guam
P.O. Box 5404
UOG Station
Mangilao, GU 96923
Phone: 671-735-2590
Fax: 671-734-2002
www.pacificsbdc.com

Pennsylvania

Pennsylvania SBDC
University of Pennsylvania
The Wharton School
Vance Hall, 4th Floor
3733 Spruce Street
Philadelphia, PA 19104-6374
Phone: 215-898-4861
Fax: 215-898-1063
http://pasbdc.org

Puerto Rico

Puerto Rico SBDC
Union Plaza 10th Floor, Ste. 1013
416 Ponce de Leon Ave.
Hato Rey, PR 00918
Phone: 787-763-6811
Fax: 787-763-6875
www.prsbdc.org

Rhode Island

Rhode Island SBDC
Bryant University
1150 Douglas Pike
Smithfield, RI 02917-1284
Phone: 401-232-6111
Fax: 401-232-6933
www.risbdc.org

South Carolina

South Carolina SBDC
USC Moore School of Business
1705 College Street
Columbia, SC 29208
Phone: 803-777-4907
Fax: 803-777-4403
http://scsbdc.moore.sc.edu

South Dakota

South Dakota SBDC
University of South Dakota
414 East Clark Street
Vermillion, SD 57069
Phone: 877-269-6837
Fax: 605-677-5427
E-mail: *jshemmin@usd.edu* or
www.usd.edu/sbdc

Tennessee

Tennessee SBDC
615 Memorial Blvd.
Murfreesboro, TN 37129
Phone: 615-849-9999
or 1-877-898-3900
Fax: 615-217-8548
www.tsbdc.org

Texas

Texas-Houston SBDC
University of Houston
2302 Fannin, Ste. 200
Houston, TX 77002
Phone: 713-752-8444
Fax: 713-756-1500
http://sbdcnetwork.uh.edu

Texas-North SBDC
Bill J. Priest Campus of
El Centro Community College
1402 Corinth Street
Dallas, TX 75215
Phone: 214-860-5831
or 1-800-350-7232
Fax: 214-860-5813
www.ntsbdc.org

Texas-NW SBDC
Texas Tech University SBDC
at Lubbock
2579 South Loop 289
Lubbock, TX 79423
Phone: 806-745-3973
Fax: 806-745-6207
www.nwtsbdc.org

University of Texas at San Antonio
501 West Durango Boulevard
San Antonio, TX 78207-4415
Phone: 210-458-2020
Fax: 210-458-2425
www.iedtexas.org

Utah

Utah SBDC
115 S. Main Street, Ste. 503
Salt Lake City, UT 84111
Phone: 801-957-3493
Fax: 801-957-2007
E-mail: *greg.panichello@slcc.edu*
or *www.utahsbdc.org*

Vermont

Vermont SBDC
P.O. Box 188
Randolph Center, VT 05061-0188
Phone: 802-728-9101
Fax: 802-728-3026
www.vtsbdc.org

U.S. Virgin Islands

Virgin Islands SBDC
University of the Virgin Islands
8000 Nisky Center, Ste. 720
St. Thomas, VI 00802-5804
Phone: 340-776-3206
Fax: 340-775-3756
www.sbdcvi.org

Virginia

Virginia SBDC
Virginia SBDC Network Drive
4031 University Drive, Ste. 200
Fairfax, VA 22030
Phone: 703-277-7700
Fax: 703-352-7730
www.virginiasbdc.com

Washington

Washington SBDC
Washington State University
534 E. Trent Avenue
P.O. Box 1495, Ste. 201
Spokane, WA 99210-1495
Phone: 509-358-7765
Fax: 509-358-7764
www.wsbdc.org

West Virginia

West Virginia SBDC
1900 Kanawha Boulevard East,
Bldg. 6, Room 652
Charleston, WV 25305
Phone: 304-558-2960
or 1-888-982-7232
Fax: 304-558-0127
www.wvsbdc.org

Wisconsin

Wisconsin SBDC
University of Wisconsin
423 Extension Building
432 North Lake Street
Madison, WI 53706
Phone: 608-263-7794
Fax: 608-263-7830
www.wisconsinsbdc.org

Wyoming

Wyoming SBDC
University of Wyoming
1000 East University, Dept. 3922
Laramie, WY 82071-3922
Phone: 307-766-3505
or 1-800-348-5194
Fax: 307-766-3406
www.uwyo.edu/sbdc

Index

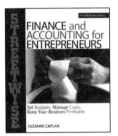
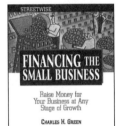

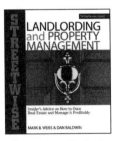

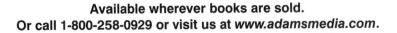

Streetwise® Managing a Nonprofit
John Riddle
$19.95; ISBN 10: 1-58062-698-X

Streetwise® Managing People
Bob Adams, et al.
$19.95; ISBN 10: 1-55850-726-4

Streetwise® Marketing Plan
Don Debelak
$19.95; ISBN 10: 1-58062-268-2

**Streetwise® Maximize
Web Site Traffic**
Nobles and O'Neil
$19.95; ISBN 10: 1-58062-369-7

**Streetwise® Motivating
& Rewarding Employees**
Alexander Hiam
$19.95; ISBN 10: 1-58062-130-9

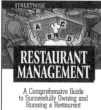

**Streetwise® Project
Management**
Michael Dobson
$19.95; ISBN 10: 1-58062-770-6

**Streetwise® Restaurant
Management**
John James & Dan Baldwin
$19.95; ISBN 10: 1-58062-781-1

**Streetwise® Sales Letters
with CD**
Reynard and Weiss
$29.95; ISBN 10: 1-58062-440-5

Streetwise® Selling on eBay®
Sonia Weiss
$19.95; ISBN 10: 1-59337-610-3

**Streetwise®
Small Business Book of Lists**
Edited by Gene Marks
$19.95; ISBN 10: 1-59337-684-7

Streetwise® Small Business Start-Up
Bob Adams
$19.95; ISBN 10: 1-55850-581-4

**Streetwise® Start Your Own
Business Workbook**
Gina Marie Mangiamele
$9.95; ISBN 10: 1-58062-506-1

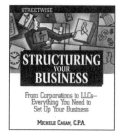

Streetwise® Structuring Your Business
Michele Cagan
$19.95; ISBN 10: 1-59337-177-2

Streetwise® Time Management
Marshall Cook
$19.95; ISBN 10: 1-58062-131-7